Guides to European Diplomatic History
Research and Research Materials

Series Editor
Christoph M. Kimmich

British Foreign Policy, 1918–1945
By Sidney Aster
ISBN: 0-8420-2176-0

French Foreign Policy, 1918–1945
By Robert J. Young
ISBN: 0-8420-2178-7

German Foreign Policy, 1918–1945
By Christoph M. Kimmich
ISBN: 0-8420-2167-1

International Organizations, 1918–1945
By George W. Baer
ISBN: 0-8420-2179-5

Italian Foreign Policy, 1918–1945
By Alan Cassels
ISBN: 0-8420-2177-9

Available from Scholarly Resources Inc.
Wilmington, Delaware

French Foreign Policy
1918–1945

A Guide to Research and Research Materials

Compiled and Edited
by
Robert J. Young

SR *Scholarly Resources Inc.*
Wilmington, Delaware

Scholarly Resources Inc.
104 Greenhill Avenue
Wilmington, Delaware 19805

Library of Congress Cataloging in Publication Data

Young, Robert J., 1942–
    French foreign policy, 1918–1945.

    Bibliography
    Includes index.
    1. France—Foreign relations—1914–1940—Library
resources—France.   2. France—Foreign relations—
1940–1945—Library resources—France.   3. France—
Foreign relations—1914–1940—Archival resources—
France.   4. France—Foreign relations—1940–1945—
Archival resources—France.   5. France—Foreign
relations—1914–1940—Bibliography.   6. France—
Foreign relations—1940–1945—Bibliography.   I. Title.
Z6465.F7Y68   [DC369]   327.44'0072044   80-53892
ISBN 0-8420-2178-7   AACR2

For My Parents

INTRODUCTION TO THE SERIES

This handbook on France is one in a series of research guides on European diplomatic history between 1918 and 1945. It is intended for scholars doing research for seminar papers, dissertations, and books. It provides information to help them plan their work and to guide them on their visits to archives and libraries. It will enable them to find their way quickly and efficiently through the voluminous research and research materials that have become available in recent years and will point them toward solutions to the problems they will encounter in the course of their work.

The handbook is organized to serve the researcher's needs. The introductory chapter describes how foreign policy was made in France: how the foreign ministry was organized and how it functioned, how it affected the conduct of foreign affairs and diplomacy, and how it was influenced by bureaucratic politics, domestic developments, and public opinion. This information will help the reader determine where to concentrate his research, how to allot research time, and, not least, how best to approach the materials in the archives. The second chapter brings together the most current information on public and private archives, on libraries, newspaper collections, and research institutes. The remainder of the volume is bibliography. Sections on general and bibliographical reference works are followed by a survey of the literature in the field, ranging from documentary series to memoirs to significant secondary sources. Arranged within a broadly chronological framework, extensively annotated, this bibliography permits ready reference to specific books and articles, historic personalities, and diplomatic events. Together with the archival information, the bibliography will suggest areas for further research and for reassessment.

There are five volumes in the series. Besides France, they cover Germany, Great Britain, Italy, and International Organizations. Each has its own distinctive features, of course, for the archival holdings and the research based on these holdings vary considerably. They are, however, meant to be complementary. They focus on materials relevant to different subject areas, and, within the limits set by the history of international relations, avoid needless repetition. They are organized along similar lines, and researchers who need to consult several volumes should have no trouble finding their way.

Each volume is prepared by an authority in the field. Each reflects experience gained on the spot in archives and libraries as well as knowlege shared by colleagues, archivists, and librarians. The volumes therefore are as current and reliable as possible.

The editors hope that these handbooks will prove to be valuable companions to all who are interested in international affairs and diplomacy.

Christoph M. Kimmich
Series Editor

CONTENTS

IV. Bibliography

V.   Appendices

Charts

I. PREFACE

Professor Kimmich, initiator of this five-volume series, has discussed the objectives of the project in his Introduction. Simply put, each contributor has sought to produce a volume of useful and up-to-date research information. Nevertheless, each volume has had to be fashioned in accordance with the current research possibilities within our respective areas. Several observations should be made in connection with this guide to French diplomatic history.

First, the volume affirms that the opportunities for primary research in France are now very considerable, particularly if one comes equipped with an appropriately broad definition of "diplomatic history". Section III, for instance, identifies something in the order of 180 sets of private papers or private collections, deriving from journalists, soldiers, bankers, industrialists, politicians, as well as from professional diplomats. Moreover, even the few references which we have selected for inclusion in this volume ought to attest to the very extensive record collections which are now available in various ministerial archives. For its part, the bibliographical component in Section IV speaks in turn to the presence of a large corpus of supporting secondary literature, including almost 400 memoir-related titles.

Second, the range of materials which have been assembled has done much to shape the volume as a whole. For example, the structure and organization of Section II were suggested by the presence of certain specific record collections in the archives of the foreign ministry. What was needed, or so it seemed, was an essay to describe the growth and operation of the French foreign ministry between the two world wars. Such an essay could become a convenient research tool if it were able to familiarize readers with the working administrative machine — the comités, the sous-directions, the cabinets — before they were faced with its archival remains. Similarly, there seemed to be a need for introducing researchers to some of the individuals who contributed to the operation of this machine between 1918 and 1945. Such is the function of the biographical data which is contained in the Appendices and in the annotations provided for the Memoirs and Biographical Studies.

Third, I have found that works of this sort seem to magnify the familiar problem of deciding what is to be included, and what not. Some of the casualties are discussed in the introduction to Section IV, but it is worthwhile alerting readers now to the fact that this volume does not deal with the French Empire or with the colonial administration. In short, it is "foreign" rather than "imperial" affairs with which we are concerned. By the same token it may be said that this volume concerns itself exclusively with research and research materials in France. Further, most of our attention is directed at the central government in Paris.

Whatever its limitations, this volume has only profited from the encouragement and assistance of many others. In France, I am deeply grateful to the members of the archival staff at the foreign ministry, including Mlle. Enjahlran, Mlle. Constans, M. Dethan and M. Lacaze. Similarly, I express my appreciation to General Delmas, Colonels Turlotte and Dutailly, and M. Nicot at the Service Historique de l'Armée de Terre; to General Christienne and Patrice Buffotot at the Service Historique de l'Armée de l'Air; and to Admiral Duval and M. Audouy at the Service Historique de la Marine. So too my thanks must go to M. François Bédarida and M. Claude Lévy of the Institut d'Histoire du Temps Présent, to Mlle. Chevignard of the Fondation Nationale des Sciences Politiques, and to Mme. Tourtier-Bonazzi of the Archives Nationales. Finally, I am profoundly indebted to Patrick Fridenson and Robert Frankenstein of the University of Paris X - Nanterre.

Appreciation and thanks are also owing to Julia Shepherd, formerly the archivist at the Liddell Hart centre for military history at King's College, London; Donald Watt and Robert Boyce of the London School of Economics; Zara Steiner of Cambridge University; Joel Blatt of the University of Connecticut; Martin Alexander, currently a doctoral candidate at Oxford University; and John Fox of the British Foreign Office Library.

In Canada, I owe a special word of thanks to Douglas Bedford, whose work as a research assistant was of the highest quality, and to John Cairns, whose scholarship could only be surpassed by his kindness. With similar gratitude I acknowledge the financial generosity of the Social Sciences and Humanities Research Council of Canada, as well as that of the University of Winnipeg. I also wish to express my thanks to Allison Sproule in the University's reference library.

Finally, I record in public a private, ever-growing indebtedness to my wife, Kathryn.

ABBREVIATIONS

A.H.R.	American Historical Review
C.F.L.N.	Comité Français de la Libération Nationale
C.N.F.	Comité National Français
C.S.D.N.	Conseil Supérieur de la Défense Nationale
C.S.G.	Conseil Supérieur de la Guerre
F.H.S.	French Historical Studies
J.M.H.	Journal of Modern History
R.D.D.M.	Revue des Deux Mondes
R.H.	Revue Historique
R.H.D.	Revue d'Histoire Diplomatique
R.H.D.G.M.	Revue d'Histoire de la Deuxième Guerre Mondiale
R.H.M.C.	Revue d'Histoire Moderne et Contemporaine
R.I.	Relations Internationales
S.D.N.	Société des Nations

II. THE FOREIGN MINISTRY AND FOREIGN POLICY

Introduction

"Diplomatic" history has been out of fashion for a long time. Caricatured as little more than vacuous inquiry into "what one clerk said to another clerk", it is often consigned to the murky backwaters of the historical discipline.[1] There it is left to the caprice of the current trendsetters, to be ignored or faulted as occasion seems to warrant. Without question, some of the criticism has been justified, but much of it has not. As a result, there are moments when some of us may be tempted to follow the example of Beverley Nichols, the author of that eloquent, anti-war tract, Cry Havoc. He wanted to abolish the word "war" on the grounds that it no longer meant what it once had. The same motive might apply in the case of "diplomatic" history, for it no longer means what it once did. Nor has it for many years. Indeed, the changes which overtook diplomatic practice, and so opened new vistas for its historians, are nowhere more in evidence than in the interwar years. Thus the years with which this volume is concerned belong to a transition period between what some have called the "old" and the "new" diplomacy.

This essay is addressed to that notion of transition. It suggests that diplomatic practice became much more sophisticated early in this century, that the meaning of diplomacy accordingly was altered by its new-found roles and, as a consequence, that diplomatic history became subject to a corresponding process of revision and growth. The truth of this is as certain as night following day, and about as novel. Nevertheless, it may be useful to re-examine what we like to think are the new conceptual approaches to diplomatic history, but to do so within a specific historical and archival context. After all, there is something fatiguing and irritating about counsels which, though theoretically intriguing, have little or no relation to specific historical experience or to the surviving historical records. This essay, complemented by the archival information in Section III, has been prepared at a time when access to the official archives in France is just beginning to permit more innovative research on the French diplomatic experience between 1918 and 1945. As a consequence, it is possible to deal more concretely and more realistically with some of the more interesting conceptual possibilities. By so doing we would hope to remind all readers of the rich potential of "diplomatic" history, and solicit the creative energies of those who have a particular interest in practicing their craft in France.

One may wish to begin with the now familiar observation that the role of the diplomat, the traditional diplomat, has been shrinking throughout the course of the twentieth century.[2] This is a judgment which few seem prepared to dispute. It is linked with the outbreak and destructive path of World War One, that first "modern" war which so prejudiced the status and ultimately the function of the diplomat. More than faintly associated with the aristocratic class, in a postwar world preoccupied with a variety of new elites, the diplomat had the uneasy look of an anachronism. Even worse, his enforced association with the guile and blunders that had served as prologue to war in 1914 meant that he was now obliged to endure suspicion — to which he was accustomed — mixed with derision — to which he was not. Finally, his traditional role as intermediary between his own government and that to which he had been accredited was being challenged by the ever more frequent recourse to what we now call summit diplomacy. As evidenced in the Congress of Paris in 1856, of Berlin in 1878, or in that of Paris in 1919, heads of state sometimes displayed an alarming predilection for diplomatic encounters with their opposite numbers, often beyond the voice and earshot of their professional diplomats or their foreign ministers. The diplomat, a professional by experience if not always by formal training, could do little but watch as the unwary moths were drawn to the flame of the international conference table.

Not much of this was of his own doing, and very little of it was within his powers to solve. He could not resist the tide which had been running against his privileged fellows for more than a half century; and none but the perverse would suggest that the diplomat had stood alone in his failure to comprehend or halt the countdown to 1914. Nor could he forbid the intrusion of amateurs into his domain, for the amateurs had become his political and institutional masters. So it is that what is sometimes called the decline of the diplomats in the twentieth century could more usefully be regarded as a redefinition of modern diplomacy. Certainly what we see in the period under study is the transformation, the continued and still-continuing transformation, of diplomatic theory and practice. Furthermore, that transformation is in itself symptomatic of some very central themes in modern western history.

One such theme is that of democratization: more people voting than ever before; more people reading than ever before; more receptivity on the part of elected legislatures to "popular" sentiment; more sensitivity on the part of executive authority to the aspirations and anxieties of legislators. In France, after 1900, the President of the

2

FOREIGN MINISTRY AND FOREIGN POLICY

Third Republic was in the process of losing his
constitutional powers in matters of foreign policy, losing
them in favor of a cabinet made up of elected deputies or
senators. Moreover, between 1902 and 1915 the Chamber of
Deputies and the Senate established their respective standing
committees for foreign affairs, thereby enlarging the
opportunities for a more active parliamentary role in the
nation's foreign policy. The democratization process, as
expressed in new franchise laws, universal education, and
civil freedoms like that of the press, thus appear at first
glance to have been complemented by a trend toward more open,
more consultative ways of formulating and conducting France's
foreign affairs.

Some will be inclined to argue that this is nothing
more than veneer. Elites change their clothes, their
rhetoric, and continue to govern. No longer able to ignore a
mass electorate, they hoodwink it instead with a torrent of
puzzling and contradictory information. In matters of
foreign policy, as is frequently said to be the case in
France, they continue to exploit the customary public
indifference to international issues, to withhold information
from the legislature, to respond to questions only when
pressed, and in general to continue all the practices and
traditions of secret diplomacy.

Neither point of view is completely satisfying. The
second will appear too cynical for some, too conspiratorial
for others. Indeed, the attribution of a conscious malice to
a handful of overseers is much too simplistic. Yet it would
be naive to think that it has been clear sailing for those
democratic forces which have demanded more open and
consultative government. Certainly in the case of France the
conduct of foreign policy was not greatly influenced by
democratic argument, at least not of the sort which has been
discussed here. The administration of French foreign affairs
remained in the hands of the few. But rather than attribute
this resistance to hostile, class conspirators, there is
something to be said for investigating the implications of
other trends in modern history. Bureaucratization and
specialization both come to mind. Here are two additional
themes which may be introduced, briefly, before embarking on
a study of their particular characteristics within the
administration of French foreign policy between the two world
wars.

This discussion can afford to be brief because both
themes are themselves symptomatic of developments within
society at large. Twentieth-century government in general,
and that of France in particular, reflects a clear and
demonstrable trend toward larger and larger bureaucracies,
with ever more specialized functionaries knowing more and
more about the particular and less and less about the
general. This is not to be explained by the machinations of

3

an ambitious few, those who are suspected of training their ambitions on great bureaucratic empires where territorial empires had once sufficed. Rather, the growth of the state apparatus and the numbers of state personnel may be explained without reference to that kind of ambition or design. Far more important is the critical impact of political centralization. Modern government has acquired more power than its historical predecessors because it has assumed far more responsibility; and it is out of the need to fulfill all of these new obligations that the extended bureaucracy has come. Furthermore, this increasingly technical age, animated by the rhetoric of scientific efficiency and highly tuned professionalism, has produced an insatiable demand for experts. Indeed, the search for experts and their "expertise" still constitutes one of the largest growth industries in the twentieth century.

In France, as elsewhere, the historical development of the ministry of foreign affairs neatly illustrates many of these changing social circumstances and perceptions. Throughout the period which interests us, both the substance of the nation's foreign policy and the manner in which it was administered were under constant review and reappraisal. For example, the ensuing pages will try to articulate an ever growing, contemporary awareness of the pivotal role which economics were coming to play in international politics. Accordingly, the first half of the twentieth century records the development of an economic counseling and assessment service within the foreign ministry as well as between it and other ministries, like that of Finance and Commerce. It is in association with this trend that one also finds the appearance of the financial attachés, the creation of special inter-ministerial economic committees, and the multiplication of communication channels between the central administration and the offices of banking, industrial, commercial and labor leaders.

Similarly, the government's increased sensitivity to the force of public opinion resulted in the growth of other specialized services within the foreign ministry. As public opinion became more important in the electoral sense, "informing" that opinion became a vital concern of the state. This "battle for the mind", an expression in use before 1914, intensified throughout the war years and the subsequent interwar period. It was a battle conducted on two fronts: the domestic, where a succession of new information services set out to ensure that the government's version of events invariably reached the electorate; the foreign, where a Paris-based version of current international affairs was always available to the governments and populace of other nations. Both campaigns, it will be appreciated, required offices full of press liaison people, linguists, translators, in-house editors, and archivists. And to these one would have to add, in the interests of various programs for cultural and educational propaganda, the external services provided by academics, jurists, writers and performing artists.

Nor was this expansion of the diplomatic service simply attributable to the new functions which foreign ministries everywhere were being asked to assume. If "modern" diplomacy meant business promotion, military intelligence, work with international organizations, and subtle propaganda campaigns, so it also involved a rethinking of traditional spatial and temporal perceptions as well. By way of illustration, the period in question demonstrates another kind of transition – from the Europe-focussed international politics of 1914, to the Europe-oriented system of the 1920s when League activity in Geneva helped deflect attention from the periodic if powerful intrusions of the United States, Russia and Japan, and finally, to the bipolar system which emerged in the course of World War Two. This extended transition period meant that foreign ministries everywhere had to adjust their internal organization and the distribution of their budgetary and personnel resources in accordance with changing geopolitical circumstances. Thus, just as the role of the financial adviser is likely to become more conspicuous in moments of economic crisis, so too the authority and influence of the ministry's Far Eastern desk might well fluctuate with the international political fortunes and ambitions of countries like China and Japan.

What happens in the spatial, geographical sense is in turn directly linked with what happens in the temporal sense. If the radio, the telegraph, the airplane, have reduced this globe to theoretically manageable proportions, they have also dramatically accelerated the pace at which affairs of any kind can be conducted. It is in the period which concerns us that messages, for the first time, could be typed en clair, scrambled in mechanical coding devices, sent by telegraph, and delivered by means of a telephone call — all within the space of a few hours. And the simple dispatch and receipt of such communications provided in turn the possibility, if not the necessity, of speeding up the entire decision-making process as well. But again, all of this required a support system of radio technicians and telegraph operators, coding and deciphering clerks, typists and telephonists. Thus the growth of these various technical services became an integral part of the ministry's bureaucratization process.

What these few examples seek to illustrate is that diplomatic practice, and hence diplomatic history, have been redefined for us. The well-orchestrated diplomatic spectacles continue as before, albeit with the ambassadors more often in supporting roles to their prime ministers and presidents. But more often than not, this is little more

5

than the publicized climax to an affair which has been initiated and conducted in private. The real work of the foreign ministry has been done in preferred silence and founded upon the counsels of specialists: those who follow the behavior of international money markets, those who study the foreign press, those who can advise on the compatability of French and international law, those whose expertise lies in new aircraft design, or shipbuilding, or ground fortifications. Such are some of the specific themes which this essay seeks to explore.

Quai d'Orsay, 1918-1945

The French ministry of foreign affairs is located at 37 Quai d'Orsay. The building in which it is housed, situated next door to the Palais Bourbon, was designed by the architect Lacornée. It was constructed during the reign of Louis Philippe in the 1840s, but was not occupied until 1853, after the fall of the Orleanist monarch. The move to the Quai d'Orsay included a transfer of the ministerial archives, a service which had become an official part of the ministry in 1822 when the ministry had taken up residence on the rue Neuve des Capucines.[3] Apart from one notably turbulent period in recent history, the ministère des affaires étrangères has remained on the Quai d'Orsay ever since its installation in 1853. Indeed, it is for that reason that the address has become as synonymous with the foreign ministry as the Elysée palace with the president of the Republic, or Downing Street with the English prime minister.[4]

Only once in modern memory has the ministry abandoned the Quai d'Orsay. In the middle of June 1940, confronted by Germany's stunning military advances across France, the cabinet of Paul Reynaud decided to sue for an armistice. Premier Reynaud then promptly resigned, recommending to President Lebrun that Marshal Pétain be asked to form a new government — the last, as it happened, of the Third Republic. One month later a parliamentary assembly, hastily convened at Vichy, voted to confer extraordinary powers upon Pétain, the new head of a new French state. At the same time, in June-July 1940, Charles de Gaulle established himself in London at the head of "Free France", a concept which gradually led to widespread de facto recognition of his "government".

Vichy, the capital of unoccupied France, soon witnessed an attempt to resume French diplomatic relations under the auspices of Pétain and Paul Baudouin, the first of the marshal's foreign ministers. Installed in the Hôtel du Parc at Vichy, but deprived of its Paris-based archives, the ministry tried to maintain the fiction of an independent foreign policy, but with rapidly faltering conviction. Baudouin, for his part, lasted only four months before being replaced by Pierre-Etienne Flandin and, in his turn, Admiral Darlan, followed by Pierre Laval. By the summer of 1944, when Laval's political career ended with his arrest, the number of states with which Vichy retained at least nominal relations had dropped to twenty-two.

Precisely the opposite pattern prevailed in the case of Free France, certainly after the creation of the Comité National Français in September 1941. De Gaulle's first two "commissioners" for foreign affairs were Maurice Dejean and René Pleven. The latter was succeeded by René Massigli who served as commissioner (1943-1944) for the Comité Français de la Libération Nationale, that uneasy, Algiers-based coalition which sought to harness de Gaulle's supporters with those of General Henri Giraud. It was in September 1944 that Massigli was succeeded by Georges Bidault, the first post-Liberation foreign minister and the man thus called upon to supervise the return of the ministry to the Quai d'Orsay.

Quai d'Orsay Before the Reforms of 1907

At the turn of the twentieth century the French foreign ministry was still functioning on a modest scale and still reflecting the assumptions and traditions of nineteenth-century diplomatic practice. The birth of the Third Republic in 1870 had done very little to alter the customs or the organization of the ministry. Indeed, the foreign office continued to operate along lines which had been established early in the century under the Restoration and July monarchies.

The ministerial brain center remained concentrated within the three principal bureaus which were supervised directly by the minister himself. These included his own personal cabinet of handpicked advisers, the office which handled the dispatch and receipt of all communications between Paris and the missions abroad, and finally the Bureau du protocole.[5] The operational apparatus which provided information to this brain center was organized bilaterally: first, a Direction des affaires politiques (engaging the diplomatic service), and second, a Direction des affaires commerciales (engaging the consular service). Both directorates, it should be noted, were organized internally into subsections determined by areas of geographical responsibility. Finally, and complementing the executive and operational branches, the ministry had two administrative divisions, one for Archives and Chancery, the other for Funds and Accounting.

This bureaucratically simple ministry was disturbed with increasing frequency in the twenty-year period prior to 1900, beginning with the reforms initiated by the Freycinet ministry in 1880. To what has been called the brain center were added three new services, one for personnel matters, one

7

for relations with the press, and one for the ciphering and deciphering of coded communications. The operational services in the ministry were enlarged by means of certain additions to the political affairs directorate: first, a new Service du contentieux (claims), second, three new geographical sous-sections (North America, South America, Far East) which were designed to facilitate the work of the two original sections, Nord and Midi.[6] Finally, the administrative machinery was overhauled by fusing into a single division the services provided by Archives, Funds and Accounting.

Even a cursory survey such as this can not fail to read the signs of expansion, the trend toward specialization, within the French foreign ministry. Attention already was being paid, however modestly at first, to matters bearing on press and public opinion, international law, and more sophisticated communications systems. At the same time, the changes made within the political affairs directorate suggest a growing awareness of Asia on the one hand, and the western hemisphere on the other. Nevertheless, in 1900, the political and commercial directorates still operated as if their professional interests were entirely distinct, one from the other; and this in turn meant that the diplomatic and consular services continued to function independently, responsible to different authorities and bereft of arrangements for the exchange of personnel. Limitations such as these clearly restricted both the functions and the resources of the foreign ministry. Its Paris-based personnel did not number much more than 100 members at the turn of the century, and its annual budget was normally far too small and politically inconsequential to provoke much interest from the legislature. There was still no provision for a standing committee on foreign affairs in either the Chamber or the Senate, nor was that a subject which often preoccupied those committees which were in place by 1900.[7] What is more, there was some reason to wonder just at that moment about the kind of future that might be in store for the French foreign ministry. Several recent presidents had been determined to uphold the constitutional laws of 1875, laws which had entrusted to the head of state a very central role in the conduct of foreign affairs. Such had been the position taken by Jules Grévy (1879-1887), Sadi Carnot (1887-1894) and Félix Faure (1895-1899). In the uncompromising words of Grévy, "Je ne permets à personne... de diriger deux choses: la Guerre et les Affaires étrangères."[8]

Quai d'Orsay, 1907-1920

Its future uncertain in 1900, the ministry of foreign affairs negotiated the next twenty years of its own history with imagination and vigor, at least from the bureaucrat's point of view. By 1920 the minister and his cabinet colleagues had managed to wrestle away most of the president's prerogatives in foreign affairs. Through parliament, the ministry had acquired what customarily were two sympathetic and supportive foreign affairs committees, one in the Chamber, the other in the Senate. Its administrative staff in Paris alone had more than doubled, as had its annual budget;[9] and the ministry was well on the way toward its own industrial revolution as pens, carriages and gaslamps slowly gave way to the typewriter, duplicating machines and telephones, electric lights and automobiles.

This process of change and adjustment was occasioned in part by prevailing social and cultural trends in the early twentieth century, and in part by the rude and particular exigencies thrown up by World War One. The changes which are to be discussed here may be grouped into three principal categories: those which reflected the steady infusion of economic calculations into diplomatic practice; those which spoke to the growing importance of informational-propaganda work at home and abroad; and those which evidenced a greater appreciation of new and more sophisticated administrative means of keeping abreast of all the changes being induced elsewhere.

1. Economics

The clearest sign that economic considerations had acquired unprecedented recognition came in the reform that fused the hitherto distinct directorates of political and commercial affairs. The result, in 1907, was the new Direction des affaires politiques et commerciales. Although the diplomatic and consular services remained separate, the constant and increasing interplay between the political and commercial interests of the state was at last being formally recognized. Moreover, whereas the system of geographic subdivisions was retained within this single directorate — principally for Europe, Levant, Asia, and America — each sous-section was now to be equipped with a team of commercial, financial and legal advisers. Thus the reform of 1907 meant a fusion of potentially competing systems of organization — one by subject, the other by geography — while it gave the margin of advantage to the thematic or subject system.[10]

The nature of this compromise confirmed the elevated status of commercial matters within the ministry, just as it promised an important role to the newly created corps of commercial and financial counselors. It was also in 1907 that yet another department emerged within the ministry, that entitled Affaires administratives et des Unions internationales. This department assumed responsibility for an array of diverse subjects, ranging from international unions, health standards and police regulations to international conventions on navigation, copyright laws and postal traffic.[11] Although these sorts of activities predictably declined with the outbreak of war in 1914, the change in attitude which they expressed certainly did not. Before long, the expressly economic demands of the war prompted the Quai d'Orsay to institute a <u>Bureau des services économiques</u>, and a companion <u>Bureau des études financières</u>.

The pattern continued after the war. A decree of May 1919 accorded to the political and commercial affairs directorate a new <u>Sous-direction des relations commerciales</u>, a subdivision exclusively concerned with the commercial problems of war-torn Europe.[12] Furthermore, the recent wedding of political and commercial affairs within the ministry greatly facilitated the process of collaboration between the Quai d'Orsay and the ministry of Commerce. These two ministries were able to work well together in their jointly sponsored <u>Office national du Commerce extérieur</u>, an agency which provided the French business community with commercial intelligence on markets and economic conditions abroad.[13] They also cooperated with the <u>Comité consultatif du Commerce</u>, a creation of 1919 which included representatives from other ministries, notably Finance, Agriculture and Public Instruction.

2. Propaganda

Just as the reforms of 1907 expressed the foreign ministry's rapidly developing interest in economics, so they also reflected a growing appreciation of propaganda. By then it was already clear that the voting public, at home and abroad, had to be informed, or conditioned, in ways which their elected governors deemed to be in the best interests of the state. Consequently, to the small press service which had been attached to the minister's <u>cabinet</u> by the Freycinet reforms of 1880 came another of the <u>1907</u> reforms. A <u>Bureau des communications</u> was created for the purpose of monitoring everything that was being written and read in the domestic and foreign press, and then for conveying the government's point of view to receptive, sometimes venal, press circles.

The war, of course, only reinforced the government's self-perceived need. With it came, in 1915, the establishment of the <u>Maison de la Presse</u> and an accompanying resolution to wage a war of propaganda that would be as intense and as ruthless as the war in the trenches. For the next three years this agency and its successors, the <u>Service de l'information à l'étranger</u> and the <u>Commissariat général de l'information et de la propagande,</u> coordinated the foreign ministry's war of words with the enemy.[14] While one branch of this service supervised all relations between journalists and the government at large, another branch monitored the foreign press, and yet another arranged for the distribution abroad of suitably francophile books, films, brochures and photographs. This latter endeavor, it should be stressed, was not simply a product of the war. Cultural propaganda of this sort was very reminiscent of work that had been undertaken by the prewar Bureau des Ecoles et des Oeuvres françaises à l'étranger. This agency, founded in 1909 as a companion to the Bureau des communications, had been charged with the promotion of French culture and civilization throughout the world — principally through the provision of educational, medical, cultural, religious or charitable services. It is here, for instance, that one might be able to determine the nature of relations between the French government and bodies such as the Alliance française or the Comité France-Amérique.[15]

3. Administration

The expansion of services within the foreign ministry meant, as a consequence, an expansion of the supporting bureaucracy. The widening geopolitical responsibilities of twentieth-century diplomacy, combined with the mounting demands of economics and propaganda respectively, seemed to necessitate a revised administrative structure. The 1907 reforms responded to this need as well. The Service du Personnel, created in 1880 and enlarged in 1891-92, was again restructured and its functions expanded. Within the decade it had acquired responsibility for all hiring and promotion within the diplomatic and consular services, as well as for all salary negotiations. So critical was its influence to become on the efficiency and morale of the ministry that it was made an explicitly autonomous service in July 1918 — theoretically, at least, removed from the clutches of the minister's own powerful cabinet.[16]

The reforms of 1907 addressed other problems. The Service des traducteurs and the Service géographique were both enlarged in keeping with their steadily increasing workload at the ministry; and the Sous-direction des Archives was reorganized in order to permit it to become an efficient reference and research service for contemporary affairs instead of simply a cataloguing department for future historians. Three years later, in 1910, the ministry created a Service des affaires militaires, an advisory body on military matters and, ironically, an early casualty of World War One. In 1912 there were some early experiments with the office of a Secrétaire d'Etat, a deputy foreign minister; and in 1915 came the extremely important introduction of the Secrétariat Général, an office which was to become in time the highest-ranking permanent civil service post in the foreign ministry.[17]

Quai d'Orsay, 1920-1940

The interwar period saw a continuation of these prewar and wartime trends, both with respect to the evolution of diplomatic function as well as to the growth of a compatible administrative structure. At the outset, attention should be drawn to the fact that one key part of the ministry's development was almost complete. It was in June 1918 that the four geographical sous-directions of the political and commercial affairs directorate were formally defined as Europe, Asie-Océanie, Afrique, and Amérique. Seven years later, in 1925, the third subdivision was renamed Afrique et Levant after some of the issues surrounding the Syrian and Palestinian mandates had been resolved and after the conclusion of the Lausanne treaty with Turkey.[18] Similarly, it was in the wake of the war and the peace settlement that another innovation appeared within the political and commercial affairs directorate. This was the Service français de la Société des Nations, the department which was to assume responsibility for handling France's relations with the new League of Nations. Less dramatic but worthy of note was the creation in 1926 of the special office of Conseiller pour les affaires religieuses, a post created for Louis Canet from which he could supervise the now-resumed relations with the Vatican. As for the other postwar changes within the ministry, reference can be made to the economic, propaganda and administrative criteria used earlier.

1. Economics

The economic dislocation caused by World War One was responsible for a series of postwar developments within the French foreign ministry. The Office des biens et intérêts privés, an agency charged with sorting out French property claims in former enemy territory, was created by a fusion of the wartime Bureau des services économiques and the Bureau des études financières.[19] This Office in turn appears to have been replaced by the Service des Réparations et de la Ruhr, which operated under the directorate of political and commercial affairs between 1923 and 1927. At the same time, the newly created Sous-direction des relations commerciales continued to function throughout the interwar period, as did the older Sous-direction des Affaires administratives et des Unions internationales. Little wonder that Jules Cambon should have remarked in 1926: "De tous les ressorts qui mettent en mouvement la machine de l'Etat les intérêts matériels sont devenus les plus puissants et ce sont eux également qui déterminent les rapports des nations entre elles."[20] Nor was this a conclusion reached only by members of the foreign ministry. Taking their lead from recent wartime experiences, other ministries demonstrated a

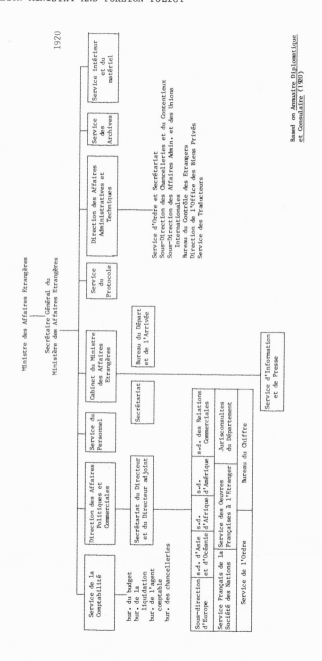

1920

Ministre des Affaires Etrangères

Secrétaire Général du
Ministère des Affaires Etrangères

Service de la Comptabilité
- bur. du budget
- bur. de la liquidation
- bur. de l'agent comptable
- bur. des chancelleries

Direction des Affaires Politiques et Commerciales

Secrétariat du Directeur et du Directeur adjoint

Sous-direction d'Europe
s.d. d'Asie et d'Océanie
s.d. d'Afrique et d'Amérique
s.d. des Relations Commerciales

Service Français de la Société des Nations
Service des Oeuvres Françaises à l'Etranger
Jurisconsultes du Département

Service de l'Ordre
Bureau du Chiffre

Service d'Information et de Presse

Service du Personnel

Cabinet du Ministre des Affaires Etrangères

Secrétariat

Bureau du Départ et de l'Arrivée

Service du Protocole

Direction des Affaires Administratives et Techniques

Service d'Ordre et Secrétariat
Sous-Direction des Chancelleries et du Contentieux
Sous-Direction des Affaires Admin. et des Unions Internationales
Bureau du Contrôle des Etrangers
Direction de l'Office des Biens Privés
Service des Traducteurs

Service des Archives

Service intérieur et du matériel

Based on Annuaire Diplomatique et Consulaire (1920)

13

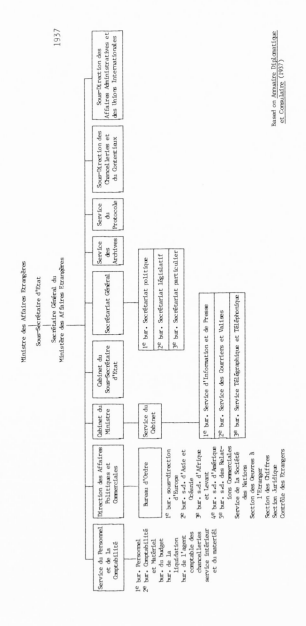

1937

Ministre des Affaires Etrangères

Sous-Secrétaire d'Etat

Secrétaire Général du
Ministère des Affaires Etrangères

| Service du Personnel et de la Comptabilité | Direction des Affaires Politiques et Commerciales | Cabinet du Ministre | Cabinet du Sous-Secrétaire d'Etat | Secrétariat Général | Service des Archives | Service du Protocole | Sous-Direction des Chancelleries et du Contentieux | Sous-Direction des Affaires Administratives et des Unions Internationales |

1e bur. Personnel
2e bur. Comptabilité et Matériel
bur. du budget
bur. de la liquidation
bur. de l'agent comptable des chancelleries
service intérieur et du matériel

Bureau d'Ordre

1e bur. sous-direction d'Europe
2e bur. s.d. d'Asie et Océanie
3e bur. s.d. d'Afrique et Levant
4e bur. s.d. d'Amérique
5e bur. s.d. des Relations Commerciales
Service de la Société des Nations
Section des Oeuvres à l'Etranger
Section des Chiffres
Section Juridique
Contrôle des Etrangers

Service du Cabinet

1e bur. Service d'Information et de Presse
2e bur. Service des Courriers et Valises
3e bur. Service Télégraphique et Téléphonique

1e bur. Secrétariat politique
2e bur. Secrétariat législatif
3e bur. Secrétariat particulier

Based on Annuaire Diplomatique et Consulaire (1937)

14

willingness to develop their own foreign services in concert
with the professional diplomats at the Quai d'Orsay. One
thinks, for example, of the Direction des finances
extérieures at the ministry of Finance or, more prominently,
the Conseil National Economique, a broadly based council
which was attached to the premier's office and funded by the
ministry of Labor.[21]

2. Propaganda

In a similar vein, the ministry of Education created a
Service universitaire des relations culturelles avec
l'étranger, an agency which was able to complement the
foreign ministry's work in the field of cultural propaganda.
To that end the Quai d'Orsay's prewar Bureau des Ecoles et
des Oeuvres françaises à l'étranger was renamed and
administratively upgraded to the Service des Oeuvres
françaises à l'étranger. The latter in turn was subdivided
into four essentially self-descriptive sections:
universitaires des écoles, artistique et littéraire, tourisme
et des sports, and oeuvres diverses.[22] The end of the war
also brought a revision of the ministerial press service. A
new Service d'Information et de Presse was fashioned out of
the various wartime agencies and placed directly under the
supervision of the Secretary-General.[23] Charged with
responsibility for all ministerial liaisons with the press,
French and foreign, and in particular for the official
defense of the 1919 peace settlement, this important new
service had acquired a very large staff of 80 members by
1921.[24] It was this service, or more accurately its internal
section d'analyse de la presse étrangère, which prepared the
important in-house publications: the Bulletins quotidiens
(and hebdomadaires) de la presse étrangère, and the Recueil
des documents étrangers.
It is worth noting that the Information service was
expected to do far more than merely monitor the press and
perform anodyne public relations functions. It was to
continue, if in more subtle form, the government's wartime
struggle on behalf of the "national interest." That is why
the ministry's annual budget always made provision for a
fonds secrets and a fonds spéciaux pour dépenses à
l'étranger, funds which could be distributed by the
Information service in exchange for favors rendered.[25] Some
of these monies are said to have gone to individual
journalists, others to editors and owners of newspapers,
still others to the French news service Agence Havas.
Indeed, Paul Allard claims that the Quai d'Orsay enjoyed a
secure "mainmise" on the Agence Havas from the moment the
government appointed Louis Rollin as Inspector of the
agency's foreign services in 1930. That appointment,
combined with healthy government funding and special

transmission privileges, is said to have given the head of the Information service almost veto power in the appointment of Havas correspondents.[26]   Given the fact that the French press relied heavily upon Agence Havas, it takes no great leap of imagination to see the potential importance of any government interference in the affairs of this key supplier of information.

More dramatic and overt was the creation in October 1936 of a Commission interministérielle pour l'Action et l'Information françaises à l'étranger. This was not simply a device of the foreign ministry, although the Quai d'Orsay clearly exercised a powerful influence within it. Rather, it was a large and unwieldy body with representatives from at least a dozen other ministries, from the premier's office, as well as from each of the ministerial cabinets. It was this step, however, which permitted the creation in December 1938 of a small secretariat for the commission, and then in July 1939 of a Commissariat général à l'Information. This new institution was entrusted to the playwright and erstwhile Inspector-general of diplomatic posts, Jean Giraudoux. With a single stroke of a pen he became responsible for a host of diverse informational services — from all public and private broadcasting agencies in France to the very particular functions carried out by groups such as the Service du contrôle des films, or the Service d'information et de propagande économique.[27] Indeed, all through the phony war period this Commissariat was a principal force in the French propaganda effort, and remained so even after it was itself placed under the direction of the new ministry of Information in April 1940.

3. Administration

Most of the administrative changes which occurred in the foreign ministry after 1920 were extensions of prewar or wartime developments. The office of Secrétaire d'Etat was filled much more frequently after the war than before it, although not on a consistent basis; and of course each deputy minister brought with him a small entourage of advisers who were akin to those in the minister's own cabinet. The latter enjoyed a healthy rate of growth in the interwar years, a prestigious and influential circle of both professional and amateur diplomatic advisers whom the minister had invited to serve on his personal staff.[28]   In 1937 this cabinet comprised one directeur (Laugier), one chef (Rochat), one chef-adjoint (Fouques-Duparc), together with the head and the deputy head of the minister's personal secretariat, and three attachés who had been seconded to the minister's staff. In addition to this team of 8 members, the Service du cabinet had 4 officers, the Service d'Information et de Presse had 21, the Service télégraphique et téléphonique had 2 and the

Bureau des courriers et valises had 7, for a grand total of 42 members. By contrast, the cabinet of the Secretary of State (Viénot) in 1937 had only 6 members — including Armand Bérard, the chef de cabinet, and Pierre Bertaux, the chef-adjoint.[29]

Three other significant administrative changes were effected between the two world wars. First came the creation of the Inspection des postes diplomatiques et consulaires. This post, introduced in May 1920, was responsible for supervising the operations of all the diplomatic and consular missions abroad, from their budget and security provisions to their archival facilities and allocation of office furnishings.[30] Second, it was in 1925 that two already important branches of the ministry were fused to make the Service du Personnel et de la Comptabilité.[31] Strengthened by this merger, and in the capable hands of Louis de Robien, its longtime director, the Personnel service went on to enjoy an even greater influence in the determination of every professional career within the diplomatic and consular services. Its growth was paralleled, though certainly not equalled, by the eventual appearance of a small secretariat for the Secrétaire Général. This, the third development, had its roots in the period between 1915 and 1920 when the office of Secretary-General was gradually transformed from temporary to permanent post. Such at least was the theory. But in fact the post only became permanent in the spring of 1925, after a three-year interval during which the office had remained unfilled and unrecognized by four successive governments. Partly because of this quite involuntary leave of absence, and partly because of resistance within the ministry, it was not until the early 1930s that the Secretary-General (Berthelot) had managed to lay claim to his own, small secretariat. Even in 1937 it had only 5 members, slightly outnumbered by the personal staff of the Secretary of State and positively overshadowed by the numbers of advisers in the minister's cabinet.[32]

Quai d'Orsay at Work (circa 1937)

The foregoing, to use a phrase from Keynes, is a bit like trying to tether a broomstick. One is confronted by constant movement as jurisdictions, functions, and personnel change according to some powerful if uncertain rhythm. Yet this evolution of "system" within the foreign ministry is potentially very important to the historical researcher. After all, he is the chief beneficiary of all the attempts since 1907 to devise systematic and predictable procedures, for the archives in which he works are essentially receptacles for the ordered remains of the past. The first thing he must learn, therefore, is how the system was designed to work. The second thing he will know by instinct,

namely that systems can malfunction and thus may defy
prediction and contradict assumption.[33]

The following hypothetical example will illustrate how
the system should have worked in 1937. The ambassador in
Washington has forwarded information derived from the
Americans on Japan's expansionist plans in the Far East. His
letter is sent directly to the service du cabinet du ministre
where copies are made for immediate distribution within the
ministry. Unlike the British system, where incoming reports
begin at the bottom of the administrative ladder and work
their way upward toward the minister, the French system is
activated from the top. In this case, the minister (Delbos),
the Secretary-General (Léger), the Secretary of State
(Viénot), and the head of the press service (Comert), all
receive copies of the ambassador's report.[34] At the same
time, additional copies are transmitted to the heads of the
sous-directions for America and Asia certainly, and quite
possibly for Europe as well. Each of these geographic
subdivisions is expected to forward its comments and
suggestions to the director of Affaires politiques et
commerciales (Bargeton). The latter may also expect to hear
from other branches of his directorate, for it is likely that
the head of the minister's cabinet (Rochat) will have asked
for copies to be sent to the Service de la Société des
Nations and possibly to the Section juridique. Armed with
the opinions of these his principal subordinates, Bargeton is
then expected to assemble a comprehensive brief for the
benefit of his immediate superior, Alexis Léger, the
Secretary-General. Léger thus advised, by his own
secretariat as well as by the director Bargeton, will then be
called upon to advise the minister on any response or course
of action that may seem appropriate. Delbos, in his turn,
cognizant of the ambassador's report from the moment of its
arrival and now amply counseled by his personal staff and
deputy minister as well as by Léger, is now free to act upon
that advice or to seek further guidance from the council of
ministers presided over by Premier Blum.[35]

Technical Services

The connection between these ministerial services and
the preceding discussion will not be immediately apparent.
However, there is a reason for the order which has been
adopted here, for the technical services include the Service
des archives; and it is with this service and its association
with the functioning of the French foreign ministry that this
section will close.

Apart from the library branch, also administered by the
archival service, the technical services included some of the
following departments. There were the staffs of the Service
géographique and the Service des traducteurs, the former

mainly attached to the various sous-sections of the political and commercial affairs directorate, the latter to the Service d'Information et de Presse or to the Service des Chiffres.

In 1937 the director of the code service was M. Bradier. Under him worked a staff of 25 cryptographers and as many stenographers, a staff large enough to handle a daily traffic of some 200-300 coded telegrams, some of them several pages in length. Furthermore, concealed within this service was a top-secret operation referred to as the Service technique. These were the men charged with intercepting and deciphering foreign telegrams and radio communications, and with delivering the translated contents — known as les Verts — to the President of the Republic, the premier, the foreign minister, and often the war minister. This clandestine work, it is worth noting, was done with the active assistance of the Service officiel (in the case of telegrams) and the Service d'écoute et d'analyse (in the case of radio signals) of the ministry of Postes, Télégraphes, Téléphones.[36]

Also included among the technical services within the ministry was the accounting department of the Service du Personnel et de la Comptabilité, and the Section juridique of the political and commercial affairs directorate. The services of the legal section, headed by M. Fromageot, were at the disposal of any branch of the ministry which required advice on matters of international law or on the compatability of such law with the constitution and legal practices of the Third Republic.[37] The director, using the parttime services of two law professors at the University of Paris — notably Jules Basdevant — is reputed to have been a critically important adviser within the ministry; indeed, one contemporary has described his influence as "second only to that of the Secretary General."[38]

Of even greater interest to the historian is the Service des archives and the attendant standing Commission des Archives Diplomatiques. To this service the contemporary diplomat looked for reference assistance in the preparation of briefs and memoranda. The historian, in his turn, looks toward the same service for help and advice in his reconstruction of the past. Regrettably, there are now limitations on what the archival service can do for us — thanks in part to the damages sustained by the archives in the course of World War Two, and in part to the failure of postwar governments to secure for the archives various collections of papers which had been carted off by retiring senior functionaries. And the events of 1940-1944 took their own heavy toll, especially on the records deriving from the period between 1935 and 1939. What was not deliberately burned in Paris in May 1940, or destroyed off Bordeaux in the vessel La Salle in June, was left to the attentions of the German occupation forces. The result of these ministrations was the dispatch to Germany of approximately 5000 cartons of documents from the French foreign ministry: principally the collections relating to the 1919 peace settlement, the work of the ministry's League of Nations' service, and, interestingly, to the work of the Service des Oeuvres françaises à l'étranger. Moreover, what remained of the diplomatic archives after this enforced exodus suffered still further damage in the course of a fire at the Quai d'Orsay during the Liberation of Paris in August 1944.[39]

Damages inflicted in the 1940s have a painful and inescapable relevance to researchers in the 1980s. Among other things, they help to explain why French record collections for the interwar period have remained closed to private scholars for so long. In the worst cases, the documentation was simply destroyed, gone forever without trace or copy. Such, tragically, was the case of many of the internal memoranda, the briefs and recommendations sent through the appropriate ministerial channels to the minister. Without rich and extensive collections of papers from the estates of the foreign ministers, and of their closest advisers, it will be forever difficult to determine with confidence the nature of the information and advice upon which the minister's policy was predicated. And the task becomes even more difficult when it is a matter of assessing the comparative importance of rival opinions within the ministry. In the latter case one can see at a glance the potential importance of papers assembled by someone like Massigli, or Bargeton, or Léger.

The picture is much brighter in the case of the incoming and outgoing dispatches. Anything that was sent into or from the ministry was supposed to have been registered in the Bureau d'Ordre of the political and commercial affairs directorate. Hence, any documents that might have disappeared in the course of the Second World War are theoretically traceable by means of the surviving registers in Paris. And it was by this method, terribly time-consuming, that the postwar archival service has managed to track down copies of missing documents in the embassy and legation archives across Europe.[40]

Diplomatic Documents

The results of these recovery efforts have been twofold. The central archives in Paris have been reconstituted, to the extent that this will ever be possible; and the salvaged documentation has been, or currently is being, organized, catalogued and prepared for the use of researchers. Second, this process of reconstitution has permitted the near-completion of a task accepted in 1961 by the Commission de Publication des Documents relatifs aux origines de la guerre, 1939-1945. Two years later, in 1963, the commission, presided over by the late Professor Renouvin, released the first volume of the published collection entitled Documents Diplomatiques Français.

This collection is divided into two series which together cover the period from July 1932 to September 1939. Having consigned the years 1930-1931 to what it regarded as a period still structured by the 1919 settlements, the commission chose to open its First Series in July 1932, in the wake of the Lausanne conference, and to close it at the height of the Ethiopian crisis in December 1935. Eight volumes have made their appearance in this series to date, taking us to 15 January 1935. The Second Series (1936-1939) currently comprises thirteen volumes — up to January 1939 — with a remaining two or three volumes expected. No comparable series as yet exists for the period from 1919 to 1931.

Each volume of the French diplomatic documents is very handsomely executed. Typically, a volume will cover a three- to four-month period and will contain from over 300 to over 500 separate documents. All volumes are organized along both topical and geographical lines, with helpful if not flawless cross-references. So too all volumes have a detailed opening index furnishing the date, provenance, and destination of each numbered document as well as a brief content description. In addition, at the back of each volume there is an alphabetical name index, including very brief identifications of the personalities mentioned, and another alphabetical index for questions of international law. Altogether, these volumes constitute an extremely valuable collection, the more so for the editors' willingness to assist readers by means of explanatory footnotes.

Even more to their credit, the publication commissioners have defined documents diplomatiques in an appropriately broad sense. Whether this was occasioned by the lacunae in the diplomatic archives or by commendable insight really does not matter. What is important is the fact that each volume has drawn upon the resources of many ministerial archives — including those of finance, colonies, and the respective armed forces — as well as upon private papers and upon the archives of the National Assembly and the Senate. In short, these published "diplomatic" documents offer a range of insights into contemporary appreciations of economic, financial and military matters. How thoroughly the editors have canvassed the available documentation at the Quai d'Orsay and elsewhere, and how judiciously they have selected those documents for publication, will remain a subject for scholarly investigation and debate for years to come. What warrants immediate recognition is this. The published documents represent but a small proportion of the reconstituted archives. The fact is that, despite the undeniable wartime damages, the diplomatic archives are much more voluminous than most scholars have come to expect.

Diplomatic Corps

The commission's decision to work from a broad definition of diplomacy is very central to the interpretive thrust of this essay. All of the preceding remarks have in common an attempt to establish a series of departure points from which diplomatic history may be approached. The more traditional perspectives remain open to us, the studies centered on the foreign ministers or their ambassadors; and they ought not elicit the derision of critics or apologies from the practitioner. But researchers may also wish to explore less travelled paths: the role which international law and its interpreters have come to play in the conduct of a nation's foreign policy; the role played and the motivations at work in the activities of propagandists in the press and cultural services; the parts played and the influence exerted by the ministry's military advisers, or its financial counselors, or its commercial attachés, or by codebreakers in the Service des Chiffres. Whether or not all of these approaches are currently practicable, the foregoing discussion may alert readers to some of the theoretical possibilities and also remind them of the range of activities in which the French foreign ministry was engaged in the period between the two world wars.

But little provision so far has been made for the diplomatic corps itself, an omission which would antagonize only those "social" historians who are prepared to countenance the study of elites. In this corps one finds a group of men who had emerged from a common if not identical process of social and political formation, who were imbued with a universally expressed belief in service to the state, but who were understandably subject to all of the petty anxieties, pressures and ambitions which shape the politics of large bureaucracies. In other words, one has a right to suppose that next to matters of career advancement, the larger issues of state often may have paled in comparison. By the same token, if it is important to know how a bureaucracy was designed to function, it is worthwhile asking who, in fact, had the ear of the minister. Similarly, it may be ventured that questions about workloads and staffing patterns are as interesting and relevant to studies of the past as they are to our contemplation of the present. In this connection it is worth recalling Armand Bérard's picture of a foreign minister too busy, or preoccupied, to read telegrams of more than three lines.[41] The members of his cabinet, accordingly, became masters of the précis, an accomplishment of sorts but only arguably a sensible way to exploit the talents of professional diplomats. In any event, in view of considerations such as these, there is something to be said for keeping the diplomats in diplomatic history. What follows, of course, is but a cryptic introduction to la Carrière.

22

FOREIGN MINISTRY AND FOREIGN POLICY

In the 1930s the Ministry of Foreign Affairs employed some 1600 people, a small staff compared to the 6000 employees in the ministry of Justice, or the 18,000 in Public Works, and positively miniscule compared to the 90,000 in Finance or the 150,000 in Post and Telegraphs.[42]   Moreover, of these 1600 public servants something like two-thirds of them were employed as secretaries, typists, doormen and other support staff.   That left between 500 and 600 professional staff serving in the still discrete diplomatic and consular services.   Altogether, including the approximately 100 professional advisers on periodic loan to the Quai d'Orsay from the justice, finance, commerce, and national defense ministries, there were some 230 professional staff stationed in Paris.[43]   The remainder served abroad, customarily in one of the 14 embassies — nine of which were in Europe — the 37 legations, 8 general consulates, or in one of the many minor consulates around the world.[44]

Most of the men who served in these missions abroad were there in their capacity as professional diplomats, the products of an extremely intense veting process.   The majority had studied at the "school for diplomats", the Ecole libre des sciences politiques, where many of the professors were members of the foreign ministry, and where the combination of high standards and high fees could be used to attract the academically gifted sons of affluent middle class families.   From there, many a graduate had gone on to write the stiff and highly competitive entrance examinations for the diplomatic service, the grand concours, in which over half of the candidates normally failed.[45]   The successful aspirants then served a three-month probationary period at the ministry before being subjected to another round of examinations which, like the first, stressed a knowledge of international law, geography and economics as well as of linguistics and diplomatic history.[46]   Only after the successful completion of this series of examinations, including a succession of oral interviews arranged by the Service du Personnel, was the new member of the service given a junior posting abroad or within the central administration at the Quai d'Orsay.

In the consular service a career began with the petit concours, a similarly devised but reputedly less rigorous entrance examination.   The very fact that it was a different examination, a different competition, was an expression of the contemporary view that the two services were and should remain distinct.   Indeed, they were not combined until 1945. In the period between the two world wars these services operated along parallel lines, both under the supervision of the Direction des affaires politiques et commerciales. Having begun at the rank of attaché, the novice diplomat progressed from third-, to second-, to first-class secretary, before becoming counselor and eventually, perhaps, minister.

The consular aspirant began as a Chancery attaché, moved from vice-consul to chancellor, and then from third-, to second-, to first-class consul, before becoming consul-general. On average, it took the diplomat eighteen years to attain the rank of plenipotentiary minister, and the consular official thirteen years to become a consul-general.[47] Until the respective ranks of counselor and consul-general were reached, there were very few crossovers or exchanges between the two services. Only after having reached the rank of consul-general was it technically possible for a member of the consular service to transfer to the diplomatic service at the rank of minister first or second class.[48] That, however, was not a common occurrence. Not more than 1 in 10 members of the consular service ever secured the rank of minister.[49] Clearly, the line was not intended to be crossed with ease or regularity.

As uncommon as it was to find a man of consular background at the head of an embassy or legation, this does not mean that French diplomats abroad were invariably products of the grand concours. Indeed, there were some very obvious exceptions. By the mid 1930s there were some 34 commercial attachés who reported directly to the ministry of Commerce, just under 50 military attachés who communicated directly with one of the three service ministries, and a handful of financial attachés — including Jacques Rueff and Emmanuel Monick — who reported directly to the director of the finance ministry's Mouvement général des fonds.[50] What is more, not all of the ambassadorial appointments were reserved for men who had made a profession of the diplomatic service. At least one had even gone to a man of consular background. Such was the case of Paul Naggiar, a member of the consular service between 1908 and 1927 before he became minister in Belgrade in 1932, in Prague in 1935, and ambassador to the Soviet Union in 1938. Léon Noel found himself ambassador to Warsaw between 1935 and 1939, following a long career in the Conseil d'Etat and a short period of service in the cabinet du ministre at the Quai d'Orsay. Léon Bérard, Vichy's ambassador to the Vatican between 1940 and 1944, had been a deputy, senator and sometime cabinet minister in the 1920s and 1930s before he received a special appointment to negotiate legal recognition of General Franco's regime in Spain in 1939. So too it was an extensive parliamentary and commercial background upon which Albert Sarraut had to draw during his ambassadorship to Turkey in 1925-1926. What these few examples suggest, therefore, is that foreign ministers were not obliged by law or custom to make their ambassadorial appointments from within professional diplomatic circles. That is hardly surprising, for the ministers themselves were politicians, not diplomats. Indeed, many were to assume office after only the briefest apprenticeship in international affairs. Surveying the range of foreign ministers who had been in office between 1870 and 1931, F.L. Schuman concluded: "In terms of vocational background and interest, twenty of the thirty-seven were lawyers or jurists, eight were primarily journalists, six were professors, one was an engineer...one a chemist...and one a business man."[51]

Another point is worth bearing in mind. Just as service through the foreign ministry was not restricted to those who had written the diplomatic examinations, neither was it necessary to choose between a post at the Quai d'Orsay and one of the previously discussed missions abroad. French diplomats could be seconded for service in other ministries, notably that of Commerce; and they were frequently called upon to serve in the administration of the French mandates. Just as commonly, they were attached to international bodies such as the Reparations Commission, or the Conference of Ambassadors, or they were posted to Geneva for service with the French delegation to the League of Nations, or with the League secretariat.[52] Such postings, especially if they involved living abroad, are said to have been received with some enthusiasm by French diplomats. This was partly because foreign postings promised substantial pecuniary benefits and partly because they opened some avenue for professional advancement within a strictly regulated system. In the first case, the salaries paid to those on mission abroad were calculated on a gold franc basis, and thus were significantly greater than salaries paid within France in depreciated paper francs. Indeed, the purchasing power of those living abroad could have been twice as great as that of their fellows stationed in Paris.[53] In the second case, service hors cadre combined the assurance of added professional experience beyond the foreign ministry with guaranteed pension and seniority rights within the diplomatic corps. Thus, as a member of a service in which promotion was known to be slow, an ambitious man might choose to advance his career by gaining experience in some of the more novel forms of diplomatic activity.

Foreign Ministry and Parliament

Whereas the material benefits which accrued from the diplomatic service were actually administered through the Service du Personnel, ultimate financial control lay in the hands of parliament. Indeed, all of the attention which has been paid to the nooks and crannies of the foreign ministry ought not cause us to forget the parliamentary character of the Third French Republic. This, too, represents another potentially important dimension of "diplomatic" history. Once again, the following remarks seek to do little more than provide some kind of foundation for more intensive analyses of this theme. For this purpose it is useful to pick up on the recent reference to the emoluments of service. The financial estimates for the foreign ministry were prepared internally by the Service du Personnel et de la Comptabilité, in cooperation with and under the supervision of the finance ministry representative, the Contrôleur des Dépenses Engagées. Once prepared, the projected budget was forwarded to the finance commissions of the Chamber of Deputies and the Senate respectively.

Throughout the interwar period the Chamber of Deputies relied upon the services of a standing committee system, sixteen commissions including one for finance and one for foreign affairs.[54] Each committee had a prescribed membership of 44 deputies and, in the case of the upper house, 36 senators. The finance commission, in both houses, was regarded as being the most influential and hence the most prestigious, since every ministerial budget had to be forwarded for its examination and approval. Each commission was presided over by an elected chairman, the président, but animated by an elected rapporteur d'information; and in the case of the finance commission, there was a series of rapporteurs, each of whom assumed responsibility for one or more ministerial budgets. Included in the work of these officers of the finance commission was the preparation of a supplementary report which described the organization of the ministry in question and, in some cases, the substance and direction of its current policies.[55] So it is that the historian is likely to have a special interest in these rapporteurs, in their exposition before parliament of the foreign ministry's budgetary requirements, as well as the role they played during the in camera meetings of the commission.[56] The same counsel holds true, of course, for the rapporteurs of the commissions des affaires étrangères and for the records of both committees in the parliamentary archives. These rapporteurs, it is worth noting, were at liberty to collect information from any source — including experts in the universities or press circles — a mandate which helped compensate for the fact that these commissions had no powers to subpoena witnesses or documentation.

A limitation as important as this amounts to an interesting comment on the historical development of French foreign policy administration since the turn of the century. The creation in 1902 of a standing committee system in the Chamber, together with the intense interest expressed in foreign policy by parliament during the war years, signaled the steady diminution of the President's role in foreign affairs. At no time was this more in evidence than during the years of the Clemenceau ministry when the not-easily-ignored President Poincaré was left to sputter angrily in neglect. In the words of Maurice Schumann, "le pouvoir théorique du président de la République irresponsable a été absorbé par le pouvoir réel du ministre responsable."[57]

But it would be fair to say that parliament gained less from the reduction of presidential powers than did the executive authority expressed by the cabinet or than the professional advisers in the permanent bureaucracy. While it is true that the foreign affairs committees were capable of marshalling parliamentary opinion against the government — as they did against Briand in 1922 or ten years later against Herriot — as a rule these committees endorsed and supported the work of the ministry. Even more to the point, while parliament could embarrass a government, either in committee or in open session, very, very rarely was it prepared to seize on a foreign issue for the purpose of toppling a ministry.

Part of this may be explained by what has variously been described as the ignorance or indifference of French legislators toward foreign issues. Politics, in descending order of importance, are said to have been municipal, regional, national and finally international. As a consequence, deputies and senators alike were prepared to leave the conduct of the nation's foreign policy to the community of proclaimed experts in the foreign ministry. Ministries could be overthrown, and that with demonstrable frequency and ease, but almost always for domestic political reasons. It is this attitude, one might assume, that explains why less than one percent of all written parliamentary questions were addressed to foreign affairs, or why there was never a single debate on the question of France's role in the Council or the Assembly of the League of Nations.[58]

A markedly different attitude, to be sure, would have required a major revision of parliamentary procedure as it had been laid down either by the constitution or by custom. For example, parliament's role in foreign affairs was forever limited until its committees acquired subpoena powers. Without teeth, the committees faced the unconcealed contempt of those like Premier Millerand who, when asked in 1920 about French support for the White Russians, would only acknowledge "un certain appui, dans certaines limites, à certains moments."[59] Similarly, the legislature's threat of an interpellation, which on domestic matters could occasion the fall of a government, was blunted by the executive's capacity to postpone the debate on the grounds of national security or national interest. Poincaré, as premier in 1923, employed this argument several times in his successful bid to postpone discussion of the Ruhr occupation.[60]

But even more serious constitutional matters had to be faced. The arbitrary powers once enjoyed by the President of the Republic under the constitution of 1875 simply had been transferred by custom to the premier and foreign minister. After 1900 it was they who could withhold from public scrutiny, even knowledge, some of the most important international engagements which had been entered into by the French state.[61] It was another case of public disclosure being judged inimical to the public or national interest, though it seemed to matter little if the argument made sense. In February 1920, for example, a number of deputies complained of one such absurdity. Was it sensible, they asked, for the government to conceal from parliament the terms of the treaty of Sèvres with Turkey, when the full text already had been published in the press?[62] Furthermore, in those cases when the executive did choose to submit treaties for parliamentary ratification — as in the case of the Washington Naval Treaty or the Locarno accords — neither the legislative assemblies nor their commissions possessed any amending powers.[63] In view of such constraints, it is unlikely that French foreign policy in this period ever could be interpreted as a conscious response to the wishes and directives of parliament and its standing committees. Rather, the published and unpublished records of parliament and its commissions are likely to reflect a widely shared set of assumptions among executors, legislators and administrators — basic assumptions about the need for promoting France's political and economic interests abroad, for ensuring her territorial integrity, for enhancing her cultural status within the world community.[64]

This conclusion notwithstanding, one must remain on the alert for the atypical, even the unusual. Herriot's resignation in December 1932, for instance, was occasioned in large part by his failure as foreign minister to carry a joint meeting of the Chamber's finance and foreign affairs committees. Not enough members were prepared to support his decision to make at least a token war debt payment to the United States.[65] In December 1938 there was a less dramatic example of parliamentary intrusion into foreign policy when foreign minister Bonnet was grilled by the Chamber's foreign affairs committee on the details of the government's "Munich" policy. Certainly the records of this commission remain the richest parliamentary resource on the Daladier government's drift toward the Munich humiliation. The parliamentary records will be equally valuable for other lines of inquiry, particularly for those researchers whose interest in foreign policy is secondary rather than primary. A case in point would be the individual who wants to study the parliamentary debates and voting records for evidence of some particular party's interest in foreign issues. Inquiries into foreign policy, as a consequence, may serve as an entrée to domestic political history, even if they do little more than confirm the near-indifference of most political parties to most foreign issues most of the time. Conversely, such inquiries may suggest that this indifference has been exaggerated. One thinks, for example, of the senators from the richest agricultural areas who displayed more than a passing interest in French immigration laws, particularly in so far as those laws affected the flow of cheap agricultural labor from Italy or eastern Europe. Or there is the case of the foreign minister Pierre Laval, the man who negotiated the mutual assistance pact with Russia in 1935. Among his reasons for so doing, it has been suggested, was the wish to undermine the electoral position of communist critics within his own constituency of Aubervilliers.

Other Approaches to the Quai d'Orsay

Considerations of the sort applied to Laval promptly return us to the question of influence, to the reasons why the past unfolded as it did. Yet how often it seems that the deeper one digs, the darker become the surroundings. Already we have the makings of an extremely complex interplay of forces which bear upon the administration of French foreign policy. There is a numerically small but highly skilled professional bureaucracy, powerful in its very permanence, and in a sense only nominally subordinate to ministers whose average tenure is less than two consecutive years in office.[66] There is a legislative body which, if normally pliable, is nevertheless capable of tightening the government's purse strings, of harassing it in committee, and ultimately of overthrowing the ministry. There is an executive branch, nominally headed by the president, in fact by a premier who very often serves as his own foreign minister, and represented by a council of ministers which seldom discusses foreign policy and never keeps an official set of minutes. Even within the bounds of this triad, the determination of motive and influence becomes a task of surpassing difficulty.

Nevertheless, even this geometry is too simple. The preceding pages have discussed at some length the expansion of the French foreign ministry — expansion of budget and personnel undeniably, but especially of services and conception. By 1920 it seemed folly to discuss foreign policy without reference to the professional counsels of the military strategists, the financial advisers, the commercial agents, and the public relations specialists. From that point on, one trick in foreign policy management was to be able to control and balance these diverse and sometimes competing counsels and ambitions. The other trick was to avoid becoming reflex-conditioned, either too responsive or too indifferent, to the recommendations of any group of experts. Whether or not either skill was acquired is a question which may be left for others to pursue at their leisure. The remarks which follow merely serve as flags for other avenues of research, each of which undoubtedly is intersected by many other thoroughfares.

A beginning has been made, though it is no more than

that, on the relationship between foreign policy and national defense considerations. Thanks to the editors of the Documents Diplomatiques Français, and to research by European and North American scholars, we have become familiar with some of the activities of the service ministries between the wars and with the proceedings of various interministerial bodies — from the Conseil Supérieur de la Défense Nationale and the Haut Comité Militaire, to the Comité Permanent de la Défense Nationale and the Conseil Suprême Interallié. The same can not be said for that plethora of committees which was the C.S.D.N. secretariat, or for the personal cabinets which altered form and sometimes direction with the comings and goings of each minister. Similarly, we have yet to penetrate very far into the field of military economics. To what extent were the international responses of French interwar governments predicated upon the slow progress toward an industrial strategy for wartime? To what extent did the nation's material needs for modern war predetermine relations with presumed allies, such as England, or presumed enemies, such as Germany? Or on a more particular note, to what extent was government policy influenced by the export and investment interests of French armament, shipbuilding and aircraft industries?

This line of investigation need not be restricted to expressly war-related industries. Nor, indeed, ought it to concentrate on the pursuit of self-interest exclusively by big business. Organized labor, the powerful industrial unions in particular, may have played their part in defining certain aspects of the government's relations with foreign states or with the international labor office of the League of Nations. Thus while work is waiting to be done on the Comité des Forges, the Comité des Houillères and the Confédération Générale du Patronat Français, so too is it needed on the Confédération Générale du Travail, the Confédération Générale du Travail Unitaire, and their respective member organizations. By the same token, research efforts in these areas are very likely to raise in their turn questions about the influence of some of the leading financial institutions, the Banque de France, the Banque de Paris et des Pays-Bas, the Crédit Lyonnais, as well as their sister institutions.

Nor should such inquiries be one-dimensional, tied to the assumption that material interests alone provide the motivation for such pressure groups and lobbying associations. One might suspect the presence of an ideological element as well, related to but not identical with economic self-interest. For example, it is possible that a profound ideological distrust of the Soviet Union, certainly inflamed by the bolshevik repudiation of czarist debts, did something to strengthen the French business community's resistance to closer ties with Russia.

Conversely, dreams of Franco-German industrial consortiums in iron, coal and chemicals may have been especially attractive to French businessmen who had more than a grudging admiration for the tough anti-communist measures implemented by Weimar and Nazi Germany. For their part, the hostility expressed by the politicized sectors of the French labor movement toward any rapprochement with the Austria of Dollfuss or the Italy of Mussolini seems to have been inspired as much by ideological distaste as by fears of deleterious economic consequences for French workers. In any event, the extent to which the biases of Right and Left intruded into foreign policy management remains a subject worthy of careful exploration.

The same may be said for the French press, a medium which conveyed the arguments of any number of pressure groups but which was also eager to offer its own counsels through the editorial column. Here again there can be a merging of the economic and the ideological, in editorials sometimes written under government direction and sometimes financed by the <u>fonds secrets</u> of various government ministries. Indeed, the marriage of journalism and politics in the Third Republic was consummated as well as celebrated in public. On balance, there is a sense that in matters of foreign policy the press was either so receptive to government suggestion that it exercised no influence at all, or so hostile that it was quietly ignored. For its part, and given the growth of services designed to "inform" public opinion, the foreign ministry may have listened only to those press versions which had been inspired at the Quai d'Orsay and which it therefore knew to be reliable. With that, of course, the question of propaganda is raised to yet another level of awareness, where the inquiry may have to turn from simple deception to the possibility of prolonged self-deception.

A Final Word

I am not at all sure whether there are any grand conclusions to be drawn from this survey of themes, issues, events. If there are, it is certainly work intended for the reader. As diverse as the content has been, some attempt has been made to fashion an interpretive essay. But it is probably fair to say that the interpretation is not especially controversial or even particularly innovative. What may be recognized as being more novel is the attempt to integrate a broader, richer notion of diplomatic history with an array of data from the specific institutions, agencies, and archives of interwar France. Indeed, to whatever extent this volume may be able to contribute to the work of other historians, for such is its sole intent, it is to be found in this integration of data and concept. Whether or not one accepts the prefix of "diplomatic" historian, regardless of

one's special skills and interests, this is our common point
of departure. This is where our craft begins.

END NOTES

1.   The phrase belongs to G.M. Young, Victorian England:
Portrait of an Age (Garden City, N.Y., 1954), 155.

2.   For example, see Gordon A. Craig, "The Professional
Diplomat and his Problems, 1919-1939," in War, Politics and
Diplomacy, edited by Gordon A. Craig (New York, 1966),
207-19; and J.B. Duroselle, "L'évolution des formes de la
diplomatie et son effet sur la politique étrangère des
Etats," in La politique étrangère et ses fondements, edited
by J.B. Duroselle (Paris, 1954), 325-49.

3.   The original service des archives and the archival depot
were products of the Torcy ministry (1696-1715). See Claude
Lebel, "L'organisation et les services du Ministère des
Affaires étrangères," in Les affaires étrangères, prepared by
the Université d'Aix-Marseille (Paris, 1959), 57-96.

4.   See also Vincent Confer, "France," in Guide to the
Diplomatic Archives of Western Europe, edited by Daniel
Thomas and Lynn Case (Philadelphia, 1959), 55-84; and Carlo
Laroche, La diplomatie française (Paris, 1946).

5.   "The procedure of official receptions of members of the
diplomatic corps and of distinguished foreigners, the rights,
privileges and immunities of diplomats, the forms of
diplomatic communications and international agreements all
fall within the scope of its activity." See F.L. Schuman,
War and Diplomacy in the French Republic (New York, 1970),
35.

6.   Ibid., 31-32; Amédée Outrey, "Histoire et principes de
l'Administration française des Affaires étrangères," Revue
Française de Science Politique 3, no. 2 (1953), 509.

7.   The Senate, for example, had more or less permanent
committees for finance, railways, customs, army and navy by
1900. A foreign affairs committee was not added until 1915.
The Chamber's Committee first appeared in 1902, one of
sixteen permanent committees which were being used to replace
the well over one hundred different ad hoc committees which
had grown up over time. See R.K. Gooch, The French
Parliamentary Committee System (New York, 1935), 76-90.

8. Maurice Schumann, "La Commission des Affaires étrangères et le contrôle de la politique extérieure en régime parlementaire," in Les affaires étrangères (Paris, 1959), 31.

9. Paul Gordon Lauren, Diplomats and Bureaucrats: The First Institutional Responses to Twentieth Century Diplomacy in France and Germany (Stanford, 1976), 95. I am very much indebted to Dr. Lauren for this fine and most useful book.

10. Outrey, "Histoire et principes," Rev. Fr. Sci. Po. 3, no. 2 (1953), 509-10.

11. Lauren, Diplomats and Bureaucrats, 90.

12. It was charged with "la reprise, réorganisation du développement des relations commerciales de la France avec les pays étrangers, de la transformation des accords de blocus, de la répartition des matières premières, du ravitaillement dans les organismes interalliés, des accords concernant le tourisme en France." See Emmanuel de Lévis Mirepoix, Le Ministère des Affaires étrangères (Angers, 1934), 132-33.

13. Among the subjects which engaged the attention of this office and its agents were "opportunities in external markets, custom regulations, import and export statistics, transportation carriers and costs, procurement of raw materials, contract law and foreign litigation, consular services, and new industrial processes and methods employed by competitors of other countries." See Lauren, Diplomats and Bureaucrats, 166.

14. Outrey, "Histoire et principes," Rev. Fr. Sci. Po. 3, no. 4 (1953), 722-23.

15. Ibid., 723-24; Lauren, Diplomats and Bureaucrats, 191-95, 204.

16. Lauren, ibid., 104; Outrey, ibid., 716.

17. Lauren, ibid., 92, 98.

18. Outrey, "Histoire et principes," Rev. Fr. Sci. Po. 3, no. 3 (1953), 510.

19. Lauren, Diplomats and Bureaucrats, 164.

20. Jules Cambon, Le diplomate (Paris, 1926), 74.

21. Outrey, "Histoire et principes," Rev. Fr. Sci. Po. 3, no. 4 (1953), 725. The Conseil was established in 1925, largely on the insistence of labor groups. It had a membership of about 50, drawn principally from labor, industry, commerce and consumer organizations. See Schuman, War and Diplomacy, 369-70.

22. Lauren, Diplomats and Bureaucrats, 191-95.

23. Schuman, War and Diplomacy, 35. See also Charles Daniélou, Les affaires étrangères (Paris, 1927), 5-98.

24. Lauren indicates as many as 80 staff members; and Paul Allard claims that there were more than 30 members in the section d'analyse alone. See Lauren, Diplomats and Bureaucrats, 194; and Allard, Le Quai d'Orsay (Paris, 1938), 61-63.

25. See Schuman, War and Diplomacy, 331-32; and John E. Howard, Parliament and Foreign Policy in France (London, 1948), 86. It does seem clear, however, that not all of these funds went to the Information service; some were set aside to finance secret, if small-scale, intelligence work.

26. Allard, Le Quai d'Orsay, 185-88.

27. M.T. Chabord, "Les services français de l'Information de 1936 à 1947," R.H.D.G.M. 16, no. 64 (1966), 81-87.

28. Henry Kittredge Norton, "Foreign Office Organization. A Comparison of the Organization of the British, French, German and Italian Foreign Office with that of the Department of State of the U.S.A.," The Annals, American Academy of Political and Social Science. Supplement to vol. 143 (1929), 13.

29. Ministère des Affaires Etrangères. Annuaire Diplomatique et Consulaire (Paris, 1937).

30. Mirepoix, Le Ministère des Affaires étrangères, 134-35.

31. Outrey, "Histoire et principes," Rev. Fr. Sci. Po. 3, no. 4 (1953), 716.

32. Annuaire Diplomatique et Consulaire (Paris, 1937).

33. Parliamentary criticism of the foreign ministry, and in particular of its administrative procedures, reached a peak in late 1932. As a result, a special commission was struck in January 1933, under the chairmanship of Senator Henry Béranger. The twenty-two-page report of this commission was

tabled in March 1933. See <u>Journal Officiel de la République Française</u>. <u>Chambre des Députés</u>. <u>Documents Parlementaires</u>. Session ordinaire de 9 Mars 1933, annexe no. 1535, 493-515.

34. Both Allard and Norton claim, in the latter's words, that the head of the Press section "sees all dispatches which come to the Quai d'Orsay and all the replies sent out by its officials." See Allard, <u>Le Quai d'Orsay</u>, 58; and Norton, "Foreign Office Organization," <u>The Annals</u>, 65-66.

35. Cf. Norton, <u>ibid</u>., 14-15.

36. Allard, <u>Le Quai d'Orsay</u>, 73-91; see also Christopher Andrew, "Déchiffrement et diplomatie: le cabinet noir du Quai d'Orsay sous la Troisième République," <u>Relations Internationales</u>, no. 5 (1976), 37-64.

37. See Howard, <u>Parliament and Foreign Policy</u>, 126-28.

38. Norton, "Foreign Office Organization," <u>The Annals</u>, 26-27.

39. Amédée Outrey, "Note sur les pertes subies du fait de la guerre par les archives du Ministère des Affaires étrangères," <u>Cahiers d'histoire de la guerre</u>, no. 2 (Oct. 1949), 31-33.

40. For more information on this massive recovery effort, see Outrey, and the general introduction prepared by Professors Renouvin and Baumont for the first volume of the <u>Documents Diplomatiques Français</u>, 2nd Series, vii-xiv.

41. Armand Bérard joined the <u>cabinet</u> of Paul-Boncour in March 1938. See his <u>Un ambassadeur se souvient</u> (Paris, 1976), 371.

42. Walter Rice Sharp, <u>The French Civil Service: Bureaucracy in Transition</u> (New York, 1931), 322-23.

43. See J.B. Duroselle, <u>La Décadence, 1932-1939</u> (Paris, 1979), 270; and his "French Diplomacy in the Postwar World," in <u>Diplomacy in a Changing World</u>, edited by S. Kertesz and and M. Fitzsimmons (Notre Dame, Ind., 1959), 204-48.

44. Duroselle, <u>La Décadence</u>, 276.

45. See Duroselle, "French Diplomacy in the Postwar World," <u>Diplomacy in a Changing World</u>, 214-15; Norton, "Foreign Office Organization," <u>The Annals</u>, 32-33; Sharp, <u>French Civil Service</u>, 145-48. Some of the most detailed information on the examination rules and the scoring system is found in

Mirepoix, Le Ministère des Affaires étrangères, 239-40, 244-49.

46. Lauren adds: "Numerous questions concerned the merchant marine, chambers of commerce, industrial property, imports and exports, customs regulations, tariffs, economic geography, civil law, and both private and public international law...." Diplomats and Bureaucrats, 101.

47. Sharp, French Civil Service, 324-26.

48. Norton, "Foreign Office Organization," The Annals, 48. Technically speaking, the rank of minister first class was the highest in the diplomatic service, the title of ambassador being regarded as a "dignity" rather than a formal rank.

49. Duroselle, "French Diplomacy in the Postwar World," in Diplomacy in a Changing World, 214.

50. Duroselle, La Décadence, 282.

51. Schuman, War and Diplomacy, 31.

52. Sharp, French Civil Service, 330-31.

53. In his long essay of 1929 Norton compares the salary of a minister first class living abroad ($12,000.00) with the salary the same man would earn in Paris ($2,400.00, plus "occasional allowances"). See "Foreign Office Organization," The Annals, 53. Schuman's work of 1931, however, places an ambassador's salary at only $8,000.00. See War and Diplomacy, 39.

54. The work of these two commissions will be of particular interest to the student of diplomacy. But attention also should be paid to the Committee on Customs and Commercial Convention, the Committee on Commerce, and the three armed forces committees. Cf. Howard, Parliament and Foreign Policy, 97.

55. Ibid., 81.

56. Whereas the meetings were held in camera, short and highly edited reports of their proceedings were subsequently circulated to members of Parliament in the form of Bulletins des Commissions. See Howard, Parliament and Foreign Policy, 101.

57. Schumann, "La Commission des Affaires étrangères," in Les affaires étrangères, 39.

58. Howard, Parliament and Foreign Policy, 62-72.

59. Schuman, War and Diplomacy, 385.

60. Howard, Parliament and Foreign Policy, 63-65; and Schuman, War and Diplomacy, 24.

61. "In fact, none of the great international agreements which have affected the balance of power and marked definite turning points in the diplomatic history of Europe have ever been submitted to, or even revealed to, Parliament, and some of them have not even been ratified by the chief executive. Neither the Franco-Russian Alliance conventions, the Franco-Italian exchange of notes of 1902, the Franco-Spanish Moroccan Convention of 1904, the Grey-Cambon letters of 1914, the Interallied Agreement of September 1914, nor the post-Versailles alliances with Poland and the Little Entente were submitted to Parliament." See Schuman, War and Diplomacy, 324.

62. Joseph Barthélemy, Essai sur le travail parlementaire et le systéme des commissions (Paris, 1934), 268.

63. Schuman, War and Diplomacy, 315-22.

64. With reference to what he calls the "tradition of national unity in foreign affairs," Schuman adds this important observation: "The Commissions of Foreign Affairs are chosen from among the Deputies and Senators on the basis of proportional representation and therefore reflect the positions and relative strength of the parties in Parliament as a whole. Party ties usually insure complete harmony between the Cabinet, the commissions, and the Chambers." War and Diplomacy, 318.

65. Howard, Parliament and Foreign Policy, 103-4.

66. Sharp, French Civil Service, 334; and Schuman, War and Diplomacy, 30-31.

III. ARCHIVES AND LIBRARIES

Introduction

This section ought to be introduced with a _caveat lector_, for the information contained here must be approached with some caution.

The most recent _loi sur les archives_ bears the date of December 1980. This is the latest government statement on French archival policy, and as such becomes an integral part of an already large corpus of earlier laws. This law, together with that of 3 January 1979, formalizes a principle that has been recognized in a fashion since 1973. In brief, it provides for a 30-year archival rule — public access to those documents, older than thirty years, which are under state jurisdiction. In other words, documents originating in or prior to 1950 are to have been opened to research by 1980. However, certain exceptions have been written into the law. Individual medical records are closed for 150 years from the birth of the individual, and personnel dossiers for 120 years. Certain court documents may be closed for 100 years, as may census and survey findings of a family or individual character. Documents deemed sensitive to state security or national defense may be closed for 60 years; and of course exceptional restrictions may be imposed on private papers by their donors.

These arrangements, on the whole, provide reasonably well for the student of foreign policy. It is true that some of the private papers remain closed or are subject to very restricted access, as is some of the documentation in the various National Defense archives; and the closure of the Riom court materials could be continued for some time under the terms of the archival law. Nevertheless, what is not subject to closure by law is, or ought to be, open to research. And theoretically it is. But practically, another law is in force, what one is tempted to call the "in progress" law. How often one still hears that phrase, _"en train de classement"_, the unwelcome news that the documents requested are still being prepared for _future_ use.

Although a stoical response is not to be recommended in moments such as this, it is important for the researcher to understand the position of the archivists. They are often under pressure from legislators and historians alike to open papers which, in point of fact, are not ready to be opened. And in the long run, it is in no one's interest to have improperly organized and uncatalogued material freely available to researchers, the more so if it is unbound material, loose documents in file folders or cartons.

The term "freely available" is used for a purpose. Rightly or wrongly, officials in French archives will distinguish between researcher A and researcher B. The former is granted the special dérogation, the latter is denied. The victim calls it discrimination, the beneficiary may be willing to acknowledge caprice. In any event, the same rules do not necessarily apply to all. One is tempted to generalize about such discretionary practices — how, for instance, the senior, published scholar has an advantage over a junior colleague or a graduate student; and yet there have been frequent cases of graduate students, French and foreign, being allowed exceptional access to documents — principally because they had satisfied the archivists over a period of time that they were serious, trustworthy scholars, not the much-feared "journalists" out for sensation and scandal. Indeed, recent experiences in the Paris archives prompt one to speak on behalf of these archivists. Certainly many of them are prepared to stretch a point in one's favor, going beyond what is required of them either by regulation or by the exigencies of their own work load. At the same time, it is only fair to say, and stress, that the initiative is left entirely to the researcher. Rarely is one told, without much prompting, of all the material that ought to be seen for one's project. The art is to discover what exists for oneself, then to make a case for being allowed to see it.

This raises the matter of indices and inventories, for very often it is not an easy matter to discover what does exist. The process of compiling comprehensive indices is not complete in many of the ministerial archives, especially for the period of the 1930s and the war years. Rather, and at best, one may find inventories for particular collections or particular series, inventories which certainly can be very useful but which are incapable of providing a broad overview of the archives as a whole. It is also possible that the inventory itself will undergo some change, either to accord with some new numbering system or to accommodate newly discovered or at least newly released documents. This is especially true of the inventories upon which this guide is based, for many of them were still in progress in 1979-1980 and as such were made available only by dérogation. The reader, therefore, is advised to treat the material in this section with discretion. The reference numbers may change; the collection may be reorganized, even physically reordered within a greater or lesser number of cartons than might be indicated here; indeed, in some cases, collections may be rehoused, shifted from one archive to another.

Above all, it ought never to be assumed that the material identified in the succeeding pages is automatically available to anyone and at a moment's notice. Whereas at times the requirement of having formal written authorization may be waived, on other occasions it will be treated as an iron law. And the act of securing written authorization, either from the archival service itself or from a private donor, may require months rather than weeks. Similarly, the reader is advised always to write in advance to the archives in question. The daily hours of opening and the annual closing periods do change from time to time, including those occasions prompted by unanticipated labour disputes or emergency repair work.

Finally, the reader is reminded of a point made in the introduction to this volume. Apart from a limited number of references to foreign or departmental archives, this work concentrates on the archives and libraries of Paris. That, by definition, is a limitation; but it is one that has been accepted for two reasons. First, and unquestionably, the national capital enjoys a preponderance of archival resources for studies concerning France's foreign relations. Second, such a focus allows for some degree of thoroughness and detail, without necessitating an even less complete volume of far greater, indeed immoderate, length.

Archives du Ministère des Affaires Etrangères

37 Quai d'Orsay, 75007 Paris. Metro: Invalides. Monday -Friday, 2-7 p.m.; Saturday, 9 a.m.-1 p.m. Annual closing, two weeks in March.

In order to obtain a reading card, one requires a letter of introduction and reference from one's university, or from one's embassy in Paris. A letter prepared by a French consul or ambassador abroad is certain to be just as effective. Advance inquiries may be addressed to: Le Ministre Plénipotentiare, Directeur des Archives. Anticipate lengthy delays in reply time.

Photocopying facilities, including microfilming, are available, but delays of up to a week are normal.

1. Outline of Some Principal Series

Series: <u>Conférence de la Paix, 1914-1931</u>. Archives du secrétariat français de la Conférence de la Paix. Vols. 1-74.

Sub-Series: <u>Recueil des Actes</u>. Cartons 1-10.

Series A: <u>Paix (1914-1920)</u>. Vols. 1-227.

Series B: <u>Amérique (1918-1940)</u>. Inventory. Organized by <u>sous-séries</u>, beginning with dossiers généraux (cartons 1-225), followed by country, alphabetically listed:

Antilles to Venezuela. Principal sous-série is for the
United States, cartons 1-503.

Series K: Afrique (1918-1940). Inventory. Organized by topic
(questions générales) and region (Afrique occidentale
anglaise to Union Sud-Africaine).

Series P: Tunisie (1917-1929). Inventory. 339 cartons,
organized by topical or regional sous-séries.

Series E: Asie. Océanie (1918-1929). Inventory. Organized by
sous-séries, beginning with Affaires Communes and
running to Turkestan Russe. Note especially the
collections under French Indochina, Japan and China.

Series Levant (1918-1929). Inventory. Organized by
sous-séries, from Arabie to Turquie, the latter being a
particularly extensive collection.

2. Series Y: Internationale, 1918-1940. Inventory.

Vols.
13-76   affaires politiques (1919-33)
77-91   affaires militaires (mainly 1920s)
92-102   droit international public et droit de la guerre
          (1919-40)
103-27   droit de la guerre sur mer et droit public maritime
          (mainly 1918-24)
128-29   droit de la guerre aérienne (mainly 1920s)
130   droit de la guerre sous-marine
131-61   comités interalliés (mainly first world war, but
          includes conseil suprême économique, 1919-20;
          comité international de relèvement économique de
          l'Europe Centrale; société pour la restauration
          économique de l'Europe, 1922-23.
162-203   questions économiques (1918-40, but mainly 1920s)
204-14   entente économique entre les alliés (1915-19)
215-376   affaires financières (1918-40)
377   sionisme
378-95   action pacifiste et révolutionnaire (1930-35)
408-28   Paix (1920-40)
429-34   Conférence des Ambassadeurs (1920-31, mainly pre-
          1923)
435-659   Société des Nations (1919-39); includes material on
          arms limitation (vols. 508-64), London Naval
          Conference (567-84) mandates (600-04).
660-91   conférences politiques, supplément (mainly 1920s),
          including San Remo, Brussels, Spa, Lausanne
693   matériel d'aviation américaine pour les alliés
          (May-June 1940)
694   accord spécial (anglo-franco-turkish, January 1940)

3. Series Z: Europe, 1918-1940. Inventory.

Organized by the following sous-séries: Albanie, Allemagne, Autriche, Balkans, Belgique, Bulgarie, Danemark, Dantzig, Espagne, Estonie, Finlande, Fiume, Grande-Bretagne, Grèce, Hongrie, Irlande, Italie, Lettonie, Lithuanie, Luxembourg, Memel, Montenegro, Norvège, Pays-Bas, Pologne, Portugal, Rhin, Elbe, Oder, Rive gauche du Rhin, Roumanie, Ruhr, Suède, Suisse, Tchéco-Slovaquie, Yougoslavie.

Sample (Allemagne): Dossiers 1-608(1918-29)
610-803(1930-40)

Dos.
1-55   divers
56-193   Armée-Guerre
194-207   Marine
208-09   Blocus
210-60   Traité de Versailles
261-345   Politique intérieure
346-66   Etats confédérés
367-71   Questions religieuses
372-420   Politique extérieure
421-36   Economie
437-56   Finances
457-513   Réparations financières
514-35   Commerce
536-48   Industrie-Travaux publics
549-67   Voies et moyens de communication
568-90   Justice
591-93   Questions juridiques
594-96   Questions culturelles
599-601   Questions sociales
602-08   Affaires diverses
610-51   divers
652-64   Armée-Guerre
665-66   Marine
666-73   Blocus
674-88   Politique intérieure
689-712   Questions religieuses
713-60   Politique étrangère
761-86   Economie-Finances
787-91   Justice - Questions juridiques
792-93   Instruction publique
794   Questions sociales
796-98   Affaires diverses
799-803   Colonies

Other Samples:	1918-29	1930-40
Autriche	1-175	176-222
Belgique	1-165	166-202
Czécho-Slovaquie	1-90	91-168
Grèce	1-175	176-247
Grande-Bretagne	1-173	174-269
Pays-Bas	1-60	61-106
Pologne	1-291	292-441
Rive gauche	1-242	243-290

4. Sous-Séries B81 and B82: Relations Commerciales, 1920-1929

There are 425 dossiers in these two sous-séries, organized as follows: Traités de Paix; Délibérations Internationales Consécutives aux Traités de Paix; Conseil Suprême Economique; Conférence de Spa - juillet 1920; Conférence Financière de Bruxelles; Conférence de Genève; Conférence Technique de Bruxelles; Sanctions; Nouvelles Sanctions; Conférence de Boulogne; Conférence de Washington; Réunion à Paris du Conseil Suprême (121); Conférence de Cannes (1922); Conférence de Gênes (1922); Réunion de La Haye; Conférence de Paris; Action de la France dans la Ruhr (1922-24; dossiers 141-405); Conférence de Londres (juillet 1924); Conférence de Paris (janvier 1925).

5. Series S.D.N.: Société des Nations, 1917-1940

One detailed inventory, one summary inventory.

Vols.
1-28	IA.	Pacte de la S.D.N.
29-176	IB.	Organisation et fonctionnement
205-26	IC.	Service français de la S.D.N.
240-431	ID.	Questions politiques
432-542	IE.	Minorités
543-625	IF.	Mandats
626-705	IG.	Dantzig et Sarre
754-824	IH.	Arbitrage, Sécurité, Désarmement
825-1151	II.	Désarmement (including Disarmament Conference)

Inventories are currently being prepared for the following:

IJ. Questions économiques et financières
IK. Communications et transit
IL. Hygiène
IM. Questions sociales
IN. Coopération intellectuelle

    IO. Presse et Information
    IP. Droit international
    IR. Réparations
    IX. Dossiers géographiques (by country)

6. Papiers d'Agents

A major collection of private and state papers, accompanied by a 4-volume general inventory and, in most cases, a detailed inventory of the separate holdings. Some expressly require written authorization. All appear subject, in the words of the general inventory, to a dérogation possible.

For selected biographical sketches consult this volume's index.

Cote
227   Alphand, Charles. 1 carton (1904-35)
6   Avenol, Joseph. 43 vols. (1920-58)
8   Barrère, Camille. 7 vols. and 2 cartons (1873-1939)
...   Bernard, Augustin. 1 carton (1933-35)
10   Berthelot, Philippe. 22 vols. (1914-34)
26   Bonin, Charles. 13 cartons (1903-31)
29   Bourgeois, Léon. 15 cartons and 45 vols. (1906-25)
36   Caillaux, Joseph. 23 cartons (1918-35)
43   Cambon, Jules. 27 cartons (1863-1934)
42   Cambon, Paul. 19 vols. (1882-1920)
37   Charles-Roux, François. 4 cartons (1900-32)
229   Chivot, Georges. 6 cartons (1922)
198   Clemenceau, Georges. 2 cartons (telegrams, 1918-20)
51   Coulondre, Robert. 2 cartons (1912-36)
40   Daeschner, Georges. 1 vol. (1925)
53   Dard, Emile. 8 cartons (1912-32)
56   Defrance, Jules. 1 carton (1908-33)
57   Dejean, François. 2 cartons (1916-27)
215   Dollot, René. 1 liasse (1914-20)
64   Doumergue, Gaston. 4 vols. (1913-36)
202   Ducrocq, Georges. 102 vols. (1898-1927)
18   Dutasta, Paul. 1 carton (1902-22)
72   Flandin, Pierre-Etienne. 1 dossier (1937-38)
...   Fleuriau, Aimé de. 3 vols. (1913-33)
206   Fouchet, Maurice. 9 cartons (1914-24)
74   Fouques-Duparc, Albert. 14 cartons (1905-32)
196   Gout, Jean. 10 vols. (1900-24)
84   Grenard, Joseph. 32 vols. (1916-23)
204   Hermite, Louis. 26 cartons and 1 liasse (1914-40)
89   Herriot, Edouard. 24 cartons (1909-42)
92   Jouvenel, Henry de. 2 cartons (1922-33)
93   Jusserand, Jules. 71 cartons (1900-28)
95   Klubukouski, Antony. 9 cartons (1886-1930)

96	Lacroix, Victor de. 2 cartons (1902-28)
97	Lagarde, Léonce. 12 vols. (1895-1935)
102	Laurent, Charles. 1 carton (1920-22)
104	Lebrun, Albert. 7 cartons (1919-23)
110	Leygues, Georges. 3 vols. (1920-21)
247	Mantoux, Paul. 1 carton (1916-19)
113	Margerie, Pierre Jacquin de. 5 cartons (1902-24)
...	Marin, Louis. 22 cartons (1871-1959)
...	Massigli, René. 5 vols. (1919)
118	Millerand, Alexandre. 94 vols. (1894-1926)
129	Ormesson, André d'. 6 cartons (1921-38)
133	Paléologue, Maurice. 5 vols. (1914-37)
265	Paul-Boncour, Joseph. 5 cartons (1924-51)
137	Pelle, General Maurice. 1 carton (1911-23)
141	Pichon, Stéphen. 8 vols. (1901-19)
252	Puaux, Gabriel. 46 cartons (1908-48)
223	Saint-Quentin, René de. 1 carton (1919-20)
166	Tardieu, André. 217 cartons and dossiers (1918-39)
241	Verchère de Refye, Paul. 1 vol. (1923-27)

Note: The following collections are not listed in the general inventory of the Papiers d'Agents. Most have been used in the preparation of the Documents Diplomatiques Français, and may well be housed in the archives of the Quai d'Orsay.

Germain-Martin, Louis. (see D.D.F. 1st Series, vols. 1 and 2.)

Hanotaux, Gabriel. 33 vols. and 10 cartons. (See Guide des Papiers des Ministres. A.N. (1978), p. 86.

Massigli, René. Reportedly a large and very significant collection on the interwar period; used in the D.D.F., 1st and 2nd Series. The ambassador's written authorization is required before consulting the inventory.

Noel, Léon. (see D.D.F., 2nd Series, vol. 7.)

Ponsot, Henry. (a collection in the name of the ambassador to Ankara in the mid-1930s; used in D.D.F. 2nd Series, vol. 10.)

Vienne, Mathieu de. (a collection in the name of the minister to Hungary in the 1930s; used in D.D.F. 1st Series, vol. 3.)

7. <u>Fonds 1940: Papiers '40</u>. General Inventory and
Particular Inventories.

<u>Papiers Dejean</u>. Papers of Reynaud's diplomatic
cabinet. 80-page typed inventory. 28 dossiers, 337 items
(Dec. 1939-June 1940).

<u>Papiers Charvériat</u>. Working papers of the Directeur
des Affaires Politiques. 3-page inventory. 8 dossiers, 27
items (1935-40).

<u>Papiers Charles-Roux</u>. 3-page inventory for cartons
numbered 32-37 (1933-45, but mainly post June 1940).

<u>Bureau d'Etudes Chauvel</u>. 11-page inventory of study
papers prepared by Jean Chauvel and colleagues after the fall
of France; and a 16-page inventory for 10 dossiers of
original documents (1935-40, but mainly late 1939 and 1940).

<u>Papiers Bonnet</u>. 8-page inventory and 3-page supplement
for 11 dossiers, 162 items (1938-42).

<u>Papiers Daladier</u>. 26-page inventory with preface by
M. Lacaze. Over 200 documents microfilmed by the Germans,
covering the period 1936-1940, mainly 1938-40.

<u>Papiers De Brinon</u>. 57-page inventory covering 3
dossiers, 321 items, for the period 1942-44. Rich in
correspondence with Laval.

<u>Papiers Abetz</u>. 4-page inventory of a dossier prepared
in 1970 from the Quai d'Orsay's collection of "Photos
allemandes" (1940-43).

<u>Papiers Bridoux</u>. 19-page inventory for 4 dossiers, 302
items, covering 1941-45, mainly 1944-45.

<u>Papiers Baudouin</u>. 83-page inventory for 4 folios, 2104
items, covering period May-October 1940. Supplemented by 3-
page inventory for 25 additional items donated in 1964.

<u>Papiers Laval</u>. A collection of papers seized in
December 1940 at Châteldon. Poor inventory identifies <u>scellé</u>
no. 1 bis, no. 4 bis, no. 5 bis, no. 6 bis. Some material
from 1935, mainly 1940.

<u>Papiers Rochat</u>. Arranged in two series. First covers
his Vichy ministry (1940-44) in 3 cartons. Second, in 17
cartons, covers period (1934-40) when Rochat was chef de
cabinet, and directeur politique. This second series
contributed to the "reconstitution" Fouques-Duparc.

noted that the F 30 series (Finances. Administration centrale) and the A(rchives) P(rivées) series are housed at the Archives Nationales. Other series numbers will be found either on the rue Saint-Honoré or at the archives center at Fontainebleau.

1. Cabinets Ministériels

74 AP	Bouthillier, Yves (1940-42)
F^{30} 4149-53	Cathala, Pierre (1942-44)
F^{30} 2390	Doumer, Paul (1921)
F^{30} 2387-89	François-Marsal, Frédéric (1920)
F^{30} 2386	Klotz, L.L. (1919)
F^{30} 2391-92	Lasteyrie, Charles de (1922-23)
5A 7-12	Pleven, René (1944-46)
74 AP	Reynaud, Paul (1938-40)
F^{30} 4154	Papiers dits du Commandant Bernard (plan Monnet, 1944)
F^{30} 4148	Divers (1933-40)

2. Bureau du Cabinet

F^{30} 4027-105	Correspondance avec les Assemblées (1870-1938)

3. Direction du Trésor: Affaires internationales

F^{30} 1432-45	Situation...des opérations en devises
F^{30} 1458-94	étrangères (1914-39)
F^{30} 1446-57	Agence comptable des avoirs du Trésor à l'étranger (1926-39)

Agences financières:

B 9678-86	Diverses (1922-57)
F^{30} 556	En Allemagne (1930-38)
B 9367-445	A Berne (1939-64)
B 19299-467	A Londres (1914-54)
B 16785-891	
B 18163-189	A Rome (1920-76)
B 19136-165	
B 9446-92	En Sarre (1928-57)
F^{30} 720	Aux Etats-Unis (1920-32)

B 21805-884   Agence financière de New York (1922-45)
F^{30} 2379   Avances aux gouvernements étrangers (1914-33)
F^{30} 2109-10   Balance des paiements (1933-51)

F^{30} 1495-545
F^{30} 2130-32   }— Commerce extérieur (1914-49)
F^{30} 2135
F^{30} 2184-290   Télégrammes adressés aux services extérieurs
                     (1914-1927)
B 12518   Réunions des conseillers financiers à Paris
F^{30} 1410-421   Crise   monétaire   et   conférences
                     internationales (1871-1942)

4. Guerres et Trésorerie aux Armées

F^{30} 1262-1379
F^{30} 1396-1401   }—Problème des réparations (1914-1952)
B 8782-785
B 12647-653
F^{30} 21786-79   Plan Dawes et dettes de guerre (1920-27)
B 12710-715   Société des Nations (1921-39)
F^{30} 2380-84   Législation du temps de guerre (1870-1941)
F^{30} 1546-584   Occupation allemande (1940-44)
F^{30} 1228-261

B 631   La France au pillage (1942-46)
F^{30} 1983-989   Négociation   d'armistice   avec   l'Italie
                     (1940-44)
B 8786-788   Armistice et traité de paix avec l'Allemagne
                     (1943-45)
F^{30} 1513-545   Commerce   extérieur,   missions   d'achat
                     (1931-45)
F^{30} 2117-125
F^{30} 2461-462   Blocus (1941-46)
F^{30} 2500
F^{30} 2113-116   Comité Français de la Libération Nationale,
                     et Gouvernement Provisoire de la République
                     Française, Alger (1943-45)

B 12728-778
B 12781-827   Missions d'achats à Londres (1938-54)
B 19299-467

B 12726, 12779
B 12780   Comité   de   coordination   franco-anglais
                     (1940-41)

5. Pays Etrangers ou Groupements d'Etats

Some select examples:

F^{30} 534–611
F^{30} 1262–1401
F^{30} 2136 ⎭ Allemagne (1914–39)
B 9679
B 12651–3

F^{30} 612–45   Autriche (1919–40)
F^{30} 1119–141   Sarre (1919–38)
B 12670
B 21805–84 ⎤ Etats-Unis (1914–44)
F^{30} 798–934
F^{30} 2836
B 12623–639
B 12672–691 ⎭ Grande-Bretagne (1914–40)
B 12702–709
B 12716–717
B 12770–771
F^{30} 533
F^{30} 1064–1118
F^{30} 2016–18
F^{30} 3297–3307 ⎭ Union des Républiques Socialistes
B 588–95   Soviétiques (1917–74)
F^{30} 12518

6. Direction des Relations Economiques Extérieures

4 D 1–9   Commission d'armistice de Wiesbaden (1940–44)

Ministère de la Défense. Archives de l'Armée de Terre

Château de Vincennes. Address inquiries to the Chef du Service Historique de l'Armée de Terre (currently General Delmas), 94300 Château de Vincennes. The section moderne is under the direction of Colonel Turlotte. It is in charge of documentation up to 1945. Open Monday–Thursday, 10 a.m. to 5:30 p.m., Friday, between 10 and 4:45. Limit of 6 cartons per day; delivered singly between 10 and 11:30, and from 1:30 to 4:30, or 4:00 on Friday.

The references which follow come principally from SERIES N (1919–1940), and are samples of materials which are likely to be of interest to the diplomatic historian.

ARCHIVES AND LIBRARIES

1. Series 1 N: Conseil Supérieur de la Guerre

Has a 30-page typed index, describing cartons 1-63.

Cartons
23-38	dossiers des séances du C.S.G. (1920-39)
41	état-major Pétain (1922-35)
42	état-major Weygand (1931-34)
43	état-major Gamelin (1935-39)
46-47	état-major Georges (1933-40)

2. Series 2 N: Conseil Supérieur de la Défense Nationale

Has a 190-page typed index, describing cartons 1-288.

4-7	délibérations du C.S.D.N. (1906-35)
8-18	délibérations de la Commission d'Etudes (1922-36)
19	Haut Comité Militaire (1932-35)
20-25	Comité Permanent de la Défense Nationale (1936-39)
26	Comité de Guerre (1939-40)
27-263	Secrétariat Général du Conseil Supérieur de la Défense Nationale
264-88	Centre des Hautes Etudes Militaires (1910-39)

3. Series 3 N: Comité de Guerre (1939-40)

See 2 N 26 above.

4. Series 4 N: Conférence des Ambassadeurs au Quai et Etat-Major de Foch

79-90	notes du secrétaire français...et documentation annexe (1921-35)
92-95	comité militaire allié de Versailles (1919-35)
96-129	commissions militaires interalliées de contrôle (1919-30)

5. Series 5 N: Cabinet du Ministre

Has a 60-page typed index. Collection is divided into two parts: A - Section de Défense Nationale, cartons 577-85; B - Correspondance des bureaux du cabinet, cartons 586-603.

577-78   organisation de la défense nationale: lois et
            décrets
579-81   politique de défense, conduite à la guerre
            (1929-40)
582   crédits et programmes d'armement (1924-36)
585   minutes de la correspondance expédiée par la
            section de défense nationale (1939-40)
586   organisation de cabinet du ministre (1920-40)
587-88   commissions   parlementaires   et   contrôle
            parlementaire (1919-40)
601   anti-militarisme
602   répression de la propagande communiste (1939-40)

6. Series 6 N: Secrétariat Général du Ministre de la
   Défense Nationale. Cartons 300-326.

300-01   organisation, attributions, composition (1920-40)
302-05   minutiers du contrôleur général Morin (1938-40)
306-13   crédits, finances (1920-40)
317-23   main d'oeuvre (1937-40)
324-26   mobilisation industrielle (1938-40)

7. Series 7 N: Etat-Major de l'Armée

The following are samples from the 63-page typed
inventory.

1er Bureau
2295-316   circulaires, notes, correspondance (1920-29)
2317-324   organisation de l'armée (1920-39)
2366-369   fortifications (1919-36)

2e Bureau
2502-540   section des armées étrangères (1919-40)
2541-560   section des missions (1919-40)
2561-568   section d'information des attachés militaires
            (1925-40)

5e Bureau
2572-76   renseignements pendant la guerre (Sept. 1939-May
            1940)

Attachés Militaires. Allemagne. 163-page index.
2583-608   rapports et correspondance (1927-39)

Documentation générale de la section allemande
2647-654   études et notes de la section allemande (1919-39)
            dossiers des manquements allemands au traité de
            Versailles (1924-33)

2655-673	documents provenant de l'Armée du Rhin (1919-30)
2674-704	renseignements sur l'armée allemande (1919-39)
	Attachés Militaires. Grande-Bretagne. 97-page index.
2794-821	rapports et correspondance (1920-40)
2822-838	renseignements sur la politique étrangère et l'Empire (1919-40)
2839-867	renseignements sur l'armée britannique (1919-40)

8. Fonds Privés. 4-volume typed index.

IK40   Fonds Regnault. 11 cartons, three of which require family permission to consult, on the careers of Generals Charles (1856-1937) and Jean (1893-1970). The latter's papers are of interest for Orient and Levant, 1922-26, pre-1939 exercises and maneuvers, and Algeria, 1942-43.

IK61   Papiers Serrigny. 2 cartons, one of which is open for research, on General Bernard Serrigny (1870-1954). Mainly for 1916-18 service on Pétain's staff. Closed carton contains original text of memoirs published in reduced form as Trente Ans avec Pétain.

IK71   Papiers Henri de Castries. Includes correspondence with Lyautey (1910-29), Mangin, Flandin, and Doumer.

IK74   Papiers Azan. 2 cartons on General Paul Azan (1874-1951). Carton 2 contains a 48-page "historique de la commission militaire interalliée de contrôle de Berlin," dated November 1924.

IK93   Fonds Fabry. 6 cartons on Jean Fabry (1893-1950). Diverse material: press clippings, some Riom court material, limited correspondence. See his journal de marche in Cabinet du Ministre, Series 5N.

IK95   Fonds Georges. 6 cartons of original and photocopied papers belonging to General Alphonse Georges. Access restricted. Microfilmed "carnets" from 1939-40, and 1943, are closed to research.

IK100   Fonds Gabriel Hanotaux. Some correspondence, but mainly working papers for his multi-volume history of World War One.

IK104   **Fonds Kastler.** 6 cartons on Colonel Kastler. Mainly on First World War, but material on the Army of the Rhine and the occupation in the 1920s.

IK110   **Papiers Malleterre.** 1 carton from General Pierre Malleterre (1858-1923); includes some material on Spa conference and post-1918 German army.

IK118   **Archives du Général Niessel** (1866-1955). 13 cartons, with a 14th on his mission to Poland in 1920-21 in the files of the 2ᵉ Bureau. Rich in correspondence, especially for the period 1917-24.

IK121   **Fonds Picard.** Material relating to General François Picard's service under Buat, Inspector-General of the Army, in the 1920s, and under General Maurin in the artillery inspectorate from 1930.

IK122   **Archives du Général Pigeaud.** 2 cartons concerning the French army, mainly in the 1920s.

IK130   **Fonds Weygand.** 13 cartons on General Maxime Weygand's collaboration with Foch (1914-18); and 28 additional dossiers covering period to 1948. Written authorization required.

IK135   **Don Pernot du Breuil.** 49-page typescript entitled, "sur l'activité du général Noguès et de son cabinet du 17 au 27 juin 1940."

IK153   **Papiers du Général Bourgeois.** 5 cartons on interwar budget, air-naval arm, and "les grandes questions politiques et le Désarmement."

IK154   **Fonds Chardigny.** Papers of General Pierre Chardigny (1873-1951), military attaché in Belgium from 1929 to 1933; include copies of his letters to 2ᵉ Bureau.

IK161   **Papiers Altmayer.** 6 cartons from General Robert Altmayer, commandant of the 8th military region (1931), inspector of cavalry (1932), recalled to service (May 1940).

IK162   **Fonds Franchet d'Esperey.** 3 cartons, mainly on 1914-18, but a range of correspondence for the interwar years.

IK174   **Fonds Keime.** 8 cartons; mainly World War Two, but some material from 1930s when General Keime was professor at the Ecole de Guerre and attached to the Chamber's army commission.

IK175   Fonds Marchal.   3 cartons on French military mission to Roumania after World War One.

IK183   Papiers du Général Noiret.   Mainly on 1939-40 operations when Noiret was in charge of Georges's 3e Bureau on the north-east front.

IK185   Fonds Jacobson.   12 cartons donated by this civilian member of the interallied control commission. Principally for the period 1918-24.   According to the inventory, "la perte des archives de l'Armée du Rhin donne à ce fonds un intérêt exceptionnel."

IK186   Fonds Reibell.   15 cartons, currently closed to research, from General Emile Reibell.   Rich in correspondence and assessed as "une bonne contribution à qui voudra étudier l'histoire coloniale de la 3eme république et surtout la période 1940-50."

IK187   Fonds Paul Reynaud.   Mainly for 1938-40.   Some personal notes, press clippings, bound volumes of speeches.

IK188   Fonds Pétain.   6 dossiers of diverse content for the period 1920-41.

IK212   Papiers Yvon.   1 carton concerning Colonel Yvon's service as military attaché in China, 1939-45.

IK213   Fonds Loizeau.   6 cartons, including unpublished memoirs, "Mes Etapes".   Good on Morocco, 1914-25.   Restricted access.

IK221   Papiers Huguet et La Panouse.   1 carton concerning service of these two military attachés to Britain, pre-1914.

IK224   Fonds Gamelin.   8 cartons, typed inventory, restricted access.   Cartons 1-5 and 8 have material on Riom court; carton 7, diverse material from 1930-40.

IK259   Archives Jocard.   8 cartons, mainly on early 1920s when General André Jocard served on a series of post-war military commissions in the Balkans.   Some material on 1939-40.

       Note: The following do not appear in the 4-volume inventory for the Fonds Privés.   Rather, these items have been identified either in the Guide des papiers des Ministres (A.N. 1978) or in the Inventaire Sommaire des Archives de la Guerre.   Série N, 1872-1919 (Troyes, 1974).   All items are located at the Château de Vincennes.

6N 53-111   Fonds Clemenceau.   59 cartons, mainly on the wartime leadership of this premier and war minister (1917-19). The collection includes the papers of General Henri Mordacq (1895-1925).

14N 48-50   Fonds Foch.   2 cartons deriving from Foch's headquarters' staff, 1916-19.

14N 1-47   Fonds Joffre.   47 cartons, mainly relating to the First World War, but with material to 1931.

6N 295-99   Fonds Lebrun.   5 cartons of parliamentary papers assembled by Albert Lebrun. Mainly on the years of World War One, but with some material on the 1920s: defense budgets and Rhenish frontier.

6N 1-6   Fonds Poincaré.   6 cartons of documents, mainly on the war years, but including material on the French military mission to Poland (1919) and German rearmament in the 1920s.

13N 1-130   Fonds Tardieu.   130 cartons concentrated mainly on the First World War and deriving principally from the commissariat général aux affaires de guerre franco-américaines. Outside dates, 1916-1921.

...   Fonds Catroux.   7 dossiers, presumably Series K, concerning international affairs in Europe, North Africa and Indochina (1919-69). Requires written authorization from family and the army historical service.

Ministère de la Défense. Archives de l'Armée de l'Air

Château de Vincennes. Address inquiries to the Chef du Service Historique de l'Armée de l'Air (currently General Christienne), 94300 Château de Vincennes. Open Monday to Friday: 8:45-11:45 a.m., 1:30-4:45 p.m. Closed for part of August.

1. Series A. Guerre, 1914-1918

This collection was badly damaged in the course of World War Two. Just under 300 cartons survived, principally for: l'aéronautique du Grand Quartier Général; l'aéronautique des armées; les formations aéronautiques. Indexed.

2. Series 2B: Etat-Major de l'Armée de l'Air (1919-40)

35-page typed index, from which the following samples are taken.

Cartons
20-25	mobilisation (1934-40)
40-96	renseignements sur les pays étrangers (mainly concentrated on late 1930s)
97-100	situation internationale
172-74	Centre des Hautes Etudes Aériennes (1934-39)
180-81	Conseil Supérieur de l'Air
183-86	achats aux Etats-Unis
187-88	missions (relations with other bodies, including Haut Comité Militaire, Conseil Supérieur de Guerre)
198-210	Société des Nations

3. Series C: Forces Aériennes Françaises d'Outre-Mer

4. Series D: Forces Aériennes de la guerre, 1939-45

ID: Grand Quartier Général Aérien (1939-40) 20-page index.

20-32	renseignements
33-36	situation internationale
37-41	forces aériennes britanniques

2D: Unités de la Guerre (1939-40) 78-page index.

3D: Secrétariat d'Etat à l'Aviation, et Secrétariat Général à la Défense Aérienne, 1940-44. 245-page typed index for a collection of 498 cartons.

1-130	cabinet militaire
131-245	cabinet civil
266-313	état-major de l'armée de l'air, 1er bureau
314-326	état-major de l'armée de l'air, 2e bureau
490-493	procès de Riom
495	historiques rédigés sous le gouvernement de Vichy

5. Series Z: Dons

Z11 275	General Vuillemin. Riom dossiers (1938-42)
Z...	Papiers de Guy La Chambre, "portant sur le procès de Riom."

6. Taped Interviews

#6   Guy La Chambre (Feb. 1975. 90 minutes)
#117   General Arnaud de Vitrolles (Nov. 1978.   120
            minutes)
...   Pierre Cot (May 1975, June 1976. 180 minutes)

Ministère de la Défense. Archives de la Marine

Château de Vincennes. Address inquiries to the Chef du
Service Historique de la Marine (currently Admiral Duval),
94300, Château de Vincennes. Open all year, Monday–Friday: 9
a.m. to 5 p.m.

Note: The information which follows must be read with
particular caution.   Of necessity, it is a synthesis
fashioned from a series of often quite inconsistent,
imprecise, undated inventories. The post–World War One
archives are indicated by the opening numeral 1, which is
followed by double lettering from AA (actes officiels)
through to GG (Private collections). The following appear to
be the most interesting items for the students of foreign
policy. The heavy wartime damage sustained by the documents
for the later 1930s may be inferred from these listings.

1. Service 1BB 2/2: Etat Major de la Marine. 2e Bureau

Cartons

65–68   diverse material, including correspondence with
            the foreign ministry (mainly 1920s, early 1930s)

2. Series 1BB 3: Ministère de la Marine

195–205   correspondence with foreign ministry (1920–24)
215–233   correspondence with war ministry (1920–27)
238   French representatives abroad (1920)
239–245   Chamber of Deputies (1920–33)
246–250   Senate (1921–33)

3. Series 1BB 7: Marines Etrangères. Attachés Navals

1–50   untitled; mainly Britain and Germany pre–1935
67–118   United States (1920–40, but mainly pre–1935)
119–122   Greece (1920–25)
123–128   Italy (1920–24)
129–133   Japan (1920–34)

134-135	Low Countries (1920-39)
136-139	Baltic and Scandinavian countries (1920-24)
140-250	Turkey (1920-39; strong on 1920s, especially 1919-23)
253-257	military attachés (1920-22)
258-267	naval missions (1920-25)

Note: Separate inventories have been prepared for the naval attachés, by country. Although they are not entirely consistent with the notes provided above, they appear to be more recent and hence are perhaps more reliable.

4. Series 1BB 8: Divers

1-19	Correspondence. Cabinet du Ministre (1920-40, mainly 1920s)
562-66	League of Nations (1920-24)
567-68	Washington Conference (1922)
569	Conference of Ambassadors (1920-21)
572	Lausanne Conference (1920-22)
576	The Hague Conference (1923)
583-97	Conseil Supérieur de la Défense Nationale (1920-33)
601-03	Haut Comité Militaire (1931-37)
715-20	Reports and correspondence; naval intelligence (1920-39)
730	Italo-Ethiopian affair (1935)

5. Series 1GG 2: papiers provenant de succession, dons et acquisitions

GG^2 142   Fonds Lacaze. 10 folders of documents from Admiral Lacaze, relating to period July 1940-July 1941, and to Vichy's relations with London, Berlin, Rome and French colonies.

GG^2 88-89   Papiers Landriau. Include some material on strategic planning and international appraisals, 1914-39.

Note: In addition to the references provided above, one is advised to consult yet other available inventories: Section d'Etudes: Correspondance; the 45-page inventory prepared for the Archives du Haut Comité Militaire; the 19-page inventory entitled Documents Internationaux.

Archives Nationales

Hôtel de Ville; Rambuteau. Open Monday—Saturday, 9 a.m. to 6 p.m. Documents for use on Saturday must be requested the day before. Closed for two weeks in July — those weeks vary — and on the first two Saturdays in August.

Foreign researchers require a letter of reference, usually from their embassy, two photographs, and their passport. Temporary reading cards (for less than a month) and permanent cards (renewable every year) are issued at the Bureau des Renseignements, on the main floor, which opens between 9:30 and 12, and between 2 and 5 in the afternoon. Readers are restricted to a maximum number of 8 cartons per day, only one of which can be used at a time.

Again the reader is reminded that the following references are simply samples of collections which may be of interest and value to the diplomatic historian.

1. <u>Series F: Administration générale de la France</u>

F^{1a}: Administration générale: objets généraux

F^{1a} 3663-70	Rapports franco-allemands (1940-44)
F^{1a} 3683-705	Ministère de l'Intérieur à Vichy (1940-44)
F^{1a} 3710-96	Commissariat à l'Intérieur de Londres et Délégation à Londres du Commissariat à l'Intérieur d'Alger (1941-44)
F^{1a} 3800-25	Commissariat à l'Intérieur d'Alger (1943-44)

F^7: Police générale

F^7 12948-13519	Relations internationales. Examples: Germany (1919 to 1936, vols. 13424-34); Italy (1925 to 1934, vols. 13453-66); Russia (1918 to 1934, vols. 13487-505)

F^{12}: Commerce et Industrie: Guerre de 1914-18

F^{12} 7762-95	Documents provenant du Comité exécutif des importations (1917-19)
F^{12} 7796-819	Documents des Services français à l'étranger (1918-19)
F^{12} 7800-807	Conseil interallié des transports maritimes (1916-20)
F^{12} 7808	Comité du ravitaillement de la Belgique (1918)
F^{12} 7809-810	Services français de Londres: Correspondance (1918-20)
F^{12} 7811-818	Haut Commissariat de France aux Etats-Unis (1917-19)

F^{12}	7819	Comité des matières premières (1910–20)
F^{12}	7822	Commission des importations (1916–19)
F^{12}	7857–858	Comité permanent international d'action économique (1916–18)
F^{12}	7859	Conseil suprême du blocus (1916–18)
F^{12}	7860	Comité de restriction du commerce avec l'ennemi (1916–18)
F^{12}	7933–962	Informations économiques provenant de différentes sources. (Classified by country, 1915–20)
F^{12}	7989–992	Bulletin économique de l'Etat-Major de l'Armée (1916–19)
F^{12}	7993–998	Etudes économiques (1914–19)
F^{12}	7999–8014	Papiers du service d'action économique (1915–18)

F^{12}: Commerce et Industrie: Après-guerre

F^{12}	8029–044	Préparation de l'après-guerre et réorganisation de l'économie française (1914–21)
F^{12}	8045–062	Comité consultatif des arts et manufactures (1917–19)
F^{12}	8063–102	Armistice: conseil suprême économique (1919–20)
F^{12}	8103–133	Armistice et traités de paix; dossiers du Ministère du Commerce (1916–20)

F^{12}: Commerce et Industrie: Service du Crédit

F^{12}	8161–62	Renseignements sur diverse banques françaises et étrangères (1922–33)

F^{12}: Commerce et Industrie: Commerce
extérieur

F^{12}	9183–198	Attachés commerciaux (1875–1937)
F^{12}	9203–284	Renseignements économiques fournis par les attachés commerciaux au ministère du Commerce (1910–39). Classified by country.

F^{30}: Administration centrale du Ministère des Finances

F^{30} See selected entries in my previous coverage of the Archives du Ministère de l'Economie et des Finances.

2. Series BB: Justice

The Riom Trial archives eventually will appear in this general series. Inquiries about this collection, which includes prosecution and defense documents as well as the trial proceedings, may be addressed to M. Pierre Cézard, Hôtel de Rohan, Archives Nationales. Access to this material currently is extremely difficult.

3. Series AJ: Fonds divers remis aux Archives

AJ 5   Délégation française à la Commission des réparations (1919-30).   A collection of 577 dossiers, with a 2-volume inventory.

AJ 6   Commission interalliée des réparations (1919-29).   A collection of 2178 dossiers, with a 2-volume inventory.

AJ 7   Commission interalliée des réparations de Bulgarie (1919-31).   A collection of 40 dossiers, with an 11-page inventory.

AJ 8   Office des paiements de réparations (1924-29).   A collection of two series: Archives de l'agent des paiements de réparations (dossiers 1-980); Archives du Comité des Transferts (dossiers 981-1045).

AJ 9   Haute   Commission   interalliée   des   Territoires Rhénans.   Haut Commissariat français dans les provinces du Rhin (1918-30).   A collection of three major fonds: Archives Interalliées HCITR (dossiers 1-1974); Archives Interalliées des Gages (dossiers 1975-2888); Archives Françaises (dossiers 2889-6596).   Detailed inventory of 556 pages.

4. Series AQ: Archives économiques

35 AQ 1-20   Siemens France (1941-44)
104-108 AQ   Entreprises allemandes ou sous contrôle
                allemand   installées   à   Paris   pendant
                l'occupation.

5. Series AR: Archives de l'Agence Havas

An important collection for both press and political history of the interwar period. See the published index, Les archives de l'Agence Havas, by Isabelle Brot. Paris, 1969.

6. Series AP: Archives Privées

Since the conditions governing access to private papers are subject to very frequent change, readers are advised to direct preliminary inquiries to the Directeur des Archives privées, Archives Nationales, 60 rue Francs-Bourgeois, 75003, Paris.

307 AP Dautry, Raoul. 260 cartons, including material from his service as Ministre de l'Armement (1939-40). Inventory. Written authorization.

151 AP Deschanel, Paul. 11 cartons, including dossiers on international politics after 1918. Inventory. Written authorization.

130 AP Dumesnil, Jacques. 30 cartons, including material on Washington, London and Geneva conference (1921-30). Inventory. Open access.

149 AP Mangin, General Charles.

317 AP Marin, Louis. 283 cartons, including material which concerns World War One and the Peace Conference as well as politics in Lorraine in the 1950s. Inventory. Cartons 1-103 are currently closed to research; the remainder may be consulted only with the written authorization of Mme Marin.

363 AP Mayer, René. 42 cartons, including material from the Commissariat aux Communications et à la Marine marchande, Alger(1943-44). Inventory. Closed until 2022.

313 AP Painlevé, Paul. 242 cartons, principally on the First World War; the last 40 cartons (approx.) concern the post-1919 period. Inventory. Open access. This collection includes the papers of Théodore Reinach (1860-1928).

... Paul-Boncour, Joseph. Currently contained in 109 cartons, including 43 cartons dealing with his interwar political career. Inventory by grandson François, whose written authorization is required.

74 AP Reynaud, Paul. 103 cartons, covering his career from 1911 to 1966, including cartons 8-29 (1913-45). Inventory divided into 2 parts. Written authorization required.

324 AP Tardieu, André. 128 cartons, principally from the First World War period; including correspondence received. Inventory. Written authorization.

94 AP   Thomas, Albert.   484 cartons, including material on his wartime ministries, his embassy in Moscow (1917-18), and the Paris Peace Conference. Inventory. Open access. There is also a microfilmed collection, 102 Mi 1, mainly on the Thomas-Lloyd George relationship (1916-18).

Note: The following are some of the private collections which have been transferred (1980) to the Archives Nationales from the Comité d'Histoire de la 2e Guerre Mondiale, formerly on the rue Leningrad, currently located at 80 b rue Lecourbe, 75015, Paris.

Barthélemy, Joseph.   1 carton of personal and administrative documents (photocopies), relating to the Riom trial and the Vichy regime.

Catroux, General.   2 cartons concerning Syria and Libya (1940-42) and Algeria (1943).

Gouin, F.   1 carton deriving from the Assemblée consultative d'Alger.

Pernot, G.   Unspecified number of documents deriving from his ministry of Blockade (1939-40).

Philip, André.   1 carton of personal papers bearing on wartime London and Algiers.

Schiffer, [].   6 cartons relating to the work of the Vichy propaganda director (1940-41).

Note: The papers of General Charles de Gaulle are shared by the Archives Nationales and the Institut de Gaulle, 5 rue de Solferino, 75007, Paris.

7. Other Private Papers

The following collections are not located at the Archives Nationales; however, most of the information on these collections is taken from the A.N. Guide des Papiers...(1978).

Baréty, Léon.   11 volumes (1920-39).   Inventory. Open access. Archives départementales des Alpes-Maritimes.

Blaisot, Camille.   2 liasses, including material on French-German relations in the 1920s. Inventory. Written authorization. Archives départementales du Calvados.

Clémentel, Etienne. Large collection of papers, including those on his ministerial career during the First World War and in the mid-1920s. Inventory in progress. Written authorization. Archives départementales du Puy-de-Dôme.

Combes, Emile. 22 cartons, 10 liasses and 1 bound volume, including some material from the First World War. Inventory. Open access. Archives départementales de la Charente-Maritime.

Eynac, Laurent. Substantial collection, particularly valuable for the interwar air ministry and air force, including a rich library collection. Inventory in progress. Written authorization. Mairie du Monastier (Haute-Loire).

François-Marsal, Frédéric. A collection that has been retained by the family, in Paris.

Jeanneney, Jules. Some 20 dossiers. Written authorization. M. Jean-Marcel Jeanneney, Rioz.

Jonnart, Charles. 22 cartons, including material on reparation commission and embassy at the Vatican (1921-23). Inventory (available at the Archives Nationales). Written authorization. Archives départementales du Pas-de-Calais.

Loucheur, Louis. Original collection at the Hoover Institute, Stanford, California. A microfilmed collection of 7 reels is available at the Institut d'histoire des relations internationales contemporaines, University of Paris I. Valuable on peace negotiations, financial problems and reparations (1916-31). Inventory. Open access.

Marchandeau, Paul. 1 malle, comprising documents from his parliamentary and ministerial career in the 1930s. Inventory in progress. Restricted access. Archives départementales du Tarn.

Mercier, Ernest. Hoover Institute, Stanford, California.

Raiberti, Flaminius. Substantial collection, including correspondence, some of which touches on his war and naval ministries in the 1920s. Authorization from Mme René Fatou, Alpes-Maritimes.

Réquin, General Edouard. A collection, housed at the Hoover Institute, Stanford, California, bearing on the career of Réquin, including years in Geneva and in Maginot's war ministry.

Sarraut, Albert. 172 liasses, covering domestic and foreign policy in the interwar period, including his years as governor-general in Indochina (1916-19) and his embassy in Turkey (1925-26). Inventory. Authorization required. Archives départementales de l'Aude.

Viollette, Maurice. 15 liasses, including material on World War One, North Africa and China (1920s and 1930s). Open access. Archives départementales d'Eure-et-Loir. Also a collection of personal papers, located at the Maison de Maurice Viollette, Dreux, Eure-et-Loir. Written authorization.

Bibliothèque Nationale

58, rue de Richelieu, 75002, Paris. Metro: Bourse, Quatre-Septembre, Palais-Royal, Richelieu-Drouot. Monday to Friday, 9 a.m. to 8 p.m.; Saturday and the month of August, from 9 a.m. to 6 p.m.; Manuscript room from 9 a.m. to 5 p.m. Closed on all legal holidays, and for two weeks following the second Monday after Easter.

To obtain a reader's card, one must present proper identification (e.g. passport), two photographs of passport size, letters of introduction from one's embassy and, commonly, from one's university. There is a fee of 10 F.

The manuscript room is to the left of the main entrance, on the second floor. Order forms may be submitted three at a time, no more than ten per day and often less during vacation periods.

1. Private Papers

Déat, Marcel. Collection donated by Madame Déat in 1973. Access to inventory and collection currently controlled by M. George Lefranc.

Flandin, Pierre-Etienne. 134 cartons; 23-page inventory. Includes material on reparations, Stresa conference, Rhineland crisis, Sudeten crisis and the Flandin trial. Principally covering 1914-1957. Authorization B.N.

Jouvenel, Henry de. 5 cartons, comprising speeches, manuscripts and notes.

Millerand, Alexandre. 102 cartons; 19-page inventory. Ranges from 1885 to 1943. Cartons 14-43 on World War I; 49-65 on his premiership and foreign ministry in 1920; 66-82 on his presidency (1920-24); 84-99 on the period from 1924 to 1940. Open access.

Poincaré, Raymond. 72 cartons. Inventory in vol.
CXXX of the Nouvelles acquisitions latines et françaises du
département des manuscrits...(1972).

Fondation Nationale des Sciences Politiques

27/30 rue Saint-Guillaume, 75007, Paris. Archives
located at 187 blvd. Saint-Germain. Metro: Sèvres-Babylone,
rue du Bac, Saint-Germain-des-Prés. Monday-Saturday, 9 a.m.
to 7 p.m. Closed last two weeks of July.
Address inquiries to Mlle Janine Bourdin, F.N.S.P., 27
rue Saint-Guillaume, 75007, Paris.

1. Private Papers

Auriol, Vincent. Approximately 230 boxes, organized
into five sections, by periods: pre-1936, 1936-40, 1940-46,
1947-54, 1954-65. Some 75 boxes for the pre-1946 period.
Access remains very restricted.

Blum, Léon. A large collection, complete with
detailed inventory. Principally a domestic political focus,
with limited value for foreign policy. Note sub-series 2 BL
(1934-40) and 3 BL (La guerre, la captivité, le procès de
Riom).

Daladier, Edouard. A collection of over 80 cartons,
accompanied by a general inventory of 5 pages, a detailed
inventory of 237 pages, and a name-subject index of 34
pages. Of particular interest for foreign policy is
sub-series 2 DA (1938-39), 3 DA (1939-40) and the Riom trial
material in 4 DA 10-30.

Kayser, Jacques. A collection addressed to the
history of the Radical Socialist party through to 1958. Of
limited interest for foreign policy, but a large press
clipping collection for the interwar years.

Roche, Emile — Caillaux, Joseph. An important
collection including material on the Agadir crisis and the
Caillaux trial of 1919, French war debts to the U.S.A
(1924-34) and correspondence between Roche and Caillaux
(1927-1944).

Schweisguth, General Victor. A collection that is
housed at the Archives Nationales (351 AP 1-). Of particular
interest is material from his service on the army staff
(1935-37), including his missions abroad.

Siegfried, André. A large collection, of limited value for questions of foreign policy; but does include his lectures to foreign ministry aspirants at the Ecole Libre des Sciences Politiques in the 1920s and 1930s.

Bibliothèque de Documentation Internationale Contemporaine

2, rue de Rouen, 92-Nanterre. Metro: RER from Auber or Etoile to Nanterre University. Monday-Saturday, 10 a.m. to 6 p.m.; from 1 July to mid-September, Monday-Friday, 10 a.m. to 5 p.m.

A photograph is required for the reading card, and a letter of reference is recommended.

1. Private Papers

Chappey, []. Some 10 cartons dealing mainly with the 1920s: reparations, several post-war missions to the Balkans, German domestic politics.

Klotz, Louis-Lucien. 38 cartons dealing with the Peace Conference of 1919. 1-17 on questions territoriales, 1-21 on questions économiques et financières. Open access. This is a collection less of private papers than of documents assembled by Klotz, many of which are now published in various forms.

Lamoureux, Lucien. 1 microfilm reel of his unpublished "Souvenirs politiques, 1919-1940." Open access.

Mantoux, Paul. 6 cartons, including 2 on the interallied conferences (1915-Nov. 1918), 1 on the Peace Conference (Feb.-June 1919), and 3 containing dossiers entitled Mantoux-A(lbert) Thomas (1915-19). Open access.

2. Additional Collections

Press clipping collection from the influential newspaper Le Temps, organized by subject heading.

"Comptes-rendus des réunions du 1er juillet 1940 au 5 août." A 10-volume collection of typed minutes prepared by the economic section of the French delegation to Wiesbaden.

ARCHIVES AND LIBRARIES

Institut d'Histoire du Temps Présent

80 b, rue Lecourbe, 75015, Paris. Metro:
Sèvres-Lecourbe, Vaugirard. Address inquiries to the
director, M. François Bédarida.

1. Private Papers

Comert, Pierre. 1 carton concerning the newspaper
France which he published in London during World War II.

Laurentie, Henri Marie. 6 cartons, including
correspondence, concerning French colonial administration
during and after World War II.

Marin, Louis. 16 cartons of press clippings
concerning his career, mainly 1938-45.

Tubert, General. 1 carton of personal documents,
including correspondence, dealing with Algeria, 1944-46.

Assemblée Nationale. Archives

Palais Bourbon, 126 rue de l'Université, 75007, Paris.
Metro: Concorde, Chambre des Députés. Monday-Saturday, 10
a.m.-12, 2 p.m.-6 p.m. No annual closing.
Address requests to the Secrétaire général des Archives
de l'Assemblée Nationale at the above address. Once
authorization is received, entrance to the archives is on the
rue Aristide Briand.
Of particular interest are the archives of the
parliamentary commissions, especially foreign affairs and
finance. This is a large collection, with but a rudimentary
inventory. Some of this material is held in a depot near
Versailles and must be brought in on request. Several days'
delay must be anticipated.

Sénat. Archives

Palais de Luxembourg, 15 rue de Vaugirard, 75006,
Paris. Metro: Odéon, Luxembourg. Tuesday-Friday, 9:30-12,
2:30-6 p.m. No annual closing.
Direct inquiries to the Directeur de la division des
archives, at the above address.
As in the case of the National Assembly, the records of
the foreign affairs, finance and military service commissions
will be of the greatest interest.

71

Other Specialized Libraries and Archives

Archives nationales, Section Outre-mer, 27 rue Oudinot, 75007, Paris.

Archives nationales, Archives privées, 60 rue des Francs-Bourgeois, 75141, Paris.

Bibliothèque. Chambre de Commerce et d'Industrie de Paris. Centre de Documentation et Archives, 16 rue Chateaubriand, 75008, Paris.

Bibliothèque. Banque de France. Service de l'Information, 43 rue de Valois, 75001, Paris.

Bibliothèque de l'Institut de France, 23 quai de Conti, 75006, Paris.

Bibliothèque du Ministère de la Défense, 231 boulevard Saint-Germain, 75007, Paris.

Bibliothèque Nordique (Fonds Finno-Scandinave de la Bibliothèque Sainte-Geneviève), 6 rue Valette, 75005, Paris.

Bibliothèque Polonaise de Paris, 6 quai d'Orléans, 75004, Paris.

Bibliothèque Sainte-Geneviève, 10 place du Panthéon, 75005, Paris.

Bibliothèque de la Sorbonne, Université de Paris, 47 rue des Ecoles, 75005, Paris.

Bibliothèque spécialisée du Centre de Documentation de l'Armement. Constructions aéronautiques, 4 avenue de la Porte d'Issy, 75015, Paris.

Centre de Documentation Juive Contemporaine, 17 rue Geoffroy-l'Asnier, 75004, Paris.

Institut d'Histoire des Relations Internationales Contemporaines, 17 rue de la Sorbonne, 75005, Paris.

Institut Historique Allemand, 9 rue Maspero, 75016, Paris.

La Documentation Française. Secrétariat général du Gouvernement, 29-31 quai Voltaire, 75007, Paris.

Press Archives

Institut Français de Presse. Centre de Documentation, 83 b, rue Notre-Dames-des-Champs, 75006, Paris.

Le Figaro. Service des Archives, 37 rue du Louvre, 75002, Paris.

Le Monde. Service de Documentation et Bibliothèque, 7 rue des Italiens, 75009, Paris.

L'Humanité. Archives, 6 boulevard Poissonnière, 75002, Paris.

L'Aurore. Archives, 100 rue de Richelieu, 75002, Paris.

IV. BIBLIOGRAPHY

Introduction

This bibliography of over 1500 entries has been prepared from an original collection of approximately 8000 titles. There are, in other words, some omissions. There are also several consequences of the attempt to maximize the utility while keeping the length within reason. First, and subject to the qualifications made in the second observation below, the need to be selective has dictated a reluctant return to a more narrow definition of diplomatic history. This should come as no surprise, for the multiple approaches which have been recommended earlier would call for a bibliography without end. Instead, and regrettably, whole categories have fallen victim to the selection process, particularly those that would have appeared under the rubric of Historical Articles or Historical Studies. So it is that the following are at best under-represented and incomplete: works on the French Empire, Algeria and the post-war mandates; works principally addressed to domestic politics and public/press opinion, or to the history of the armed services; works of the sort which broadly survey international relations and "Great Power" politics, treating France certainly, but seldom with much confidence or authority; finally, the countless works which concentrate on the Occupation, the Collaboration, the Resistance, within France between 1940 and 1944.

Second, it is fitting for the author to be the first to comment on the sometimes inconsistent and always arbitrary criteria that have been used to structure each sub-section. For instance, I have cast a wider net for Memoirs from the period than for Biographies. On balance, and since decisions had to be made, it seemed preferable to have a more comprehensive list of Memoirs than of the biographical works, many of which were written without benefit of much documentation and thus are now very dated. Even that decision, it should be noted, was based on solely French memoir material and as such has made no provision for the memoirs of foreigners who may have played prominent if indirect roles in French foreign affairs. Attention might also be drawn to the fact that the subject matter represented in the completed Dissertations is more varied, diverse, than what is found under Historical Studies. In this case I reasoned that researchers were less likely to locate the unpublished but often excellent dissertation than they were the published piece.

Third, the right to annotate these entries has been
exercised with discretion. I have kept to a minimum both
judgmental and descriptive comments. The volume may suffer
for it, for one would hardly question the utility of accurate
and judicious annotations. But even those which may be so
appraised can be misleading, the judgmental because they
cannot possibly speak to the needs and interests of all
researchers, the descriptive because their unavoidably
incomplete quality may divert potential readers from a source
that might have proven rich, even indispensable. Instead,
most of my annotations take the form of brief identifications
— biographical data principally for the authors of Memoirs
or the subjects of Biographies. The end result has been a
miniature Who Was Who in French diplomacy.

A. REFERENCE WORKS

General

1. An Index to Book Reviews in the Humanities.
    Detroit, 1963-1980.

2. Bibliographie annuelle de l'histoire de France. 25
    vols. Paris, 1955-1978.

    The most thorough guide to periodical literature in
    French. Includes some French books and theses.

3. Book Review Index. Detroit, 1965-1980.

4. French Historical Studies.

    See listings under "Recent Books on French History"
    in this biannual journal.

5. Historical Abstracts, 1450-Present. Bibliography of
    the World's Periodical Literature. Santa
    Barbara, 1955-quarterly.

    Currently 26 volumes. Abstracts now being grouped
    according to subject and geographical headings. Not
    as thorough for French publications.

6. Revue d'Histoire de la Deuxième Guerre Mondiale.

    See extensive bibliographies in each issue.

7. Social Sciences Index. New York, 1975-.

    Successor to Social Sciences and Humanities Index.

REFERENCE WORKS

International Relations

8. Foreign Affairs Bibliography: A Selected and
    Annotated List of Books on International
    Relations. New York, 1933-1976-.

    Volumes cover 1919-1932, 1932-1942, etc. to 1972.
    Emphasis on contemporary affairs, but includes
    coverage of recent history.

9. Foreign Affairs 50-Year Bibliography. New
    Evaluations of Significant Books on International
    Relations, 1920-1970. New York, 1972.

    Extensive comments on "significant" works.

10. League of Nations. Catalogue of Publications,
    1920-1935. Geneva, 1935. 5 Supplements
    (1936-1945).

11. Moussa, Farag. Diplomatie Contemporaine. Guide
    Bibliographique. Geneva, 1964.

12. Political Science, Government and Public Policy
    Series. Princeton, 1967-.

    Index to American periodical literature.

13. Wright, M., Davis, J., and Clark, M. Essay
    Collections in International Relations: A
    Classified Bibliography, 1977.

14. Zawodny, J.K. Guide to the Study of International
    Relations. San Francisco, 1966.

    Excellent, annotated guide to research and reference
    materials.

Biographical

15. Cooke, James J. France 1789-1962. Newton Abbot,
    1975.

    Principally a collection of brief biographies.

16. Coston, Henry, ed. Partis, journaux et hommes
    politiques d'hier et d'aujourd'hui. Paris,
    1960.

17. Coston, Henry, ed. Dictionnaire de la politique
    française. Paris, 1967.

Biographical

18.   Current Biography. New York, 1941-1980-.

        Annual volumes which include a reasonable number of
        French personalities. Usually press pieces, often
        with photograph. Brief obituaries of those
        discussed in previous volumes.

19.   Dictionnaire de biographie française. Paris,
        1933-1980-.

        Authoritative work, currently in 14 volumes
        (covering A to F). Excludes those born after 1925.
        Often includes military men and diplomatic
        personnel, although on occasion deletes obvious
        choices, like Daladier.

20.   Dictionnaire des parlementaires français,
        1889-1940. 8 vols. Paris, 1960-1977.

21.   Obituaries from The Times, 1961-1970. Reading,
        1975.

        Reproduces only those of the most prominent
        individuals, the majority of whom apparently were
        British.

22.   Obituaries from The Times, 1971-1975. Compiled as
        above by Frank C. Robert. Reading, 1978.

23.   Phrangoules, A.P., ed. Dictionnaire diplomatique.
        2 vols. New York, 1968.

24.   Pierrard, Pierre. Dictionnaire de la IIIe
        République. Paris, 1968.

25.   Who's Who in France. Paris, 1953-1980.

        Published in French, every second year. Coverage is
        brief, rather haphazard, but still very useful.

Guides to French Libraries and Archives

26.   Archives Nationales. Guide des Papiers des
        Ministres et Secrétaires d'Etat de 1871 à 1974.
        Vol. 1. compiled by Chantal de Tourtier-Bonazzi
        and François Pourcelet. Paris, 1978.

REFERENCE WORKS

Guides to French Libraries and Archives

27.   Archives Nationales. Etat Général des Fonds. Vol.
        1. l'Ancien Régime. Vol. 2. 1789-1940. Paris,
        1978.

28.   Archives Nationales. Guide du Lecteur. Paris,
        1978.

29.   Astorkia, Madeline. "Les sources de l'histoire de
        l'armée de l'air pendant la deuxième guerre
        mondiale au service historique de l'armée de
        l'air." R.H.D.G.M. 28 (1978): 123-130.

30.   Bégué-Diziain, Mme. Guide bibliographique sommaire
        et méthodique d'histoire militaire. Vol. 6
        (1919-45). Paris, 1967.

31.   Carbone, Salvatore. "Gli Archivi Francesi."
        Quaderni della Rassegna degli Archivi di Stato,
        3(1960): 1-127.

32.   Cezard, Pierre. "Fonds d'Archives relatifs à
        l'emploi pendant la seconde guerre mondiale
        conservés aux Archives Nationales." R.H.D.G.M.
        15(1965): 84-88.

33.   Chapon, C. "Documentation; l'armée de terre
        française: 2 septembre 1939 et 9 mai 1940."
        Revue Historique des Armées 6(1979): 164-192.

34.   Confer, Vincent. "France." in Guide to the
        Diplomatic Archives of Western Europe, pp.
        55-84. Edited by D. Thomas and L. Case.
        Philadelphia, 1959.

35.   Delmas, J. "Le service historique de l'armée de
        terre et la deuxième guerre mondiale."
        R.H.D.G.M. 28(1978): 113-121.

36.   Devos, J.D., et al. Inventaire sommaire des archives
        de la Guerre Série N, 1872-1919. Troyes, 1974.

37.   Fabre, Devos, et al. Inventaire des archives
        conservées au service historique de l'état-major
        de l'armée. Archives modernes. Paris, 1954.

38.   Fournier, Jean. "Les archives militaires et leur
        exploitation par les historiens contemporains."
        Revue des travaux de l'académie des sciences
        morales et politiques 124(1971): 129-145.

Guides to French Libraries and Archives

39.   Hartmann, Peter Claus. Archives, bibliothèques et centres de documentation à Paris pour l'histoire des XIXe et XXe siècles. Paris, 1978.

40.   Hubert, Jean-Paul. "Les possibilités de la recherche et les archives aux ministères de l'économie et des finances." Revue d'Histoire Economique et Sociale 49(1971): 161-179.

41.   Kaspi, André. "Le centre de documentation juive contemporaine." Revue d'Histoire moderne et contemporaine 23(1976): 305-311.

42.   Ministère des Affaires Etrangères. Archives diplomatiques. Guide du Lecteur. Paris, 1977.

43.   Ministère des Armées. Service Historique. Guide bibliographique sommaire d'histoire militaire et coloniale française. Paris, 1969.

44.   Ministère de l'Economie. Ministère du Budget. Archives Economiques et Financières: état des fonds au 31 mars 1978. Paris, 1978.

45.   Outrey, Amédée. "Note sur les pertes subies du fait de la guerre par les archives du ministère des affaires étrangères." Cahiers d'histoire de la guerre(1949): 31-33.

46.   Posner, Ernst. "Manual of Archives Administration: Theory and Practice of Public Archives in France." American Archivist 35(1972): 51-58.

47.   Sheppard, Julia. "Vive La Différence?! An Outsider's View of French Archives." Archives 14(1980): 151-62.

48.   Vale, M.G.A. "Libraries and Archives. 3. France." History 55(1970): 65-68.

49.   Welsch, Erwin K. Libraries and Archives in France: A Handbook. New York, 1979.

As general guides which contain an enormous amount of useful information, this and Hartmann, #39, are to be recommended.

REFERENCE WORKS

Guides to Dissertations

50. American Doctoral Dissertations. Ann Arbor, 1973-.

The most comprehensive of its kind; includes Canadian dissertations.

51. Bibliographie analytique des thèses de doctorat des universités de France (1966-1974). Paris, 1978.

52. Catalogue des thèses de doctorat, soutenues devant les universités françaises. Nouvelle Série. Paris, annual.

53. Dissertation Abstracts International. Ann Arbor, monthly.

Prior to vol. 30(1970) series entitled Dissertation Abstracts. The abstracts themselves are excellent, although not all dissertations are abstracted.

54. Doctoral Dissertations in History. 4 vols. Washington D.C. 1976-1980.

55. Historical Research for University Degrees in the United Kingdom. London, annual.

56. Index to Theses: Accepted for Higher Degrees by the Universities of Great Britain and Ireland. London, 1973-1980.

57. Jacobs, Phyllis M. History Theses 1901-1970: Historical research for higher degrees in the universities of the United Kingdom. London, 1976.

58. Kuehl, Warren F. Dissertations in History. An Index to Dissertations Completed in History Departments of United States and Canadian Universities. 2 vols. 1. (1873-1960), 2. (1961-1970). Kentucky, 1972.

59. List of Doctoral Dissertations in History in Progress or Recently Completed in the United States, May 1970-May 1973. Washington D.C., 1974.

Guides to Dissertations

60.   Ministère des Universités. Répertoire raisonné des doctorats d'état en cours. 2 vols. Paris, 1978.

61.   Register of Post-Graduate Dissertations in Progress in History and Related Subjects. Ottawa, annual.

B. DISSERTATIONS

Dissertations Completed

62.   Adams, D.B. "The Role of Military Considerations in Anglo-French Decision-Making in the Munich Crisis." University of Denver, Ph.D., 1971.

63.   Adams, W.E. "André Tardieu and French Foreign Policy, 1902-1919." Stanford, Ph.D., 1959.

64.   Allen, D.R. "French Views of America in the Nineteen Thirties." Boston University, Ph.D., 1970.

65.   Atkinson, J.L.B. "Camille Barrère, Ambassador to Rome: The First Eight Years of a Mission." Pennsylvania State University, Ph.D., 1951.

66.   Balzarini, S.E. "Britain, France and the 'German Problem' at the World Disarmament Conference, 1932-1934." Washington State University, Ph.D., 1979.

67.   Birn, D.S. "Britain and France at the Washington Conference, 1921-1922." Columbia, Ph.D., 1964.

68.   Blacksburg, L. "Bankruptcy of Appeasement: Anglo-French Acquiescence of Italian Expansion in Africa during the 1930s." City University of New York, Ph.D., 1974.

69.   Blatt, J.R. "French Reaction to Italy, Italian Fascism and Mussolini, 1919-1925." University of Rochester, Ph.D., 1977.

70.   Boyle, T.E. "France, Great Britain, and German Disarmament, 1919-1927." State University of New York, Ph.D., 1972.

71.   Brandstadter, M. "Paul Reynaud and the Third French Republic, 1919-1939." Duke University, Ph.D., 1971.

Dissertations Completed

72.   Burnett, R.A. "Georges Clemenceau in the Paris Peace Conference, 1919." University of North Carolina, Ph.D., 1968.

73.   Carley, M.J. "The French Intervention in the Russian Civil War, November 1917-April 1919." Queen's University, Ph.D., 1976.

74.   Carré, C. "Les attachés militaires français, 1920-1945. Rôle et influence." Paris I, maîtrise, 1976.

75.   Casset, J.M. "L'attitude française vis-à-vis de l'Italie (octobre 1938-mai 1939)." Paris I, maîtrise, 1967.

76.   Cleveland, R.E. "French Attitudes toward the 'German Problem', 1914-1919." University of Nebraska, Ph.D., 1957.

77.   Colin de Verdière, J.F. "La politique financière de la France pendant la seconde guerre mondiale, 1939-1945." Paris, Thèse science économique, 1964.

78.   Connors, J.D. "Paul Reynaud and French National Defense, 1933-1939." Loyola (Chicago), Ph.D., 1977.

79.   Cooke, W.H. "Joseph Caillaux and International Relations, 1911-1920." Stanford, Ph.D., 1928.

80.   Cox, F.J. "French Strategy at the Paris Peace Conference: A Study of the Conflict between Foch and Clemenceau over the problem of Security." University of California, Ph.D., 1947.

81.   Dutailly, Henry. "Les problèmes de l'armée de terre française, 1935-1939." Paris I, 3e cycle, 1980.

82.   Duvivier, P.F. "A Study in Diplomacy from Disarmament to Rearmament: Franco-German Relations from February 1932 through June 1935." Georgetown University, Ph.D., 1976.

83.   Fitzgerald, S.E. "A Vision of Future War: France 1919-1940." California (Berkeley), Ph.D., 1974.

DISSERTATIONS

Dissertations Completed

84.   Flynn, J.F.   "The 1923 Ruhr Crisis as a Two-Front
        War: Intra-German   and   German-French
        Confrontations." Ohio State, Ph.D., 1977.

85.   Frankenstein, R.   "Le financement du réarmement
        français, 1935-1939." Paris I, 3e cycle, 1978.

86.   Friedberg, R.M.   "French Radical Opinion and French
        Foreign Policy, 1933-1939." Connecticut, Ph.D.,
        1972.

87.   Gay, A.C.   "The Daladier Administration,
        1938-1940." North Carolina (Chapel Hill), Ph.D.,
        1970.

88.   Gazet, M.   "L'Assemblée consultative provisoire,
        Alger, 3 novembre 1943-25 juillet 1944." Paris,
        3e cycle, 1970.

89.   Girard, C.S.M. "The Effects of Western Hemisphere
        Issues upon Franco-American Relations during the
        Second World War." Bryn Mawr, Ph.D., 1968.

90.   Goldman, A.L.   "Crisis in the Rhineland: Britain,
        France and the Rhineland."   Indiana, Ph.D.,
        1967.

91.   Gombin, R.   "La S.F.I.O. et la politique étrangère
        française entre les deux guerres mondiales."
        Paris, Thèse science politique, 1967.

92.   Goodman, R.E.M.   "The Rhineland Crisis and the
        Politics of Dependence: A Case Study in
        Bureaucratic   Government   and   Irresponsible
        Leadership." Princeton, Ph.D., 1978.

93.   Goold, J.D. "'Old Diplomacy': The Diplomatic Career
        of Lord Hardinge, 1910-1922." Cambridge, Ph.D.,
        1976.

94.   Gordon, R.A.   "France and the Spanish Civil War."
        Columbia, Ph.D., 1971.

95.   Grayson, J.G. "The Foreign Policy of Léon Blum and
        the Popular Front Government in France." North
        Carolina, Ph.D., 1962.

96.   Greene, F. "French Military Leadership and Security
        against Germany, 1919-1940." Yale, Ph.D., 1950.

Dissertations Completed

97.   Ground, R.P.   "The Political Record of Maurice Paléologue." Oxford, B. Litt., 1962.

98.   Hall, H.H.   "The Eastern Question in Anglo-French Relations, 1920-1922." Vanderbilt, Ph.D., 1971.

99.   Harvey, J.C.   "The French Security Thesis and French Foreign Policy from Paris to Locarno, 1919-1925." Texas University, Ph.D., 1955.

100.   Hauser, J.D.   "Britain, France, and the United States at the World Economic Conference of 1933: A Study in Futility." Washington State, Ph.D., 1973.

101.   Holder, F.B.   "André Tardieu, Politician and Statesman of the French Third Republic: A Study of His Ministries and Policies, 1929-1932." Berkeley, Ph.D., 1962.

102.   Hood, R.C.   "The French Naval Officer Corps, 1919-1939." Maryland, Ph.D., 1979.

103.   Hood, R.E.   "Sanction Diplomacy: Britain and French Rhine Policy, 1920-1924." Georgetown, Ph.D., 1975.

104.   Hunt, H.H.   "Edouard Daladier, the Radicals and the Formation of the Popular Front, 1934-1936." Case Western, Ph.D., 1976.

105.   Hyde, J.M.   "Pierre Laval: The Illusions of a Realist, 1939-1940." Harvard, Ph.D., 1963.

106.   Jasperson, M.   "Laval and the Nazis: A Study of Franco-German Relations." Georgetown, Ph.D., 1967.

107.   Jeanmougin, G.   "Les relations franco-turques de 1925 à 1935." Nice, 3e cycle, 1972.

108.   Joliet, P.V.   "French-American Relations and the Political Role of the French Army, 1943-1945." State University of New York (Binghamton), Ph.D., 1978.

109.   Jones, J.R.   "The Foreign Policy of Louis Barthou, 1933-1934." North Carolina, Ph.D., 1958.

DISSERTATIONS

Dissertations Completed

110. Kaiser, D.E. "Germany, Britain, France and Eastern Europe, 1930-1939: Political and Economic Diplomacy in the Successor States." Harvard, Ph.D., 1976.

111. Kaplan, J.L. "France's Road to Genoa: Strategic, Economic, and Ideological Factors in French Foreign Policy, 1921-1922." Columbia, Ph.D., 1974.

112. Karter, S.M. "Coercion and Resistance-Dependence and Compliance: The Germans, Vichy, and the French Economy." Wisconsin (Madison), Ph.D., 1976.

113. Kaspi, A. "Les Etats-Unis et la formation du Comité français de libération nationale: la mission de Jean Monnet à Alger." Nanterre, 3e cycle, 1969.

114. Keeton, E.D. "Briand's Locarno Policy: French Economics, Politics, and Diplomacy, 1925-1929." Yale, Ph.D., 1975.

115. Kooker, J.L. "French Financial Diplomacy: The Interwar Years." Johns Hopkins, Ph.D., 1975.

116. Lenoir, N.R. "The Ruhr in Anglo-French Diplomacy: From the Beginning of the Occupation until the End of Passive Resistance." Oklahoma, Ph.D., 1972.

117. Ling, B. "Parliaments and the Peace Treaty: A Comparative Study of the Reactions of the British and French Parliaments to the Treaty of Peace of 1919." London, Ph.D., 1938.

118. Loyrette, J.E.L. "The Foreign Policy of Poincaré: France and Great Britain in Relations with the German Problem, 1919-1924." Oxford, B. Litt., 1955.

119. McClare, A.D. "Vincent Auriol in the Interwar Years." Duke, Ph.D., 1974.

120. Mageli, P.D. "The French Radical Party and the Problem of French Relations with Russia, 1917-1939." University of Chicago, Ph.D., 1978.

Dissertations Completed

121.   Mealy, K. "De Gaulle et les Etats-Unis, 1940-1945." Strasbourg, 3^e cycle, 1969.

122.   Melby, E.D.K. "Oil and the International System: The Case of France, 1918-1969." Johns Hopkins, Ph.D., 1978.

123.   Melton, G.E. "Admiral Darlan and the Diplomacy of Vichy, 1940-1942." North Carolina, Ph.D., 1966.

124.   Miller, D.J. "Stephen Pichon (1857-1933) and the Making of French Foreign Policy (1906-11)." Cambridge, Ph.D., 1977.

125.   Miller, J.L. "Henry de Jouvenel and the Syrian Mandate." Bryn Mawr, Ph.D., 1970.

126.   Nies, J.L. "Franco-American Relations, 1917-1918." Nebraska (Lincoln), Ph.D., 1973.

127.   Payne, D.S. "The Foreign Policy of Georges Clemenceau, 1917-1920." Duke, Ph.D., 1970.

128.   Peake, T.R. "The Impact of the Russian Revolution upon French Attitudes and Policies toward Russia, 1917-1918." North Carolina, Ph.D., 1974.

129.   Perett, W.G. "French Naval Policy and Foreign Affairs, 1930-1939." Stanford, Ph.D., 1977.

130.   Pitts, V.J. "France and the German Problem: Politics and Economics in the Locarno Period, 1924-1929." Harvard, Ph.D., 1975.

131.   Pitz, A.H. "United States Diplomatic Relations with Vichy France from 1940 to 1942." Northern Illinois, Ph.D., 1975.

132.   Poitrineau, A. "Les idées politiques d'André Tardieu." Algiers, Thèse de Droit, 1953.

133.   Prévost, F. "L'opinion français après la conférence de Munich, octobre-décembre 1938." Paris, maîtrise, 1967.

134.   Rakowsky, J. "Franco-British Policy toward the Ukranian Revolution, March 1917 to February 1918." Case Western, Ph.D., 1974.

DISSERTATIONS

Dissertations Completed

135.   Redman, M.E. "Franco-American Diplomatic Relations, 1919-1926." Stanford, Ph.D., 1946.

136.   Resovich, T. "France in Transition: Pre-Vichy Diplomatic and Political Realignments, May 10-June 25, 1940." Wisconsin, Ph.D., 1966.

137.   Ruby, M. "La vie et l'oeuvre de Jean Zay." Paris, 3e cycle, 1967.

138.   Sable, S.K. "The French Nationalists and the Collapse of the Third Republic (1938-1941)." Case Western, Ph.D., 1978.

139.   Safford, J.O. "French Attitudes toward Impending War, 1935-1939." Cornell, Ph.D., 1976.

140.   Sakwa, G. "Franco-Polish Relations, 1935-1938: A Study in Policy and Opinion." London, M. Phil., 1968.

141.   Santore, J.F. "The Foreign Policy of the French Communist Party, 1931-1935." Columbia, Ph.D., 1976.

142.   Schadler, A.L. "Anglo-French Economic Coordination in World War II: The Anglo-French Coordinating Committee, 1939-1940." Lehigh University, Ph.D., 1975.

143.   Schrecker, E.W. "The French Debt to the United States, 1917-1929." Harvard, Ph.D., 1974.

144.   Serota, M.I. "The Effect of the War Debt Question upon French Internal Politics and Diplomacy, 1924-1926." University of Chicago, Ph.D., 1976.

145.   Sharp, A.J. "Britain and France and the Execution of the Peace of Versailles, 1919-23, with Special Reference to Disarmament and Reparations." Nottingham, Ph.D., 1975.

146.   Silvestri, G.D. "Paul Reynaud and the Fall of France." Syracuse, Ph.D., 1969.

147.   Sinanoglou, I. "France Looks Eastward: Perspectives and Policies in Russia, 1914-1918." Columbia, Ph.D., 1974.

Dissertations Completed

148. Solo, R. "André François-Poncet: Ambassador of France." Michigan State, Ph.D., 1978.

149. Steinfels, P. "French Left-Wing Intellectuals and Foreign Policy: The Ligue des Droits de l'Homme, 1933-1939." Columbia, Ph.D., 1976.

150. Szaluta, J. "Marshal Pétain between Two Wars, 1918-1940." Columbia, Ph.D., 1969.

151. Tadesse, F. "La politique éthiopienne de la France de 1933 à 1936." Strasbourg, 3e cycle, 1966.

152. Thayer, P. "Locarno and its Aftermath: A Study of the Foreign Policy of Aristide Briand and Gustav Stresemann, 1925-1928." North Carolina, Ph.D., 1956.

153. Trafford, D.W. "A Study of the Problem of French Security and the British and French Presses, 1919-1925." Indiana, Ph.D., 1947.

154. Verich, T.M. "The European Powers and the Italo-Ethiopian War, 1935-1936: A Diplomatic Study." Duke, Ph.D., 1973.

155. Waites, N.H. "British Foreign Policy towards France regarding the German Problem from 1929-1934." London, Ph.D., 1972.

156. Weigold, M.E. "National Security versus Collective Security: The Role of the 'Couverture' in Shaping French Military and Foreign Policy (1905-1934)." St. John's University (N.Y.), Ph.D., 1970.

157. Welch, E.J. "France and her East European Allies in the League of Nations, 1920-1926." Fordham, Ph.D., 1958.

158. White, D.S. "Franco-American Relations in 1917-1918: War Aims and Peace Prospects." Pennsylvania State University, Ph.D., 1954.

Dissertations in Progress (supervisor's name in brackets)

159. Agostino, M. "L'Image du Pape Pie XI dans la presse française et dans la presse italienne (1922-1929)." Lyon III (Gadille), d'Etat.

DISSERTATIONS

Dissertations in Progress

160. Ahmedov, A. "Les relations franco-turques entre les deux guerres mondiales." Paris VIII (Castellan), d'Etat.

161. Alexander, M.S. "Maurice Gamelin and the Defence of France: French Military Policy, the U.K. Land Contribution and Strategy towards Germany, 1935-1940." Oxford (Parker), Ph.D.

162. Bogdan, H. "La politique française à l'égard de la Hongrie, 1919-1929." Paris I (Duroselle), d'Etat.

163. Boulesteix, "La mobilisation de 1939." Paris I (Duroselle), d'Etat.

164. Burford, G.E. "The Allied Military Control and Disarmament of Germany, 1919-1922." London (Robertson), Ph.D.

165. Butler, J.E. "The Conference of Ambassadors, 1920-1931." London (Dakin), Ph.D.

166. Cointret-Labrousse, M. "Le Conseil National, 1940-1944." Paris X (Rémond), d'Etat.

167. Couder, L. "Les relations franco-italiennes entre 1919 et 1926." Paris I (Duroselle), d'Etat.

168. Debeir, J.C. "Les dévaluations du franc dans l'entre-deux-guerres." Paris I(Bouvier), d'Etat.

169. Du Réau, E. "Edouard Daladier et le problème de la sécurité de la France." Paris I (Duroselle), d'Etat.

169A. Frankenstein, R. "Les relations franco-britanniques, 1935-1947." Paris X (Girault), d'Etat.

170. Gardiner, J. "De Gaulle and the Free French In London, 1940-1943." London (Johnson), Ph.D.

171. Groseillers, G. "Les buts de guerre de la France, 1939-1940." Montréal (Seager), Ph.D.

Dissertations in Progress

172.   Hennebicque, A. "Economie de guerre et préparation
        de l'après-guerre en France, 1914-1924." Paris
        VIII (Bouvier), d'Etat.

173.   Jordan, N.T. "The Breakdown of France's Eastern
        Alliances: The 'Petite Entente' and Poland,
        1935-1937." London (Robertson), Ph.D.

174.   Kassem, S. "Le Sandjak d'Alexandrette entre la
        France, la Turquie et la Syrie de 1918 à 1940."
        Paris VIII (Castellan), d'Etat.

175.   Kirkland, F.R. "The French Officer Corps and the
        Fall of France: Psychological Factors Influencing
        the Attitudes and Behavior of French Officers,
        1920-1940." Pennsylvania State University,
        Ph.D.

176.   Lacaze, Y. "La France et Munich." Paris I
        (Duroselle), d'Etat.

177.   Larmaillard, "L'influence de l'Etat-Major sur
        l'élaboration de la politique extérieure
        française." Paris X (Girault), 3ᵉ cycle.

178.   Le Motheux, "L'Image des Etat-Unis et des
        Américains en France de 1944-1945." Paris X
        (Girault), 3ᵉ cycle.

179.   Maga, T.P. "The United States, France and the
        Refugee Crisis, 1933-1945." McGill (Randall),
        Ph.D.

180.   Manning, P.M. "Britain and the Free French in the
        Second World War." London (Watt), M. Phil.

181.   Marchal, J. "La reconstruction des régions
        dévastées de la France et les réparations du
        lendemain de la première guerre mondiale." Paris
        I (Duroselle), d'Etat.

182.   Mares, A. "Aspects ⟨des relations franco-
        tchécoslovaques dans l'entre-deux-guerres."
        Paris I (Snejdarek), d'Etat.

183.   Martin, M. "La presse parisienne et l'information
        économique et financière, 1890-1939." Paris X
        (Levy-Leboyer), d'Etat.

DISSERTATIONS

Dissertations in Progress

184. Masuzoe, Y. "La sécurité de la France, sa recherche par Aristide Briand, 1921 à 1932." Paris I (Duroselle), d'Etat.

185. Moss, J. "Soviet Diplomatic Relations with France, 1917-1924." North Carolina, Ph.D.

186. Néant, H. "Les relations économiques entre la France et la Grande-Bretagne de 1919 à 1931." Paris X (Girault), d'Etat.

187. Nouschi, M. "La politique navale française, 1919-1939." Rennes II (Thobie), d'Etat.

188. Ormos, M. "La France et les états successeurs de l'Autriche-Hongrie de 1918 à 1923." Paris VIII (Castellan), d'Etat.

189. Rouge, P. "La politique française et la formation de la Yougoslavie, 1914-1920." Paris VIII (Castellan), d'Etat.

190. Salmon, P.J.K. "Allied Strategy and Diplomacy in Scandinavia, 1939-1940." Cambridge (Hinsley), Ph.D.

191. Salvatore, A.T. "Evolution of a Pacifist, Paul Faure, 1918-1940." New York, Ph.D.

192. Saly, P. "Le financement public de l'économie française, 1918-1940." Paris VIII (Bouvier), d'Etat.

193. Sarvis, A.R. "The French Right and the Franco-Soviet Pact, 1934-1938." Case Western, Ph.D.

194. Schaeffer, P. "La presse française et l'Allemagne Hitlérienne (1933-1939)." Metz (Poidevin), d'Etat.

195. Schwedes, J.T. "Great Britain, De Gaulle, and the Future of France, 1940-1944." Minnesota, Ph.D.

196. Shearson, A.J. "Public Debate in France on Disarmament and its Influence on Diplomacy of Arms Control, 1925-1935." Georgetown, Ph.D.

Dissertations in Progress

197.   Silberstein, B.   "Raoul Dautry, ministre de l'armement, 1939-1940." Paris I (Bouvier), 3e cycle.

198.   Soutou, G.   "Les buts de guerre économiques des grandes puissances, 1914-1920." Paris I (Duroselle), d'Etat.

199.   Stevenson, D.   "French War Aims towards Germany, 1914-1919." Cambridge (Andrew), Ph.D.

200.   Szych, "Les relations militaires franco-polonaises de 1919 à 1939." Lille (Nordmann), 3e cycle.

201.   Vaisse, M.   "L'Attitude de la France à l'égard du désarmement, 1919-1939." Paris I (Duroselle), d'Etat.

202.   Wolikow, S.   "L'activité étatique et le développement économique: l'exemple du secteur pétrolier en France de la première guerre mondiale aux lendemains de la seconde." Paris VIII (Bouvier), d'Etat.

203.   Woollard, N.W.   "Anglo-Franco-Russian Relations in 1939." Belfast (Blair), Ph.D.

C. DOCUMENTARY COLLECTIONS

Introduction

The most important published collection of documents relating to French foreign policy in this period is the multi-volume, official series Documents Diplomatiques Français. The reader is reminded that this collection has been discussed in Section II of the present volume.

The principal foreign collections must be treated here with comparable brevity. The following official series, each of them multi-volume in character, must be regarded as important companions to the French diplomatic documents. Certainly they contribute significantly to an understanding of French policy, its motivation and its impact abroad. Particularly noteworthy are the Documents Diplomatiques Belges, the Documents on British Foreign Policy, the Foreign Relations of the United States, the Documenti Diplomatici Italiani, the Documents on German Foreign Policy, and the Akten zur Deutschen Auswärtigen Politik. Attention also should be paid to the various series of League of Nations publications, including the Official Journal, the Treaty Series, and the Armaments Year-Book.

For all of its limitations, the Serre report (#205), and the accompanying nine volumes of testimony, remains a key source for interwar and wartime France. This collection was the work of a parliamentary commission that was charged with an inquiry into Les événements survenus en France de 1933 à 1945. Under the guidance of its rapporteur, M. Charles Serre, the commission conducted its hearings between 1947 and 1951. Witnesses were interviewed, written depositions were received, and a certain amount of original documentation was collected from state and private archives. The deficiencies of this collection are as obvious as its contributions. Too often, it may be said, the commission members did not pursue their interrogation of the witnesses as intensely as the historian might have wished; and certainly far too often potentially key witnesses were either overlooked entirely or at any rate were not compelled to appear before the commission. Not only was this the case for the former foreign minister Delbos, the former premier Chautemps, and the Quai d'Orsay's long-serving secretary-general, Alexis Léger, but it applied to such prominent ambassadors as Coulondre, Corbin and Naggiar, and to most of the foreign ministry's senior functionaries — Bargeton, Massigli, Charvériat, Renom de la Baume, Hoppenot. Nevertheless, the

testimonies which the commission did gather from some of the
Third Republic's diplomatic and consular personnel, and many
of its cabinet ministers and senior military officers,
continue to make this collection very worthwhile.

Finally, some mention must be made of the Trial
literature which emerged from Vichy's court of Riom or from
the Provisional Government's trial proceedings against
alleged collaborators. It goes without saying that these
investigations in courts of law were not addressed
exclusively, even primarily, to matters of foreign policy.
But by the same token, that subject was frequently raised;
and the defendants, accordingly, were obliged to address it.
The post-war trials of Laval and Flandin, both interwar and
wartime foreign ministers, are useful in this respect. So,
too, certain volumes deriving from the Riom trials are likely
to benefit the student of diplomatic history. In particular,
one might single out the documentary material assembled by
Ribet (#238) and by Michel (#236), the latter being the most
recent study based on documentation which is preserved at the
Archives Nationales but which remains closed to the
attentions of most scholars. In the absence of the complete
Riom archives, instructions as well as the trial proceedings,
one must rely on these published works, and on the Riom
materials contained in the Daladier and Blum papers at the
Fondation Nationale des Sciences Politiques.

General

204.   Chambrun, René and Josée de. France during the
        German Occupation, 1940-1944; A Collection of 292
        Statements on the Government of Maréchal Pétain
        and P. Laval. 3 vols. Stanford, 1959.

205.   France. Assemblée Nationale, 1946-1958. Session de
        1947. Commission chargée d'enquêter sur les
        événements survenus en France de 1933 à 1945.
        No. 2344. Rapport fait au nom de la
        commission...par M. Charles Serre, rapporteur
        général. 2 vols. Paris, 1952.

        Annexes (Dépositions). Témoignages et documents
        recueillis par la commission d'enquête
        parlementaire. 9 vols. Paris, 1951-1952.

206.   France. Délégation française auprès de la
        Commission d'armistice. La délégation française
        auprès de la Commission allemande d'Armistice.
        Recueil de documents publiés par le gouvernement
        français. 5 vols. Paris, 1947-1959.

DOCUMENTARY COLLECTIONS

General

> This published collection may be supplemented by an
> unpublished 10-volume collection of minutes prepared
> by the economic branch of the French delegation to
> Wiesbaden. See Section Three, under Bibliothèque de
> Documentation Internationale Contemporaine.

207.   France. Journal officiel de la république
        française, 1870-1940. Chambre des députés.
        Débats parlementaires. Paris, 1881-1940.

208.   France. Journal officiel de la république
        française. Chambre des députés, 1876-1940.
        Documents parlementaires. Annexes aux
        procès-verbaux des séances. Paris, 1881-1939.

209.   France. Journal officiel de la république
        française. Sénat, 1876-1940. Débats
        parlementaires. Paris, 1881-1940.

210.   France. Journal officiel de la république
        française. Sénat, 1876-1940. Documents
        parlementaires. Annexes aux procès-verbaux des
        séances. Paris, 1881-1939.

211.   France. Journal officiel de l'Etat Français,
        1940-1944. Lois et décrets, 4 janvier 1941-24
        août 1944. Vichy, 1941-1944.

212.   France. Lois et décrets, 5 septembre 1870-3 janvier
        1941. Paris, Vichy, 1870-1941.

Diplomatic Documents

213.   Basdevant, J. Recueil de traités en vigueur entre
        la France et les puissances étrangères. 4 vols.,
        Paris, 1918-1922.

214.   France. Ministère des Affaires Etrangères.
        Annuaire diplomatique et consulaire de la
        République française. Paris, annual.

215.   France. M.A.E. Bulletin périodique de la presse.
        Paris, in-house ministerial publication.

216.   France. M.A.E. Bulletin quotidien de la presse
        étrangère. Paris, in-house ministerial
        publication.

Diplomatic Documents

217. France. M.A.E. Commission de publication des documents relatifs aux origines de la guerre, 1939-45. Documents diplomatiques français. First Series (1932-1935) and Second Series (1936-1939). Paris, 1963-.

See remarks under "The Diplomatic Documents" in Section Two.

218. France. M.A.E. Compte définitif des dépenses de l'exercise, 1881-1938. Melun, 1897-1942.

219. France. M.A.E. Documents diplomatiques. Conférence de Washington, juillet 1921-février 1922. Paris, 1923.

220. France. M.A.E. Documents diplomatiques. Conférence économique internationale de Gênes, 9 avril-19 mai 1922. Paris, 1922.

221. France. M.A.E. Documents diplomatiques. Documents relatifs aux réparations. 2 vols. Paris, 1922-24.

222. France. M.A.E. Documents diplomatiques. Demande de moratorium du gouvernement allemand à la commission des réparations du 14 novembre 1922. Paris, 1923.

223. France. M.A.E. Documents diplomatiques. Documents relatifs aux notes allemandes du 2 mai et 5 juin 1923 sur les réparations. Paris, 1923.

224. France. M.A.E. Documents diplomatiques. Documents relatifs aux négociations concernant les garanties de sécurité contre une agression de l'Allemagne (10 janvier 1919-7 décembre 1923). Paris, 1924.

225. France. M.A.E. Le livre jaune français. Documents diplomatiques, 1938-1939. Paris, 1939.

226. France. M.A.E. Négociations relatives à la réduction et à la limitation des armements, 14 octobre 1933-17 avril 1934. Paris, 1934.

227. France. M.A.E. Office des biens et intérêts privés. Guide pratique. Paris, 1920.

DOCUMENTARY COLLECTIONS

Diplomatic Documents

228.   France. M.A.E. Réponse du gouvernement français à
        la lettre du gouvernement britannique du 11 août
        1923 sur les réparations. Paris, 1924.

229.   Lacaze, Yvon. De l'Anschluss à la crise de mai
        1938: contribution des documents diplomatiques
        français à l'étude du problème tchécoslovaque.
        Paris, 1976.

230.   Mennevée, Robert. Documents politiques,
        diplomatiques et financiers, 1921-1923. Paris,
        1923.

Trial Literature

231.   Haute Cour de Justice. Procès du Maréchal Pétain.
        Compte rendu in extenso des audiences. Paris,
        1945.

232.   Léon Blum devant la Cour de Riom, février-mars
        1942. Paris, 1945.

233.   Le procès Flandin devant la Haute Cour de Justice,
        23-26 juillet, 1946. Paris, 1947.

234.   Le procès Laval. Compte rendu sténographique.
        Paris, 1946.

235.   Les procès de collaboration. Fernand de Brinon,
        Joseph Darnand, Jean Luchaire. Paris, 1948.

236.   Michel, Henri. Le procès de Riom. Paris, 1979.

        The author draws attention to a large dossier which
        was prepared for the trial, specifically bearing on
        foreign policy between 1930 and 1939. Entitled "La
        guerre de 1939 est une résultante," the dossier
        includes testimonies from Bonnet, Marchandeau,
        Weygand, Caillaux, de Monzie, Denain, Dautry, Fabry
        and Pomaret.

237.   Noguères, Louis. Le véritable procès du maréchal
        Pétain. Paris, 1955.

238.   Ribet, Maurice. Le procès de Riom. Paris, 1945.

239.   Tissier, Pierre. The Riom Trial. London, 1942.

D. MEMOIRS/MEMOIR RELATED

Note. Those individuals whose names are preceded by an * are
examined in greater detail in the Appendices.

240.   Albord, General Tony. Pourquoi cela est arrivé, ou
         les responsabilités d'une génération militaire,
         1919-1939. Paris, 1946.

         Staff officer to General Héring, the military
         governor of Strasbourg, in the mid-1930s.

241.   *Alphand, Hervé.   L'Etonnement d'être: journal
         1939-1973. Paris, 1977.

242.   Armengaud, General J.   Batailles politiques et
         militaires sur l'Europe: Témoignages 1932-40.
         Paris, 1948.

         Deputy chief of air staff (1932) and director of the
         Centre d'études aériennes (1931-32); Inspector-
         General of the air force (1936). Retired (1936) but
         active publicist.

243.   Arnal, Pierre.   "Souvenirs de Haute-Silésie
         (1920-1921)." R.H.D. 80 (1966): 46-72, 149-179.

         Entered diplomatic service (1919); Upper Silesia
         (1920); 2nd sec. in Berlin embassy (1922-24);
         sous-directeur des relations commerciales (1925-32);
         conseiller, Berlin (1932-37); head of S.D.N. service
         at Quai (1937-40); director of economic affairs
         (1940-44); ambassador to Venezuela in 1950s.

244.   Astier de la Vigerie, Emmanuel d'. Les dieux et les
         hommes, 1943-1944. Paris, 1964.

245.   — De la chute à la libération de Paris (25 août
         1944). Paris, 1965.

         Naval officer turned journalist; a leader of Free
         French resistance movement; commissioner for the
         Interior (1943) under the C.F.L.N.

99

246.   Auphan, Admiral Paul.   "Un témoin à la barre de
         l'histoire."   Ecrits de Paris (April 1949):
         62-70.

247.   — Les grimaces de l'histoire, suivie de l'histoire
         de mes "trahisons". Paris, 1951.
         1921.

248.   — "De la mystification en histoire."   Ecrits de
         Paris 161 (1958): 122-27.

249.   — "La guerre de 1939 et le gouvernement de Vichy."
         Cahiers Charles Maurras 33 (1970): 19-29.

250.   — Histoire élémentaire de Vichy. Paris, 1971.

251.   — L'honneur de servir. Paris, 1978.

         Auphan was deputy chief of the naval staff and
         minister of the Merchant Marine under Vichy.

252.   Auriol, Vincent.   Hier...demain.   2 vols.   Tunis,
         1944.

         Deputy (1919-); minister of Finance (1936) of
         Justice   (1937-38);   house   arrest   under   Vichy
         (1940-42); member of Consultative Assembly, Algiers
         (1943-44) and Paris (1944-45); postwar ministries;
         elected President of 4th Republic in 1947.

253.   Baeyens, Jacques.   Au bout du Quai: souvenirs
         d'un retraité des postes. Paris, 1975.

254.   — Etranges affaires étrangères. Paris, 1978.

         Diplomat, successively attached to embassy in
         Bucharest (1930), Tokyo (1933), Washington (1938);
         delegate of C.F.L.N. in Washington (1943); directed
         cabinet of Resident General in Tunis (1943);
         attached to consulate in San Francisco (1945);
         distinguished postwar career within the Quai and
         abroad.

255.   Bainville, Jacques.   Journal, 1919-1926.   Paris,
         1949.

         Historian of monarchist persuasion; active in
         circles of Action Française and a friend of Maurras.

256.   Baraduc, Jacques.   Dans la cellule de Pierre Laval.
         Paris, 1948.

One of Pierre Laval's three appointed lawyers for the trial of 1945.

257.   Bardoux, Jacques. De Paris à Spa; la bataille diplomatique pour la paix française. Paris, 1921.

258.   — "La rupture franco-britannique." Revue des Deux Mondes (July 1940): 54-62.

259.   — "L'accord franco-japonais d'août-septembre 1940." R.D.D.M. (Oct. 1940): 392-401.

260.   — Journal d'un témoin de la Troisième, 1 septembre 1939-15 juillet 1940. Paris, 1957.

261.   — La délivrance de Paris. Paris, 1958.

262.   — "La réoccupation militaire de la Rhénanie par Adolphe Hitler le 7 mars 1936: un épisode inconnu." Revue des travaux de l'Académie des sciences morales et politiques (1959): 130-39.

Professor at Ecole des Sciences Politiques and at Ecole Supérieure de Guerre; journalist with special interest in diplomacy, contributing often to Journal des Débats, Le Temps, Figaro; senator (1938); deputy to Constituent Assemblies (1944-45) and postwar National Assemblies.

263.   Barrès, Maurice. L'oeuvre de Maurice Barrès. xix and xx, Mes cahiers, janvier 1919-décembre 1923. Paris, 1969.

Intellectual of the political right, a nationalist and traditionalist; and a vociferous spokesman for a French Rhineland; died 1923.

264.   Barthélemy, Joseph. Mémoires d'un ministre du Maréchal. Auch, 1948.

Professor at the Faculty of Law and the Ecole des Sciences Politiques; onetime French delegate to the League of Nations, and frequent contributor to the press; leading constitutional expert, and minister of Justice under Vichy.

265.   *Baudouin, Paul. Neuf mois au gouvernement, avril-décembre 1940. Paris, 1948.

266.   — "Un voyage à Rome: février 1939." R.D.D.M. (1 May 1962): 69-85.

267.   Beaufre, General André. Le drame de 1940. Paris, 1965.

268.   — La revanche de 1945. Paris, 1966.

269.   — Mémoires, 1920-1940-1945. Paris, 1969.

270.   — La France combattante, 1939-1945. Paris, 1972.

         Member of military mission to Moscow (1939); army staff headquarters (1940); permanent-secretary of National Defense in Algeria (1940-41); helped in the preparation of the 1942 landings; distinguished postwar career as serving officer and military writer.

271.   Belin, René. Du secrétariat de la C.G.T. au gouvernement de Vichy: Mémoires, 1933-1942. Paris, 1978.

         A union leader of the postal workers and executive officer of the Confédération générale du Travail from mid-1930s; minister of Production and Labor under Vichy.

272.   Benoist, Charles. Souvenirs. 3 vols. Paris, 1934.

         Deputy, and rapporteur-général on the political clauses of the Versailles treaty in 1919.

273.   Bérard, Armand. Un ambassadeur se souvient. Vol. i: Au temps du danger allemand; vol. ii: Washington et Bonn, 1945-1955. Paris, 1976-78.

         Diplomat, attached to Berlin embassy (1931-36); chef de cabinet for the Under Sec. of State (1936-37); posted to Washington (1938) and Rome (1939); served on French delegation to Wiesbaden (1940-42); chef de service of the foreign affairs commissariat, Algiers (1944); Washington embassy (1945); distinguished postwar diplomatic career within the Quai and abroad.

274.   Béraud, Henri. Les derniers beaux jours, 1919-1940. Paris, 1953.

Journalist who contributed regularly to Carbuccia's right-wing Gringoire.

275.   Berl, Emmanuel. La fin de la IIIe République: 10 juillet 1940. Paris, 1968.

Journalist, and editor of the Radical weekly Marianne in the 1930s.

276.   Bernanos, Georges. Les enfants humiliés: journal 1939-1940. Paris, 1968.

Catholic, royalist writer; active for a time in the Action Française.

277.   Béthouart, General Antoine Emile. Des hécatombes glorieuses au désastre, 1914-1940. Paris, 1972.

Attached to Yugoslav army (1931-33), then military attaché (1934-36); commander of Narvik force (1940); divisional commander, Morocco (1940-42); military mission to U.S.A. (1942); chief of national defense, Algiers (1944); postwar senator.

278.   Beuve-Méry, Hubert. Réflexions politiques, 1932-1952. Paris, 1951.

Journalist; a director of the Institut Français de Prague (1928-39) and a correspondent for Le Temps; director-general of Le Monde (1944).

279.   *Bidault, Georges. D'une résistance à l'autre. Paris, 1965.

280.   Bidault, Suzanne (née Borel). Souvenirs de guerre et d'occupation. Paris, 1973.

The first woman to serve in the French diplomatic corps; wife of Georges Bidault.

281.   Billotte, General Pierre. Le temps des armes. Paris, 1972.

French military representative in Moscow (1941); de Gaulle's chief of staff in London (1942) and secretary to the Comité de la Défense Nationale (1942); armored brigade commander (1944); deputy chief of staff of national defense (1945-46).

282.   Bloch, Marc. L'étrange défaite. Témoignage écrit
         en 1940.   Suivi   des   écrits   clandestins,
         1942-1944. Paris, 1957.

         Historian and a founder of the Annales; reserve
         officer and Resistance leader; executed 1944.

283.   Bloch-Lainé, François. Profession: fonctionnaire.
         Entretiens avec François Carrière. Paris, 1976.

         Entered Finance Inspectorate (1936); financial
         attaché, China; financial counselor, Indo-China
         (1945-46); directed Robert Schuman's cabinet
         (1946).

284.   *Blondel, Jules. Ce que mes yeux ont vu de 1900 à
         1950. Récit d'un diplomate. 2 vols. Arras,
         n.d.

285.   — Au fil de la carrière. Récit d'un diplomate,
         1911-1938. Paris, 1961.

286.   Blum, Léon. Extraits de discours et articles de L.
         Blum. Paris, n.d.

287.   — L'exercice du pouvoir. Paris, 1937.

288.   — L'histoire jugera. Montreal, 1945.

289.   — Le dernier mois. Paris, 1946.

290.   — L'oeuvre de Léon Blum. 4 vols. Paris, 1955-65.

         Deputy (1919-42); premier (1936-37); vice-premier
         (1937-38); premier (1938); defendant at Riom (1942);
         deported to Germany (1943-44); president of the
         provisional government (1946-47).

291.   Bois, Elie-Joseph. Truth on the Tragedy of France.
         London, 1941.

         Journalist and editor of Petit-Parisien; and close
         friend of Paul Reynaud.

292.   Boisanger, Claude de. "Une tentative de dialogue
         entre Hanoi et Alger (1943): la mission
         François." Ecrits de Paris 314 (1972): 10-19.

293.   — "On pouvait éviter la guerre d'Indochine."
         Ecrits de Paris 368 (1977): 75-82.

294.   — On pouvait éviter la guerre d'Indochine: souvenirs 1941-45. Paris, 1977.

Diplomat, posted to a number of European capitals in the 1920s and 1930s; head of Information and Press section at Quai (1936); Baudouin's chef de cabinet (1940); head of the diplomatic service in Indochina (1941-45).

295.   Boislambert, Claude Hettier de. "Juin-Juillet 40: A Londres avec De Gaulle." Nouvelle Revue des Deux Mondes 4 (1978): 50-58.

Cavalry officer; assistant director of de Gaulle's cabinet (1940); delegate to provisional consultative assembly (1944); postwar deputy and ambassador.

296.   *Bonnet, Georges. Défense de la paix. 2 vols. Geneva, 1946.

297.   — "La France et la Méditerranée." Rivista di studi politici internazionali 17 (1950): 373-87.

298.   — "Il y a vingt-cinq ans, la seconde guerre mondiale commençait." Historia 154 (1959): 221-28.

299.   — Le Quai d'Orsay sous trois Républiques, 1870-1961. Paris, 1961.

300.   — "L'occupation de la Rhénanie en 1936." Ecrits de Paris 238 (1965): 14-17.

301.   — Quai d'Orsay: 45 Years of French Foreign Policy. Isle of Man, 1965.

302.   — Vingt ans de vie politique, 1918-1938: de Clemenceau à Daladier. Paris, 1969.

303.   — Dans la tourmente: 1938-1948. Paris, 1970.

304.   — "La politique extérieure de la France avant la deuxième guerre mondiale." Académie des sciences, belles-lettres et arts de Besançon, 179 (1972): 117-20.

305.   Bonte, Florimond. De l'ombre à la lumière: souvenirs. Paris, 1965.

306.   — Le chemin de l'honneur: de la Chambre des députés
         aux prisons de France et au bagne d'Afrique.
         Paris, 1970.

         Member of the central committee of the communist
         party (1924-64); editor-in-chief of Humanité
         (1929-32); elected deputy (1936).

307.   Bordeaux, Henry.   "Souvenirs de Versailles
         (1931-32)." Ecrits de Paris (Jan. 1954): 8-14.

308.   — Histoire d'une vie. 12 vols. Paris, 1956-1970.

309.   — "Mes visites au maréchal Pétain (1940-43)."
         Ecrits de Paris 238 (1970): 72-87.

         Journalist, man of letters, historian.

310.   Boris, Georges.   Servir la République; textes et
         témoignages. Paris, 1963.

         Journalist of early anti-fascist persuasion;
         associated with Cartel des Gauches in 1920s, and
         with Popular Front in 1930s; an early supporter of
         de Gaulle.

311.   Bourget, General Paul-Alexandre.   De Beyrouth à
         Bordeaux: La guerre de 1939-40 vue du P.C.
         Weygand. Paris, 1946.

         Weygand's chief of staff in the Levant (1939-40),
         and a senior officer of the Armistice Army.

312.   Bourret, General Victor.   La tragédie de l'armée
         française. Paris, 1947.

         Head of Daladier's military cabinet at the war
         ministry (1936-37).

313.   Bouscat, General René. De Gaulle, Giraud. Dossier
         d'une mission. Paris, 1967.

         Chief of French air staff (1944-45).

314.   Bouthillier, Yves.   Le drame de Vichy.   2 vols.
         Paris, 1950-51.

Chef de cabinet of finance minister (1931); secretary-general of the ministry (1938); minister of finance, and of finance/commerce (1940); finance minister under Vichy (1940-41); minister of national economy/finance (1941-42).

315. Brasillach, Robert. <u>Notre avant-guerre: Mémoires</u>. Paris, 1941.

Journalist, and editor of the right-wing <u>Je suis partout</u> (1937); frequent contributor to newspaper <u>Action française</u>.

316. Bret, Paul-Louis. <u>Au feu des événements: mémoires d'un journaliste, Londres-Alger, 1929-1944</u>. Paris, 1959.

Journalist (pseud. Saint-Martin); editor and director of Agence Havas (1928-43); director-general of Agence France-Presse in Paris (1947-50).

317. *Briand, Aristide. <u>Paroles de paix</u>. Paris, 1927.

318. Brinon, Fernand de. <u>Mémoires</u>. Paris, 1949.

Journalist; Vichy's representative to the German authorities in occupied France.

319. Brisson, Pierre. <u>Vingt ans de "Figaro", 1938-1958</u>.

Journalist, and postwar editor of <u>Figaro</u>.

320. Brugère, Raymond. <u>Mémoires</u>. <u>Veni, vidi, Vichy</u>. Paris, 1944.

Diplomat; interwar minister/ambassador to Ottawa, Belgrade, Brussels; postwar secretary-general at the Quai d'Orsay.

321. Bugnet, Colonel Charles. <u>En écoutant le maréchal Foch (1921-1929)</u>. Paris, 1929.

Aide-de-camp to Foch.

322. Bührer, General Jules E. <u>Aux heures tragiques de l'Empire, 1938-1941</u>. Paris, 1947.

Chief of the colonial general staff (1938-40).

323. Caillaux, Joseph. <u>Mes mémoires</u>. 3 vols. Paris, 1942-47.

324.   — "Mon dernier entretien avec Aristide Briand sur
les origines de la guerre de 1914-18." Nouvelle
Revue des Deux Mondes 10 (1978): 83-90.

Deputy (1898-1919); senator (1925-44); prewar
premier; finance minister (1928) (1935); chairman of
Senate finance commission (1935-40).

325.   *Cambon, Paul. Correspondance, 1870-1924. 3 vols.
Paris, 1940-46.

326.   Carbuccia, Horace de. Le massacre de la victoire.
i, 1919-1934. Paris, 1973.

Owner of the right-wing newspaper Gringoire.

327.   Carcopino, Jérôme. Souvenirs de sept ans:
1937-1944. Paris, 1953.

Historian at the Sorbonne (1920-37); director of the
French School in Rome (1937-40); minister of
Education (1941-42).

328.   Carpentier, General Marcel. "Avec Weygand au
Moyen-Orient (1939-1940)." Revue militaire
générale, 9, 2 (1961): 245-60; 9, 4 (1961):
497-512.

Headed military mission to Brazil (1930-35); chief
of Juin's staff (1943-44); de Lattre's aide-de-camp
(1944).

329.   Cassin, René. "Churchill et la France pendant la
deuxième guerre mondiale, 1939-1945." Annales du
Centre Universitaire Méditerranéen 15 (1961-62):
77-98.

330.   — "Comment furent signés les accords Churchill-de
Gaulle de 7 août 1940." Revue de la France libre
154 (1965): 4-10.

331.   — "L'appel du 18 juin et le rôle de la France
libre." Revue de la France libre 187 (1970):
14-15.

National Commissioner for Justice and Education in
the Free French government in London (1940-42).

332.   Cathala, Pierre. Face aux réalités: La direction
des finances sous l'occupation. Paris, 1948.

Finance minister in Laval's government formed in April 1942; friend of Mussolini, exsyndicalist.

333.　Catoire, General Maurice. La direction des services de l'Armistice à Vichy. Paris, 1955.

334.　Catroux, General Georges. Deux missions en Moyen-Orient, 1919-1922. Paris, 1958.

Officer with extensive Norh African and Middle East experience during interwar years; governor-general of Indochina (1940); early Gaullist; commanded Syrian campaign (1941); Free French representative in Algiers (1943); minister of State (1943-44); ambassador to Moscow (1945-48).

335.　Cerf-Ferrière, René. L'Assemblée consultative vue de mon banc, novembre 1943-juillet 1944. Paris, 1974.

President of the group "Résistance" at the consultative assembly, and member of the 4e bureau of de Gaulle's C.F.L.N. (1943).

336.　Chambe, General René. "Weygand à l'heure d'Alger." R.D.D.M. 16 (1965): 492-511.

337.　── "Le maréchal Pétain à l'heure d'Alger." Revue de Paris 73 12 (1966): 20-28.

338.　── Au carrefour du destin. Weygand, Pétain, Giraud, De Gaulle. Paris, 1975.

Air force officer; joined Giraud (1942) whom he served as minister of Information, then as chef de cabinet; joined Juin's staff in Italy (1944).

339.　*Chambrun, Comte Charles Pineton de. Traditions et souvenirs. Paris, 1952.

340.　Chambrun, Comte René de. I Saw France Fall. Will She Rise Again? New York, 1940.

Lawyer specializing in international law; married Josée Laval (1935).

341.　*Charles-Roux, François. Huit ans au Vatican, 1932-1940. Paris, 1947.

342.   — Cinq mois tragiques aux Affaires étrangères (21
         mai-1 novembre 1940). Paris, 1949.

343.   — Souvenirs diplomatiques d'un âge révolu. Paris,
         1956.

344.   — Souvenirs diplomatiques. Rome-Quirinal. Paris,
         1958.

345.   — Une grande ambassade à Rome, 1919-1925. Paris,
         1961.

346.   Chastenet, Jacques. Quatre fois vingt ans. Paris,
         1974.

         Journalist, historian, businessman; director of
         Union des mines (1925-30); editor of Le Temps
         (1931-42).

347.   Chautemps, Camille. "Lettre d'un condamné." Ecrits
         de Paris (June 1946): 117-22.

348.   — Cahiers secrets de l'armistice (1936-1940).
         Paris, 1963.

         Deputy (1919-34); senator (1935-41); succession of
         cabinet posts between the wars, including three
         premierships (1930) (1933-34) (1937-38);
         vice-premier (1938-40).

349.   *Chauvel, Jean. Commentaire. 3 vols. Paris, 1971-73.

350.   Claudel, Paul. Journal. 2 vols. Paris, 1968-69.

351.   — Mémoires improvisées. Paris, 1969.

         Diplomat and author; ambassador to Japan (1921-26),
         U.S.A. (1927-33), Belgium (1933-35).

352.   Clemenceau, Georges. Grandeurs et misères de la
         victoire. Paris, 1930.

353.   — Au soir de la pensée. 2 vols. Paris, 1930.

354.   — Discours de guerre. Paris, 1968.

355.   — Lettres à une amie, 1923-1929. Paris, 1970.

         French premier (1917-1919).

356.   Clémentel, Etienne. La France et la politique

économique interalliée. Paris, 1931.

French minister of Commerce and Industry (1915-20); minister of Finance (1924-25).

357. Closon, François-Louis. Commissaire de la République du général de Gaulle, Lille, septembre 1944-mars 1946. Paris, 1980.

Entered Finance ministry (1932); head of financial services for French purchases from USA (1939); director for the commissioner of the Interior, C.F.L.N., Algiers (1943); regional commissioner of the provisional government, Lille (1944-46).

358. Comert, Pierre. "Lettres d'il y a trente ans sur Munich." Politique aujourd'hui (Jan. 1969).

Attached to Quai press bureau (1916); headed press section of mission to London (1917); headed League information section in Geneva (1919-33), and Quai press department (1933-38); edited daily newspaper France in London during war years.

359. Conquet, General Alfred. Trente ans avec Pétain. Paris, 1959.

360. — Autour du maréchal Pétain; lumières sur l'histoire. Paris, 1963.

361. — Auprès du maréchal Pétain. Paris, 1970.

Professor at Ecole de Guerre (1923-24); army staff (1924-34); secretary to Pétain as war minister (1934); Pétain's chief of staff and director of his cabinet (1934-37); head of army historical service (1943); deported to Germany (1943-45).

362. Cot, Pierre. Le procès de la République. 2 vols. New York, 1944. Translated as Triumph of Treason. New York, 1944.

363. — "Compte rendu de mission en U.R.S.S. (mars-juillet 1944)." Cahiers d'histoire de l'Institut Maurice Thorez 8 (1974): 262-77.

Deputy (1928-40); professor of law; Under-Secretary of State at Quai (1932); minister of Air (1933-34) (1936-37) and Commerce (1938); member of Provisional Consultative Assembly (1944-45), and the Constituent Assemblies (1945-46); deputy (1946-58).

364.   *Coulondre, Robert. De Staline à Hitler: souvenirs
        de deux ambassades, 1936-1939. Paris, 1950.

365.   Crusoé (pseud. for Jacques Lemaigre-Dubreuil).
        Vicissitudes d'une victoire. Paris, 1946.

        Businessman; one of the "Group of Five" who prepared
        the "deal" between General Giraud and Robert Murphy,
        Roosevelt's delegate in North Africa, in 1943.

366.   *Daladier, Edouard. The Defence of France. London,
        1939.

367.   — "Munich: vingt-trois ans après." Le Nouveau
        Candide (Sept.-Oct. 1961).

368.   Dampierre, Robert de. "Dix années de politique
        française à Rome (1925-1935)." R.D.D.M.   21
        (1953): 14-38; 21 (1953): 258-83.

        Diplomat; posted to Tokyo (1917-19), the Quai
        d'Orsay (1919-24), Rome (1924-35), Belgrade
        (1935-37), Ottawa (1937-40), Oslo (1940), Budapest
        (1940-42); interned by Germans (1944-45); series of
        postwar ambassadorships.

369.   *Darlan, Admiral François. L'Amiral Darlan Parle.
        Paris, 1953.

370.   Daudet, Léon. Souvenirs politiques. Paris, 1974.

        Right-wing journalist and one-time editor of Action
        française; elected deputy (1919); period of exile in
        Belgium in mid-1920s; supporter of Vichy regime.

371.   Dautry, Raoul. "Note au président du conseil (13
        juin 1940)." R.H.D.G.M. 1 (June 1951): 56-58.

        Minister of Armaments (1939-40); and of
        Reconstruction and Urbanism (1944-46).

372.   Debû-Bridel, Jacques. L'agonie de la troisième
        république, 1929-1939. Paris, 1949.

373.   — De Gaulle et le Conseil national de la
        Résistance. Paris, 1978.

        Journalist associated with Emile Buré's l'Ordre; led
        the right-wing Fédération République into de
        Gaulle's C.N.F. (1942).

374.   Decoux, Admiral Jean.   A la barre d'Indochine.
        Paris, 1949.

375.   — Sillages dans les mers du sud.   Paris, 1953.

        Commander-in-Chief of French naval forces in the Far
        East (1939-40); Governor-General of Indochina and
        French High Commissioner in the Pacific (1940-45).

376.   Degoutte, General Jean.   L'occupation de la Ruhr.
        Dusseldorf, 1924.

        Commander of the French Army of the Rhine (1919-25).

377.   Desgranges, Abbé Jean.   Journal d'un prêtre député,
        1936-1940.   Paris, 1960.

        Deputy from Morbihan; christian democrat, and
        frequent contributor to the post-1945 Ecrits de
        Paris.

378.   Dhers, Pierre.   Regards nouveaux sur les années
        quarantes.   Comment M. Benoist-Mechin écrit
        l'histoire....Paris, 1958.

        Professor; member of the two Constituent Assemblies
        (1945-46); member of the postwar commission of
        inquiry into "les événements de 1933 à 1945"; deputy
        (1946-51).

379.   Donnay, Maurice.   Mon journal, 1919-1939.   Paris,
        1953.

        Playwright and intellectual.

380.   Duclos, Jacques.   Mémoires.   3 vols.   Paris,
        1968-70.

        Deputy (1926-40); vice-president of the Chamber of
        Deputies (1936-39); secretary of the Communist party
        (1931-64); delegate to provisional consultative
        assembly (1944-45).

381.   Du Moulin de Labarthète, Henry.   Le temps des
        illusions. Souvenirs (juillet 1940-avril 1942).

        Head of Pétain's civilian cabinet at Vichy.

382.   Elie, Hubert.   Souvenirs d'un diplomate, 1920-1950.
        Paris, 1978.

383.   Erlanger, Philippe. La France sans étoile.
        Souvenirs de l'avant-guerre et du temps de
        l'occupation. Paris, 1974.

        Secretary-general (1930-38), then director (1938-68)
        of the Association française d'action artistique;
        headed service for artistic exchange at Quai
        (1948-68). Diplomat, historian, art critic and
        journalist.

384.   Fabre-Luce, Alfred. Journal de la France, mars
        1939-juillet 1940. Paris, 1940.

385.   — Histoire de la révolution européenne, 1919-1945.
        Paris, 1954.

386.   — Vingt-cinq années de la liberté. 2 vols. Paris,
        1962-64.

387.   — Journal de la France (1939-1944). Paris, 1969.

        Brief diplomatic career (1919-20); thereafter
        journalist and historian.

388.   Fabry, Jean. Février 1934-Juin 1940. De la Place
        de la Concorde au cours de l'Intendance. Paris,
        1942.

389.   — J'ai connu, 1934-1945. Paris, 1960.

390.   — "D'Edouard Herriot à Raymond Poincaré." Ecrits
        de Paris 194 (1961): 54-64.

        Journalist; deputy (1919-36); senator (1936-45);
        minister of Colonies (1923-24) and War (1934)
        (1935-36); long-standing chairman of the army
        commission in the Chamber of Deputies.

391.   Faucher, General Louis. "Some Recollections of
        Czechoslovakia." International Affairs xviii
        (May-June 1939): 343-60.

        Headed French military mission to Czechoslovakia in
        the 1920s and 1930s, until his resignation over
        Munich in 1938.

392.   Faure, Paul. De Munich à la cinquième République.
        Paris, 1949.

        Socialist deputy (1924-32) (1938-42); minister of
        State (1936-38).

114

MEMOIRS/MEMOIR RELATED

393.   Fernet, Admiral Jean Louis. <u>Aux côtés du maréchal</u>
        <u>Pétain. Souvenirs (1940-1944)</u>. Paris, 1953.

        Member of the C.S.D.N. secretariat in the 1930s;
        charged with the General Secretariat of the
        premier's office under Vichy.

394.   Ferry, Abel. <u>Les carnets secrets (1914-1918) d'Abel</u>
        <u>Ferry</u>. Paris, 1957.

        Deputy for the Vosges (1909-18); Under-Secretary of
        State at the foreign ministry (1914-15).

395.   *Flandin, Pierre-Etienne. <u>Discours</u>. Paris, 1937.

396.   — <u>Politique française, 1919-1940</u>. Paris, 1947.

397.   Fleury, Comte Serge. <u>Du haut de ma falaise.</u>
        <u>Souvenirs d'un diplomate</u>. Angers, 1963.

        Diplomat and writer; interwar posting to Syria,
        Bulgaria, Canada and U.S.A.; service within Quai in
        commercial relations and press sections; deputy
        director of protocol at the U.N.

398.   Foch, Marshal Ferdinand. <u>Mémoires pour servir à</u>
        <u>l'histoire de la guerre</u>. Paris, 1931.

        Chief of the general staff (1917); generalissimo of
        allied armies (1918).

399.   *François-Poncet, André. "France and the Rhine."
        <u>Spectator</u> (March 1946): 267-68.

400.   — "France and the Ruhr." <u>Economist</u> 150 (April
        1946): 570-72.

401.   — <u>Souvenirs d'une ambassade à Berlin: septembre</u>
        <u>1931-octobre 1938</u>. Paris, 1946.

402.   — "Poincaré tel que je l'ai vu." <u>Figaro littéraire</u>
        (June 1948).

403.   — <u>De Versailles à Potsdam; la France et le problème</u>
        <u>allemand contemporain</u>. Paris, 1948.

404.   — <u>Carnets d'un captif</u>. Paris, 1952.

405.   — "Souvenirs d'audiences privées." <u>Historia</u> 81
        (1953): 219-21.

406.   — "Les nazis ont-ils participé à l'assassinat du roi Alexandre?" Historia 95 (1954): 465–68.

407.   — "Il y a trente ans: ce que fut Locarno." Historia 107 (1955): 401–10.

408.   — "Hitler et Mussolini." Historia 105 (1955): 121–30.

409.   — "J'ai assisté à la conférence de Munich." Historia 142 (1958): 239–48.

410.   — Au Palais Farnèse. Souvenirs d'une ambassade à Rome, 1938-1940. Paris, 1961.

411.   — Au fil des jours, propos d'un libéral, 1942-1962. Paris, 1962.

412.   — "Le traité de Versailles, 1919." Plaisir de France 31 (1965): 12–19.

413.   Frossard, L.O. "Les carnets de L.O. Frossard." L'Aurore (4–16 Feb. 1949).

Deputy who sat alternately as a Socialist, Communist, then Independent; minister of Labor (1935-36); minister of State (1938), Propaganda (1938), Public Works (1938-40).

414.   Galtier-Boissière, Jean. Mémoires d'un Parisien. 3 vols. Paris, 1960–63.

Journalist with long associations with Canard Enchaîné and La Flèche; director of Crapouillot.

415.   Gamelin, General Maurice. Servir. 3 vols. Paris, 1946–47.

Chief of staff to Joffre (1916); military mission to Brazil (1919-25); commander-in-chief in Levant (1925-28); chief of army staff (1931-35); vice-pres. of C.S.G. (1935-40); chief of general staff of national defense (1938-40); commander-in-chief of French land forces, and allied forces in France (1939-40); defendant at Riom; deported (1943); liberated (1945).

416.   Garnier, Jean-Paul. Excellences et plumes blanches, 1922-1946. Paris, 1961.

Diplomat, posted to Warsaw (1928), to the foreign minister's cabinet at the Quai (1932), to Rome (1934-1940); minister's cabinet (1940); active in "Libération-Nord" (1943); series of postwar missions abroad and senior postings at the Quai.

417. Gauché, General Maurice. Le deuxième bureau au travail, 1935-1940. Paris, 1953.

Head of French military intelligence, both "open" and clandestine.

418. Gaulle, General Charles de. Discours et messages, 1940-1946. Paris, 1946.

419. — Mémoires de guerre. 3 vols. Paris, 1954-57.

420. — Mémoires d'espoir, 1958-. Paris, 1970.

Veteran of WWI (1914-18) and Russo-Polish war (1920-21); professor at St. Cyr and Ecole Supérieur de Guerre (1920s); headed military missions to the Middle East (1929-32); Under-Secretary of State for War in Reynaud cabinet (June 1940); formed provisional Free French government (June 1940); joined with Giraud to form C.F.L.N. (1943) in Algiers. President of the Provisional Government (1944-46); President of the Fifth Republic (1959-69).

421. Génébrier, Roger. "Edouard Daladier, président du Conseil," pp. 75-84. Edouard Daladier, Chef de Gouvernement. Paris, 1977.

Head of Daladier's cabinet militaire (1938-40).

422. Giraud, General Henri. Mes évasions. Paris, 1946.

423. — Un seul but, la victoire. Alger 1942-1944. Paris, 1949.

Veteran of 1914-18, and of Riff campaign (1920s); military governor of Metz (1936); captured 1940; escaped 1942; appointed commander of all French forces in North Africa (November 1942); succeeded Darlan as high-commissioner (December 1942).

424. Giraudoux, Jean. Armistice à Bordeaux. Paris, 1945.

Author, dramatist, diplomat; general commissioner of Information (1939-40); Free French naval officer

(1940-44); attached to de Gaulle's personal cabinet (1945).

425.   Green, Julien. Journal, 1928-1966. 8 vols. Paris, 1961-67.

Man of letters; American nationality but permanent residence in France since 1922.

426.   Groussard, Colonel Georges.   Chemins secrets. Mulhouse, 1948.

427.   — Service secret, 1940-1945. Paris, 1950.

428.   — Service secret, 1940-1945. Le double jeu de Vichy. Paris, 1964.

Officer in Huntziger's war ministry at Vichy; mission to Churchill (1941); arrested by Darlan, but escaped to Switzerland where he helped organize Resistance work in France.

429.   Guerin, André. La vie quotidienne au Palais-Bourbon à la fin de la troisième République. Paris, 1978.

Journalist for l'Oeuvre and Aurore; editor-in-chief of latter post-1945.

430.   Guitard, Louis. La petite histoire de la 3e république. Paris, 1959.

431.   — Lettre sans malice à François Mauriac sur la mort du général Weygand et quelques autres sujets. Avignon, 1966.

Lawyer and frequent contributor to Ecrits de Paris; active in the Union des Intellectuels Indépendants, a group which, among other things, urged amnesty for imprisoned Vichy leaders.

432.   Hanotaux, Gabriel. "Les carnets de Gabriel Hanotaux." R.H.D. (1977): 5-142; (1979): 47-182.

Deputy and foreign minister before 1914; delegate to the League (1918) and ambassador extraordinaire to Rome (1920).

433.   Henry-Haye, Gaston. "La fin d'une ambassade." Ecrits de Paris (April 1954): 55-68.

434. — La grande éclipse franco-américaine (1940-1942). Paris, 1972.

Deputy (1928-35); senator (1935-44); Vichy's ambassador to Washington.

435. *Herriot, Edouard. Episodes 1940-1944. Paris, 1950.

436. — "Souvenirs d'entre deux guerres." Les Annales. Conférencia (15 Jan. 1950): 1-16.

437. — Jadis. ii, D'une guerre à l'autre, 1914-1936. Paris, 1952.

438. Isorni, Jacques. Souffrance et mort du maréchal Pétain. Paris, 1951.

439. — Ainsi passent les républiques. Paris, 1959.

440. — Pétain a sauvé la France. Paris, 1964.

441. — Je hais ces impostures. Paris, 1977.

442. — and Annie Pétain. Correspondance de l'Isle d'Yeu (Lettres de Jacques Isorni et de la maréchale Pétain). Paris, 1966.

Lawyer in Paris Court of Appeal since 1931; engaged in Pétain's trial (1945); deputy in the 1950s.

443. Jacomet, Robert. L'Armement de la France, 1936-1939. Paris, 1945.

Technical adviser to French delegation to the League and the Disarmament Conference; secretary-general of the ministry of National Defense and War (1936-39).

444. Janin, General. Ma mission en Sibérie, 1918-1920. Paris, 1933.

French commander of the Czech forces in Russia (1918).

445. Jauneaud, General Jean-Henri. De Verdun à Dien-Bien Phu. Paris, 1959.

Entered Flying Corps (1915); head of the military cabinet of air minister Cot (1933) (1936-37); and deputy chief of air staff (1936-37).

446.   Jeanneney, Jules. Journal politique, 1939-1942.
        Paris, 1972.

        Senator (1909-1944); Under-Secretary of State to
        Clemenceau (1917-20); president of the Senate
        (1932-40); minister of State (1944-45).

447.   Joffre, Marshal Joseph. Mémoires du maréchal
        Joffre. 2 vols. Paris, 1938.

        "Victor of the Marne" (1914); commander-in-chief of
        all French forces (1915); replaced by Nivelle
        (1916); subsequent wartime missions to U.S.A. and
        Japan.

448.   Jouhaud, General Edmond. La vie est un combat.
        Paris, 1974.

        Commanded air reconnaissance force (1939); deputy
        chief of air staff (1946) and chief (1958).

449.   Jourdan, Henri. "Souvenirs d'un Français en poste à
        Berlin de 1933 à 1939." Mémoires de l'Académie
        des sciences, belles-lettres et arts de Lyon, 29
        (1975): 125-37.

        Professor; lecturer in Germany (1925-33); director
        of Institut français de Berlin and cultural attaché
        to Berlin embassy (1933-39); attached to mission in
        Berne (1939-41); post-war director of French
        Institute in London (1945-60).

450.   Jouvenel, Bertrand de. D'une guerre à l'autre. 2
        vols. Paris, 1940-41.

451.   — Un voyageur dans le siècle. I, 1903-1945.
        Paris, 1980.

        Journalist; diplomatic correspondent in 1930s;
        distinguished postwar career as journalist and
        university lecturer; son of Henry, ambassador,
        senator.

452.   Juin, Marshal Alphonse. Mémoires. 2 vols. Paris,
        1959-60.

        Commander-in-chief of French forces in North Africa
        (1941); commanded French army in Tunisia (1942-43),
        and French Expeditionary Corps in Italy (1943-44);
        chief of the general staff of national defense
        (1944-47).

453.   Kayser, Jacques. "Edouard Herriot et les dettes américaines." Les cahiers français 18 (1957): 20-21.

454.   — "Souvenirs d'un militant." Cahiers de la République 3 (1958): 69-82.

455.   — De Kronstadt à Khrouchtchev: Voyages franco-russes, 1891-1960. Paris, 1962.

Journalist; frequent contributor to La République, l'Oeuvre, Marianne between the wars; postwar editor of Le Monde; vice-president of Radical party in 1930s; counselor in London embassy (1943-44).

456.   Klotz, Louis-Lucien. De la guerre à la paix; souvenirs et documents. Paris, 1924.

Deputy, then senator (1898-1928); finance minister (1910-13) (1917-20).

457.   *La Baume, Comte Robert Renom de. Souvenirs, 1918-1950. Tours, 1970.

458.   — "L'Espagne 'non belligérante' (1940)." Revue d'histoire diplomatique 69 (1955): 126-29.

459.   *Laboulaye, André. "Rencontre avec quelques hommes d'état." R.H.D. 79 (1965): 97-112.

460.   Lacour-Gayet, Robert. "Le problème de la dette française envers les Etats-Unis après la première guerre mondiale (1917-32)." R.H.D. 75 (1961): 10-24.

French financial attaché in Washington in 1920s; Inspector-General of Finance (1939).

461.   Lagardelle, Hubert. "Histoire du Pacte à Quatre." Ecrits de Paris 126 (1955): 15-28.

462.   — Mission à Rome. Paris, 1955.

Syndicalist; well connected in Mussolini's Italy; attached to French embassy staff (1932-37); minister of Labor in Laval's cabinet formed April 1942.

463.   Lamoureux, Lucien. "Une crise financière sous la IIIe République (1933-34)." Revue politique et parlementaire 723 (1962): 25-31; 724 (1962): 29-37.

464. —— "La politique des changes en 1934." Revue politique et parlementaire 762 (1965): 66-71.

465. —— Mes souvenirs. Moulins, 1969.

Deputy (1919-43) and lawyer; minister of Education (1926), Colonies (1930); series of cabinet posts in 1930s, mainly Commerce and Colonies; Reynaud's minister of Finance (March-June 1940); member of the Conseil National (1941-44).

466. Laniel, Joseph. Jours de gloire et jours cruels: 1908-1958. Paris, 1971.

Deputy (1932-40) and industrialist; Under-Secretary of State in Finance ministry (1940); delegate to Provisional Consultative Assembly (1944); member of the two Constituent Assemblies (1945-46); postwar deputy.

467. Lapie, Pierre-Olivier. De Léon Blum à de Gaulle. Paris, 1971.

Socialist deputy (1936-40); rallied early to de Gaulle; governor of Chad (1940-42); member of Consultative Assembly, Algiers (1943) and Paris (1944); postwar deputy.

468. Larminat, General Edgard de. Chroniques irrévérencieuses. Paris, 1962.

Interwar service in Morocco and Indochina; chief of staff to C-in-C Eastern Mediterranean (1940); governor-general of French Equatorial Africa, and High Commissioner of Free France in Africa (1940-41); commanded Free French in Syria (1942-43); chief of de Gaulle's staff (1943); Inspector-General of Overseas Forces (1945-47).

469. *Laroche, Jules. La Pologne de Pilsudski. Souvenirs d'une ambassade, 1926-1935. Paris, 1953.

470. —— "Une occasion perdue; la question des zones franches." R.H.D. 69 (1955): 106-25.

471. —— "La grande déception de Cannes; souvenirs de 1922." Revue de Paris 64 (1957): 39-51.

472. —— Au Quai d'Orsay avec Briand et Poincaré, 1913-1926. Paris, 1957.

473.   La Rocque, Colonel Annet François de. <u>Au service de l'avenir</u>. Paris, 1948.

Liaison officer between French and Polish commands (1921-23); retired from army (1928); president of Croix de Feu (1933-36) then of Parti social français (1936); owner of <u>Le Flambeau</u> and <u>Le Petit Journal</u>.

474.   *Laval, Pierre. <u>Laval Parle...Notes et mémoires rédigés à Fresnes d'août à octobre 1945</u>. Paris, 1948.

475.   —— <u>The Unpublished Diary of Pierre Laval</u>. London, 1948.

475A.   Lazareff, Pierre. <u>Dernière Edition</u>. Montreal, 1942.

Journalist; associated between the wars with <u>Paris-Midi</u> and <u>Paris-Soir</u>; head of French services in the American War Information department during the Second World War.

476.   Lebrun, Albert. <u>Témoignages</u>. Paris, 1945.

Deputy (1900-20); senator (1920-32); President of the Republic (1932-40); minister of Blockade and Liberated Territories (1917-19).

477.   Lémery, Henry. <u>D'une république à l'autre; souvenirs de la mêlée politique, 1894-1944</u>. Paris, 1964.

478.   —— "Clemenceau comme je l'ai vu." <u>Histoire de notre temps</u> 6 (1968): 159-77.

Deputy (1914-19); senator (1920-40); Under Secretary for Maritime Transport (1917-19); vice-premier in Doumergue cabinet (1934); minister of Colonies (1940).

479.   Lemonnier, Admiral André-Georges. <u>Les cents jours de Normandie</u>. Paris, n.d.

Naval officer attached to Senate naval commission (1936-39); liaison officer with Belgium (1939-40); directed office of Merchant Marine, Algiers (1942); chief of naval staff (1943-50).

480.   Loiseau, Charles. "Ma mission auprès du Vatican (1914-1918)." <u>Revue d'histoire diplomatique</u> 74 (1960): 100-115.

Diplomat; ambassador to the Vatican during World War One.

481.   Loizeau, General Lucien. "Une mission militaire en U.R.S.S." R.D.D.M. 18 (1955): 252-76.

Deputy chief of the army general staff (1935); military governor of Metz; commanded 6th Army Corps (1939-40).

482.   Loucheur, Louis.   Carnets secrets, 1908-1932. Paris, 1962.

Deputy (1919-31); Under-secretary, then minister, of Armaments and War Manufacture (1916-17); of Industrial Reconstitution (1917-20); of Liberated Regions (1921-22); of Commerce and Industry (1924); of Finances (1925); Commerce (1926); Labor (1928-30); National Economy, Commerce and Industry (1930-31).

483.   Loustaunau-Lacau, Colonel Georges. Mémoires d'un Français rebelle, 1914-1948. Paris, 1948.

Post-1918 service on staffs of Debeney, Pétain, Franchet-d'Esperey; staff officer at war ministry; military writer under pseudonym "Navarre".

484.   Lyautey, Marshal Louis Hubert. La Renaissance du Maroc (1912-1922). Dix ans de protectorat. Rabat, 1922.

485.   — Lyautey, Pierre. ed. Lyautey l'africain; textes et lettres du Maréchal Lyautey. 4 vols. Paris, 1953-57.

War minister (1916-17); Resident-General of the French Republic in Morocco (1917-1925).

486.   Mangin, Lt. Colonel Louis-Eugène. La France et le Rhin, hier et aujourd'hui. Geneva, 1945.

Organized paramilitary operations of French resistance groups in occupied France (1943-44); attached to several defense ministry cabinets in 1950s; son of General Charles Mangin, from whose notes this volume is partly written.

487.   Mantoux, Paul Joseph. Les délibérations du Conseil des quatres (24 mars-28 juin 1919). 2 vols. Paris, 1955.

Interpreter for the Supreme Council in 1919; director of the political section of the League secretariat (1920-27); headed the British section of Giraudoux's Information commissariat (1939).

488. Marin, Louis. "Contributions à l'histoire des prodromes de l'Armistice." R.H.D.G.M. (July 1951): 1-26.

489. — "Gouvernement et Commandement; conflits, différends, immixtions qui ont pesé sur l'Armistice de juin 1940." R.H.D.G.M. (Oct. 1952): 1-28; (Jan. 1953): 1-14.

Deputy (1905-51); very frequent cabinet minister, from Poincaré's government (1924) to that of Reynaud (1940); President of the Fédération Républicaine (1925-); member of Consultative and Constituent Assemblies (1944-46).

490. Maritain, Jacques. A travers le désastre. New York, 1941.

Writer and philosopher; professor of philosophy at Catholic Institute of Paris; ambassador to Vatican (1945-48).

491. Martet, Jean. Monsieur Clemenceau peint par lui-même. Paris, 1929.

492. — Le silence de Monsieur Clemenceau. Paris, 1929.

493. — Le tigre. Paris, 1930.

Wartime chief of Clemenceau's private secretariat.

494. Martin du Gard, Maurice. La chronique de Vichy, 1940-1944. Paris, 1948.

495. — Les Mémorables. 2 vols. Paris, 1957-60.

Essayist and critic; cousin of Roger.

496. *Massigli, René. "De Versailles à Locarno." Revue de Paris 64 (1957): 24-39.

497. — La Turquie devant la guerre: mission à Ankara, 1939-1940. Paris, 1964.

498. — "Anthony Eden et la France." Nouvelle Revue des Deux Mondes 3 (1977): 594-98.

499.   Mast, General Charles. "Comment j'ai conduit l'opération clandestine d'aide française au débarquement allié en Algérie." Miroir de l'histoire 5 (1954): 83–91, 734–42.

500.   — Histoire d'une rébellion, Alger: 8 novembre 1942. Paris, 1969.

Military attaché in Tokyo (1932–37); key figure in preparations for allied landings (Nov. 1942); wartime missions to Egypt and Syria (1943); Resident-General at Tunis (1943–47).

501.   Mauriac, François. Mémoires politiques (1933–1953). Paris, 1967.

Journalist and man of letters; post-1945 administrator of Le Figaro.

502.   Maurois, André. Mémoires. Paris, 1970.

Man of letters, and member of the Academy (1938); lecturer in U.S.A. (1940–42) and North Africa (1943–44).

503.   Maurras, Charles. La seule France. Chronique des jours d'épreuve. Lyon, 1941.

Founder of the review, later daily, Action française; philosopher and activist of the anti-parliament Right; warned of Hitler's menace but rallied with enthusiasm to Pétain.

504.   Mendès-France, Pierre. Liberté, liberté chérie: 1940–1944. Paris, 1977.

Deputy (1932–1940); Under Secretary of Finance (1938); Commissioner of Finance, Algiers (1943); minister of National Economy (1944–45); postwar deputy and premier.

505.   Mermeix (pseud. of Gabriel Terrail). Le combat des trois; notes et documents sur la conférence de la paix. Paris, 1922.

506.   Messimy, General Adolphe. Mes souvenirs. Paris, 1937.

Deputy (1902–19); senator (1923–35); colonial and war minister before 1914; president of the Senat commission on Colonies (1926–31).

507. Minart, Colonel Jacques. <u>P.C. Vincennes, secteur 4</u>. 2 vols. Paris, 1945.

508. — <u>Le drame du désarmement français, 1918-1939</u>. Paris, 1959.

A member of the C.S.D.N. secretariat in the 1930s; head of Pétain's personal cabinet at Vichy.

509. Moch, Jules. "Souvenirs sur Vincent Auriol." <u>Revue socialiste</u> (1966): 80-93.

510. — <u>Rencontres avec I: Darlan, Eisenhower</u>. Paris, 1968.

511. — <u>Rencontres avec II: Léon Blum</u>. Paris, 1970.

512. — <u>Rencontres avec III: De Gaulle</u>. Paris, 1971.

513. — <u>Le Front populaire; grande espérance</u>. Paris, 1971.

514. — "Léon Blum et son oeuvre." <u>Annales du Centre universitaire méditerranéen</u> (1972-73): 105-115.

515. — <u>Une si longue vie</u>. Paris, 1976.

Socialist deputy (1928-42); Under Secretary in the premier's office (May-June 1937); minister of Public Works (March-April 1938); voted against giving Pétain constitutional powers (July 1940).

516. Mollet, Guy. <u>Témoignages, 1905-1975</u>. Paris, 1977.

Professor of English; joined Resistance after two years of imprisonment (1940-42); Secretary of the Comité de Libération (1944); postwar deputy and premier.

517. Monick, Emmanuel. <u>Pour mémoire</u>. Paris, 1970.

Inspectorate of Finance; financial attaché, Washington (1930-34), London (1934-40); secretary-general of French government in Morocco (1940); secretry-general of finance ministry (1944); governor of Bank of France (1945-49).

518. Monnerville, Gaston. <u>Témoignage</u>. Paris, 1975.

Deputy (1932-40); Under-Secretary of State for Colonies (1937-38); deputy to Consultative Assembly

(1944) and the Constituent Assemblies (1945-46); postwar senator.

519.   Monnet, Jean. Mémoires. Paris, 1976.

Businessman and economic adviser; representative in allied executive committees (1914-18); deputy secretary-general of the League (early 1920s); member of British Supply Council in Washington (1940); commissioner for Armaments and Reconstruction at Algiers (1943); creator and architect of Monnet Plan (1946) and Schuman Plan (1950).

520.   Montigny, Jean. Toute la vérité sur un mois dramatique de notre histoire. De l'armistice à l'Assemblée nationale, 15 juin-15 juillet, 1940. Clermont-Ferrand, 1950.

521.   — Le complot contre la paix, 1935-1939. Paris, 1966.

Deputy and lawyer; French delegate to League of Nations; a friend of Bonnet and Caillaux.

522.   Monzie, Anatole de. Ci-devant. Paris, 1941.

523.   — La saison des juges. Paris, 1943.

Deputy (1909-19) (1929-40); senator (1920-29); minister of Finance (1925), of Public Works (1925-26, 1938-40), of Education (1932-34).

524.   Morand, Paul. Journal d'un attaché d'ambassade. Paris, 1963.

525.   — "Saint-John Perse à Londres en 1940." La nouvelle revue française 278 (1975): 103-05.

Diplomat and man of letters; diplomatic posting to Madrid (1918), Siam (1925); head of French mission for economic warfare in Britain (1939-40); minister to Bucharest (1943); ambassador to Berne (1944).

526.   Mordacq, General Henri. La mentalité allemande; cinq ans de commandement sur le Rhin. Paris, 1926.

527.   — La vérité sur l'armistice. Paris, 1929.

528.   — Le ministère Clemenceau; journal d'un témoin. 4 vols. Paris, 1930-31.

529.　　　— L'armistice du 11 novembre 1918; récit d'un témoin. Paris, 1937.

Clemenceau's personal aide and chief military adviser.

530.　　　Moreau, Emile. Souvenirs d'un gouverneur de la Banque de France. Histoire de la stabilisation du franc (1926-1928). Paris, 1954.

Served in finance ministry before 1914; appointed to the Committee of Experts (1926); president of the Bank of France (1926-30); president of the managing board of the Banque de Paris et des Pays-Bas (1936-).

531.　　　Muselier, Admiral. De Gaulle contre le Gaullisme. Paris, 1946.

Commander-in-Chief of the Free French Navy and Air Force (1940-42).

532.　　　Navarre, General Henri. Le service des rensignements, 1871-1944. Paris, 1978.

Head of the German section in the special services of French military intelligence (1936-40); head of Weygand's intelligence staff (1940); principal figure in Resistance work of intelligence officers.

533.　　　Noel, Léon. Un témoignage: le diktat de Rethondes et l'armistice franco-italien de juin 1940. Paris, 1945.

534.　　　— Une ambassade à Varsovie, 1935-1939. L'agression allemande contre la Pologne. Paris, 1946.

535.　　　— Conseils à un jeune français entrant dans la diplomatie. Paris, 1948.

536.　　　— "Il y a dix ans était signé l'Armistice de 1940." Historia (May 1950): 322-32; (June 1950): 416-24.

537.　　　— "Le projet d'union franco-britannique de juin 1940." R.H.D.G.M. 6 (1956): 22-47.

538.　　　— La guerre de 39 a commencé quatre ans plus tôt. Paris, 1979.

Diplomat; director of premier's cabinet (1932); posted to Prague (1932-35), Warsaw (1935-40); plenipotentiary minister to Armistice negotiations with Germany and Italy (1940).

539. Nolde, General André. "Une mission militaire française auprès de Tchang-kai-Chek en 1939. Un épisode peu connu de l'histoire diplomatique de l'immédiate avant-guerre." Revue de défense nationale 27 (June 1971): 976-85.

540. Nollet, General Charles. Une expérience de désarmement. Cinq ans de contrôle militaire en Allemagne. Paris, 1932.

President of the Interallied Military Control Commission (1919-1924).

541. Ormesson, Wladimir d'. "Grand corps et grands commis: la carrière diplomatique." R.D.D.M. (July 1958): 50-73.

542. — De Saint-Pétersbourg à Rome. Paris, 1969.

Journalist and diplomat; editorial writer for Figaro and foreign policy specialist for Temps in 1930s; ambassador to the Vatican (1940, 1948-56) and to Argentina (1945-48).

543. Paillole, Paul. Services spéciaux, 1935-1945. Paris, 1975.

Army counter-intelligence officer (1935-40); principal figure in intelligence work for wartime Resistance.

544. Painlevé, Paul. Paul Painlevé, paroles et écrits. Paris, 1936.

Deputy (1910-33) and professor of mathematics; variety of prewar ministries, then premier (1925), war minister (1925-1926, 1929); finance (1925); air minister (1930-31, 1932-33).

545. *Paléologue, Maurice. La Russie des tsars pendant la grande guerre. 3 vols. Paris, 1921-22.

546. Pange, Jean de. Mes prisons, pages de journal (1938-1941). Paris, 1958.

547.   — Journal. 3 vols. Paris, 1966-70.

548.   — "Mission en Erythrée (1941)." Revue de la France
         libre 224 (1978): 9-11.

         Historian and man of letters.

549.   Passy, Colonel (pseud. for A.E.V. Dewavrin).
         Souvenirs. 3 vols. Monte Carlo, 1947-.

         Head of Free French counter-intelligence in London
         (1940); chief of staff to General Koenig, de
         Gaulle's delegate to the allies (1944).

550.   *Paul-Boncour, Joseph. Entre deux guerres. 3 vols.
         Paris, 1945-46.

551.   *Peretti de la Rocca, Emmanuel. "Briand et Poincaré
         (souvenirs)." Revue de Paris 43 (1936): 775-88.

552.   Pétain, Marshal Philippe.   Quatre années au
         pouvoir. Paris, 1949.

553.   — Actes et écrits. 2 vols. Paris, 1974.

         Commander-in-chief of the French armies on the
         Western Front (1917); war minister (1934);
         ambassador to Spain (1939-40); last premier of the
         Third French Republic (June-July 1940); chief of
         state of the Vichy regime (1940-44).

554.   Peyrouton, Marcel. Du service public à la prison
         commune. Souvenirs; Tunis-Rabat-Buenos Aires-
         Vichy-Alger-Fresnes. Paris, 1950.

         Official in colonial administration in Paris
         (1920s); deputy head of the minister's cabinet
         (1929); Resident-General, Tunisia (1933), Morocco
         (1936); ambassador to Argentina; Governor-General of
         Algeria (1943).

555.   Piétri, François. Mes années d'Espagne (1940-
         1944). Paris, 1954.

556.   — "Souvenirs de Barthou." R.D.D.M. 5 (1961):
         65-75.

557.   — "La question des dettes interalliées." R.D.D.M.
         15 (1963): 379-89.

558.   — "Le 7 mars 1936." R.D.D.M. (1966): 181-87.

Deputy (1924-42); Under-Secretary of Finance (1926); minister of Colonies (1929, 1930, 1933); of the Budget (1931-32); of National Defense (1932); of Finance (1934); of Marine (1934-36); ambassador to Spain (1940-44).

559.   Pineau, Christian. La simple vérité: 1940-1945. Paris, 1960.

Economist, with Banque de France then Banque de Paris et des Pays-Bas (1931-38); attached to cabinet of his father-in-law Jean Giraudoux, commissioner of Information (1939); postwar deputy and foreign minister.

560.   Pinot, Robert. Le comité des forges au service de la nation. Paris, 1919.

Secretary-general of the Comité des Forges during World War One.

561.   *Poincaré, Raymond. Histoire politique. Chroniques de quinzaine (du 15 mars 1920 au 15 janvier 1922). 4 vols. Paris, 1920-22.

562.   — Au service de la France: neufs années de souvenirs. 10 vols. Paris, 1926-33.

563.   Pomaret, Charles. Le dernier témoin; fin d'une guerre, fin d'une république, juin et juillet 1940. Paris, 1968.

Deputy (1928-42); minister of Labor under Daladier and Reynaud (1938-40); of Interior in Pétain's cabinet (June-July 1940).

564.   Portmann, Georges. Le crépuscule de la paix. Bordeaux, 1955.

Medical doctor, and senator (1932-40); secretary-general of Information at Vichy (1941); postwar senator.

565.   Prételat, General André. Le destin tragique de la ligne Maginot. Paris, 1950.

Chief of staff, Levant Army (1920-22); commander of Paris Region (1930-34); member of C.S.G. (1934-39).

566.   Prioux, General René. <u>Souvenirs de guerre,</u>
        <u>1939-1943.</u> Paris, 1947.

        Commander of French Cavalry Corps (1939-40).

567.   Puaux, Gabriel. <u>Deux années au Levant. Souvenirs</u>
        <u>de Syrie et du Liban, 1939-1940.</u> Paris, 1952.

568.   — <u>Mort et transfiguration de l'Autriche.</u> Paris,
        1966.

569.   — "La conférence de la paix et le traité de
        Versailles." <u>Revue de Paris</u> 76 (1979): 29-39.

570.   — "La conférence de la paix et traité de
        Versailles: Souvenirs d'un collaborateur d'André
        Tardieu." <u>Revue des travaux des sciences morales</u>
        <u>et politiques.</u> 122 (1969): 335-50.

        Diplomat; secretary-general of Tunisian government
        (1920-22); consul-general in Rhine provinces
        (1922-24); minister to Lithuania (1926-28), Roumania
        (1928-33), Austria (1933-38); High-Commissioner to
        Syria (1939-40·); Resident-General in Morocco
        (1943-46).

571.   Raissac, Guy. <u>De la Marine à la Justice.</u> Paris,
        1972.

        Lawyer-magistrate; historian; secretary-general of
        the Haute Cour de Justice (1948) in which position
        he supervised the reordering and assembling of the
        Vichy government archives.

572.   Raphael-Leygues, Jacques. <u>Chroniques des années</u>
        <u>incertaines, 1935-1945.</u> Paris, 1977.

        Attached to premier's cabinet (Daladier) in 1938-39;
        Commissioner-General of the Navy; postwar deputy and
        ambassador; grandson of Georges Leygues.

573.   Recouly, Raymond. <u>Le mémorial de Foch; mes</u>
        <u>entretiens avec le maréchal.</u> Paris, 1929.

        Journalist and historian; frequent contributor to
        the Rightist weekly <u>Gringoire.</u>

574.   Regnault, General Jean. "Une mission française à
        Berlin (octobre-novembre 1920)." <u>Revue de la</u>
        <u>Société des amis du Musée de l'Armee</u> 65 (1962):
        4-14.

575.   Reibel, Charles. Pourquoi et comment fut décidée la
         demande d'armistice. Vanves, 1940.

575A.   — Les responsables. Paris, 1941.

         Deputy (1919-35); senator (1935-44); Under-Secretary
         of State under Premiers Millerand and Leygues
         (1920); minister of Liberated Regions (1924).

576.   Rémy, Colonel (pseud. for Léon Gilbert). On
         m'appelait Rémy. Paris, 1951.

577.   — Mémoires d'un agent secret de la France libre. 6
         vols. Paris, 1964-68.

578.   — Dix ans avec de Gaulle (1940-1950). Paris, 1971.

         Attached to Bank of France between the wars; joined
         de Gaulle (June 1940); organized intelligence
         networks in occupied France.

579.   Réquin, General Edouard. Combats pour l'honneur
         (1939-1940). Paris, 1946.

580.   — D'une guerre à l'autre, 1919-1939: Souvenirs.
         Paris, 1949.

         Staff officer with Foch and Joffre (1916-18);
         technical adviser to Paris Peace Conference (1919);
         head of war minister's cabinet (1930-32); military
         representative to League (1930-32); member of
         C.S.G. (1938-39); commanded 4th Army in 1939-40.

581.   *Reynaud, Paul. La France a sauvé l'Europe. 2
         vols. Paris, 1947.

582.   — Au coeur de la mêlée, 1930-1945. Paris, 1951.

583.   — Mémoires. 2 vols. I Venu de ma montagne.
         Paris, 1960; II Envers et contre tous. Paris,
         1963.

584.   Ribot, Alexandre. Journal et Correspondances
         inédites, 1914-1922. Paris, n.d.

585.   — Lettres à un ami. Souvenirs de ma vie
         politique. Paris, 1924.

         Several times premier before 1914; successively
         finance minister, premier and foreign minister
         between 1914 and 1917.

586.   Ristelhueber, René. "Mackenzie King et la France. Souvenirs d'une mission diplomatique au Canada." R.D.D.M. (1, 15 March, 1 April 1954): 116-35; 287-305, 459-73.

Vichy minister to Ottawa, 1940-1942.

587.   Roche, Emile. "Caillaux: Le premier cabinet Léon Blum: La guerre d'Espagne." Nouvelle Revue des Deux Mondes 2 (1978): 348-54.

588.   — "Le Pacte à Quatre et Henry de Jouvenel." Nouvelle Revue des Deux Mondes 9 (1978): 557-85.

589.   — "Caillaux et Briand." Nouvelle Revue des Deux Mondes 10 (1978): 74-82.

Journalist; vice-president of the Radical Socialist party in the 1930s; directed finance minister's cabinet (Caillaux) in 1935.

590.   Roché, Louis. "Paul Claudel à l'ambassade de Bruxelles (1933-34)." Revue d'Histoire Diplomatique 85 (1971): 65-85.

Diplomat, posted to Warsaw (1931), Brussels (1932), Vienna (1934), London (1937), Dublin (1940); member of B.B.C. French Services (1942-43); counselor to French delegation in London (1943-44).

591.   Roton, General B. Années cruciales. Paris, 1947.

Chief of staff to General Georges (1940).

592.   Rougier, Louis. Mission secrète à Londres (les accords Pétain-Churchill). Montreal, 1945.

593.   — Les accords secrets franco-britanniques de l'automne 1940: Histoire et imposture. Paris, 1954.

594.   — "De la documentation par l'absurde en histoire, à propos d'un livre du général Schmitt." Ecrits de Paris (1958): 15-40.

Professor; emissary of Vichy government to London (November 1940).

595.   Rueff, Jacques. Oeuvres complètes. I De l'aube au crépuscule; Autobiographie. Paris, 1977.

Entered Inspectorate of Finance (1923); attached to
Poincaré's cabinet (1923-24); League's financial
section (1927-30); financial counselor to embassy in
London (1930-36); deputy governor of Bank of France
(1939-40); headed economic and financial delegation
to C-in-C, Germany (1944-45).

596.   *Saint-Aulaire, Comte Auguste Félix Charles de
         Beaupoil. <u>Confession d'un vieux diplomate</u>.
         Paris, 1953.

597.   — <u>Je suis diplomate</u>. Paris, 1954.

598.   Sarraz-Bournet, Ferdinand. <u>Témoignage d'un
         silencieux</u>. Paris, 1948.

         A staff member of the French delegation to the
         Franco-Italian Armistice Commission (1940).

599.   Sault, Jean du. "Les relations diplomatiques entre
         la France et le Saint-Siège." <u>R.D.D.M.</u> (1971):
         115-22.

         Diplomat, and secretary to the embassy at the
         Vatican; posted to the Quai (1931-34); minister then
         ambassador to Portugal (1945-51).

600.   Sauvy, Alfred. <u>De Paul Reynaud à Charles de
         Gaulle</u>. Paris, 1972.

         Economist-statistician; periodic economic adviser to
         government, especially during Reynaud's premiership
         and finance ministry.

601.   Serrigny, General Bernard. <u>Trente ans avec Pétain</u>.
         Paris, 1959.

         Attached to Pétain's staff throughout World War One;
         retired (1932) into business career, but remained a
         close personal friend and adviser to Pétain during
         the Vichy period.

602.   Seydoux, François. "Aux Affaires étrangères, de
         Jules Cambon à Geoffroy de Courcel." <u>Nouvelle
         Revue des Deux Mondes</u> (1973): 380-90.

603.   — <u>Mémoires d'Outre Rhin</u>. Paris, 1975.

604.   — "Sur les relations franco-allemandes (1920-25)."
         <u>Nouvelle Revue des Deux Mondes</u> 11 (1977):
         329-34.

Diplomat, attached to French delegation to League (1927-32), then to Berlin embassy (1933-36); member of Bureau d'études clandestin des Affaires étrangères (1943); distinguished postwar career at Quai and ambassadorships abroad.

605. *Seydoux, Jacques. De Versailles au plan Young; réparations, dettes interalliées, reconstruction européenne. Paris, 1932.

606. Soustelle, Jacques. Envers et contre tout. Souvenirs et documents de la France libre (1940-44). 2 vols. Paris, 1947-50.

Professor; joined de Gaulle (1940); several wartime missions for Free France in Latin America; national commissioner for Information (1942); director-general of the Services spéciaux in Algiers (1943-44); minister of Information, and of Colonies (1945).

607. Stehlin, General Paul. "Réalités stratégiques en 1939 et vingt ans après." Revue de défense nationale 15 (1959): 749-62.

608. — Témoignage pour l'histoire. Paris, 1964.

609. — "Fin septembre 1938, Munich." Dix leçons sur le Nazisme (1976): 155-79.

Air attaché in Berlin (1936-39); special mission to Finland and Norway (1939-40).

610. Tabouis, Geneviève. They Called Me Cassandra. New York, 1942.

611. — Vingt ans de suspense diplomatique. Paris, 1958.

612. — "Août 1939...". R.D.D.M. (1972): 599-607.

Journalist with particular interest in foreign affairs; associated principally with l'Oeuvre and l'Information.

613. *Tardieu, André. The Truth about the Treaty. Indianapolis, 1921.

614. — L'année de Munich. Paris, 1939.

615. Thorez, Maurice. <u>Fils du peuple</u>. Paris, 1938.
Communist deputy; secretary general of the
Communist party (1930-); delegate to Provisional
Consultative Assembly (1944-45) and member of
Constituent Assemblies (1945-46); minister of
State in de Gaulle government (1945-46).

616. Tirard, Paul. <u>La France sur le Rhin; douze années d'occupation rhénane</u>. Paris, 1930.

French high commissioner in the Rhineland
(1918-30).

617. Tissier, Pierre. <u>I Worked with Laval</u>. London,
1942.

Principal private secretary to Laval, when latter
was minister of Labor, of Interior, and Premier
(1930-31).

618. Tournelle, G. de la. "A Dantzig de décembre 1934 à
septembre 1939." <u>R.H.D.</u> (1978): 321-47.

French consul in Danzig in 1939.

619. Vallat, Xavier. <u>Le nez de Cléopâtre. Souvenirs d'un homme de droite, 1919-1944</u>. Paris, 1957.

Deputy (1919-40) and journalist; member of far Right
groups, <u>Le Faisceau</u> (1925-26) and <u>Croix de Feu</u>
(1928-36); secretary-general for Veterans Affairs
(July 1940) and commissioner-general for Jewish
Questions (April 1941); seconded to staffs of
Pétain, then Laval (1942); editorialist on state
radio (1944).

620. Vaux Saint-Cyr, C. de. "Ma mission en Finlande;
souvenirs." <u>R.D.D.M.</u> (15 Oct. 1953): 721-31.

Consul-general, Cologne (1937); chargé d'affaires,
Berlin (1939).

621. Vendroux, Jacques. <u>Souvenirs de famille et journal politique</u>. I <u>Cette chance que j'ai eue, 1920-1957</u>. Paris, 1974.

Industrialist from Calais; brother-in-law of Charles
de Gaulle.

622. Vernoux, General Marcel. <u>Wiesbaden, 1940-1944</u>.
Paris, 1954.

138

A staff member of the French delegation to the Franco-German Armistice Commission.

623. Villelume, General Paul de. _Journal d'une défaite, août 1939- juin 1940_. Paris, 1976.

Liaison officer between foreign ministry and general staff (1935-40); directed military cabinet of the national defense minister (Reynaud) in May-June 1940; secretary-general of the Army ministry (1946).

624. Weiss, Louise. _Mémoires d'une Européenne_. 3 vols. Paris, 1972-74.

Journalist; director of _l'Europe Nouvelle_ (1918-34); editor of clandestine _Nouvelle République_ (1942-44).

625. Weygand, Commandant Jacques. _The Role of General Weygand: Conversations with his Son_. London, 1948.

626. —— _Le serment. Récit_. Paris, 1960.

627. Weygand, General Maxime. "Souvenirs de 1918." _R.D.D.M._ (1953): 3-25, 193-214.

628. —— _En lisant les mémoires de guerre du général de Gaulle_. Paris, 1955.

629. —— _Mémoires_. 3 vols. Paris, 1950-1957.

630. —— "En juin 1919, le traité de Versailles était signé." _Historia_ (1959): 617-22.

Chief of staff to Foch (1914-23); high commissioner in Syria (1923-24); chief of the army staff (1930); vice-president of C.S.G. (1931-34); c-in-c of French forces in the theatre of the Eastern Mediterranean (1939-40); chief of general staff and commander-in-chief (May-June 1940); minister of National Defense (June-Sept. 1940); Governor of Algeria (1941); arrested and imprisoned by the Germans (1942-45).

631. Zay, Jean. _Carnets secrets_. Paris, 1942.

632. —— _Souvenirs et solitudes_. Paris, 1945.

Deputy (1932-40); minister for Education (1936-39); assassinated (1944).

E. BIOGRAPHICAL STUDIES

The criteria used in selecting these works have been more narrow and exclusive than those used in the selection of the Memoirs. Included, for obvious reasons, are studies of diplomats and foreign ministers and, given their constitutional or de facto influence, presidents and premiers. So too provision has been made for politicians who took a particular interest in foreign policy (e.g. Bardoux or de Monzie) or who may have been entrusted with some extraordinary diplomatic mission (e.g. Bérard). Expressly, if reluctantly, eliminated are many studies of military or naval officers (e.g. Foch), press figures, and politicians whose interests and energies normally were confined to domestic and regional issues.

Note. The number (#....) following many of these entries will direct the reader to brief career data on the subject of these biographical studies.

633.   Allier, Jacques. "In memoriam M. Gabriel Puaux, président honoraire de la S.H.F.P.." Société de l'histoire du protestantisme français. Bulletin. (Jan.-March 1970): 1-6. See #567.

634.   Amouroux, Henri. Pétain avant Vichy; la guerre et l'amour. Paris, 1967. #552.

635.   Antériou, J. and Baron, J. Edouard Herriot au service de la république. Paris, 1957. See Appendix B.

636.   Aron, Robert. Charles de Gaulle. Paris, 1964. #418.

637.   Arrighi, Jean-François, Maurice Schumann and Georges Clancier. "Hommage à Wladimir d'Ormesson." Nouvelle Revue des Deux Mondes 12 (1973): 537-47. #541.

638.   Aubert, L. et al. André Tardieu. Paris, 1957. See Appendix B.

639.   Aubert, Octave. Louis Barthou. Paris, 1935. See Appendix B.

640.   Aubertin, Jean. Le colonel de Gaulle. Paris,
        1965. #418.

641.   — Charles de Gaulle. Paris, 1966.

642.   Audry, Colette. Léon Blum, ou la politique du
        juste. Paris, 1955. #286.

643.   Auffray, Bernard. Pierre de Margerie (1861–1942) et
        la vie diplomatique de son temps. Paris, 1976.

        De Margerie was ambassador in Berlin (1922–31). See
        Appendix D.

644.   Baholli, Zia. Portrait de Léon Blum. Gentilly,
        1970. #286.

645.   Baraduc, Jacques. Pierre Laval devant la mort.
        Paris, 1970. See Appendix B.

646.   Barrès, Philippe. Charles de Gaulle. New York,
        1941. #418.

647.   Barros, John. Betrayal from Within. Joseph Avenol,
        secretary-general of the League of Nations
        (1933–1939). New Haven, 1969.

        Inspectorate of Finance; financial delegation to
        London (1916–23); member of financial committee of
        the League, before becoming secretary-general.

648.   Bauchard, Philippe. Léon Blum: le pouvoir pour quoi
        faire? Paris, 1976. #286.

649.   Baumont, Maurice. Aristide Briand. Diplomat und
        Idealist. Göttingen, 1966. See Appendix B.

650.   Beauphan, R. de. "Fernand de Brinon; ambassadeur de
        France." Illustration 207 (1940): 272. #318.

651.   Bechtel, Guy. Laval, 20 ans après. Paris, 1963.
        See Appendix B.

652.   Bemont, P.J. "Charles de Gaulle, la légende et
        l'histoire." Ordre français (1969): 21–39. #418.

653.   Benjamin, René. Clemenceau dans la retraite. Paris
        1930. #352.

654.   Berl, Emmanuel. "Paul Reynaud dans l'épreuve."
        Preuves 16 (1966): 27–32. See Appendix B.

655.   Besseige, Henri. Herriot parmi nous. Paris, 1960.
          See Appendix B.

656.   Bibesco, Marthe.   "Deux vrais amis: Claudel et
          Berthelot." Revue de Paris 72 (1965): 12-25.
          #350 and Appendix C.

657.   Billard, Colonel André. Philippe Pétain. Chef de
          guerre, chef d'Etat, martyr et saint de France.
          Orléan, 1958. #552.

658.   Billiau, Mme. and A. Jardillier. "Aristide Briand,
          1862-1932." Nouvelles de l'Eure 52-53 (1974):
          32-47. See Appendix B.

659.   Binion, Rudolph. Defeated Leaders: The Political
          Fate of Caillaux, Jouvenel and Tardieu. West-
          port, Conn., 1975. #s 323, 767, and Appendix B.

660.   Blond, Georges. Pétain, 1856-1951. Paris, 1966.
          See #552.

661.   Boisdeffre, Pierre de.   De Gaulle malgré lui.
          Paris, 1978. See #418.

662.   Bolton, Glaney. Pétain. London, 1957. #552.

663.   Bonafé, Félix. "Le souvenir de Jacques Bardoux."
          L'Auvergne littéraire, artistique et historique
          53 (1976): 1-22. #257.

664.   — Jacques Bardoux, une vocation politique. Tulle,
          1977.

665.   Bonheur, G.   Charles de Gaulle.   Paris, 1958.
          #418.

666.   Bonnet, Georges.   "Léon Bérard diplomate."
          R.D.D.M. 8 (1961): 605-12.

          Deputy (1910-27); senator (1927-44); minister of
          Public Instruction (1919-20, 1921-24); minister of
          Justice (1931-32, 1935-36); negotiated recognition
          of Franco's Spain (1939); ambassador to Vatican
          (1940-44).

667.   Bordes, Robert. "René Mayer." Nouvelle Revue des
          Deux Mondes (1973): 329-337.

Appointed to Conseil d'Etat (1920); Under-Secretary of State to Premier Briand (1925-26); secretary-general of Railways Advisory Board; head of the armaments mission to London (1939-40) and member of the Anglo-French Coordinating Committee; commissioner of Communications and Merchant Marine, Algiers (1943); minister of Transport and Public Works in de Gaulle's provisional government (1944).

668. Bouleaux-Jossoud, M.T. Raymond Poincaré, 1860-1934. Bar-le-Duc, 1960. See Appendix B.

669. Bourget, Pierre. Un certain Philippe Pétain. Paris, 1966. #552.

670. Bréal, Auguste. Philippe Berthelot. Paris, 1937. See Appendix C.

671. Bredin, Jean-Denis. Joseph Caillaux. Paris, 1980. #323.

672. Brichant, Colette. Charles de Gaulle, artiste de l'action. New York, 1969. #418.

673. Brissaud, André. Pétain à Sigmaringen. Paris, 1966. #552.

674. Brooks, R. "The Unknown Darlan." United States Naval Institute Proceedings 81 (Aug. 1955): 879-92. See Appendix B.

675. Bruun, Geoffrey. Clemenceau. Cambridge, Mass., 1943. #352.

676. Cameron, Elizabeth R. "Alexis Saint-Léger Léger." In The Diplomats, 1919-1939, pp. 378-405. Edited by Gordon A. Craig and Felix Gilbert. Princeton, 1953. See Appendix C.

677. Cassin, René. "Herriot et l'honneur." In Edouard Herriot: études et témoignages, 9-16. Paris, 1975. See Appendix B.

678. Castex, Henri. "Un portrait d'Aristide Briand." Information historique 34 (1972): 120-23. See Appendix B.

679. Cattaui, Georges. Charles de Gaulle. L'homme et son destin. Paris, 1960. #418.

680. — "Claudel Intime." Annales du Centre Universitaire Méditerranéen 21 (1968): 99-112. #350.

681. Chabannes, Jacques. Aristide Briand. Paris, 1973. See Appendix B.

682. Chaigne, Louis. Paul Claudel: The Man and the Mystic. Westport, Conn., 1978. #350.

683. Challener, Richard D. "The French Foreign Office: The Era of Philippe Berthelot." In The Diplomats, 1919-1939, pp. 49-85. Edited by Gordon A. Craig and Felix Gilbert. Princeton, 1953. See Appendix C.

684. Chastenet, Jacques. Raymond Poincaré. Paris, 1948. See Appendix B.

685. — "Voici cent ans naissait Poincaré." R.D.D.M. (1960): 385-402.

686. — Inauguration du monument de Louis Barthou, à Pau, 4 mai 1963. Discours. Paris, 1963. See Appendix B.

687. Chiroux, René. "Jacques Bardoux, témoin de la Troisième République." Revue d'Auvergne 89 (1975): 113-57. #257.

688. — "Jacques Bardoux (1874-1959), un libéral sous la République parlementaire." Revue politique et parlementaire 78 (1976): 9-27.

689. Clair-Guyot, Jean. "Le voyage extraordinaire du président Deschanel." Miroir de l'histoire 38 (1953): 223-34.

690. — "L'extraordinaire voyage (la chute du président Deschanel)." Aux carrefours de l'histoire 2 (1957): 127-36.

Deputy (1885-1920); president of the Chamber of Deputies (1898-1902) (1912-20); senator (1921-22); President of the Republic (Feb.-Sept. 1920).

691. Clark, Stanley F. The Man Who Is France: The Story of General de Gaulle. New York, 1960. #418.

692.   Claudel, Pierre.   "Paul Claudel diplomate."   Paul
        Claudel zu seinem hundertsten Geburtstag (1970):
        11-15.   #350.

693.   Clemenceau,   Madeleine.   Georges   Clemenceau.
        Aurillac, 1966.   #352.

694.   Coblentz, P.   Georges Mandel.   Paris, 1946.

        Chef de cabinet to Premier Clemenceau (1917-20);
        deputy   (1919-24,   1928-42);   minister   of   Postal
        Affairs (1934-36); minister of Colonies (1938-40);
        imprisoned and assassinated (1940-44).

695.   Cole, Hubert.   Laval: A Biography.   London, 1963.
        See Appendix B.

696.   Colton, Joel.   Léon Blum: Humanist in Politics.   New
        York, 1966.   #286.

697.   ── "The Poetry, Prose, and Politics of Léon Blum,
        1872-1950."   A.H.R. 79 (1974): 1491-98.

698.   Crawley,   Aidan.   De   Gaulle: A   Biography.
        Indianapolis, 1969.   #418.

699.   Crozier, Brian.   De Gaulle.   New York, 1972.   #418.

700.   Dalby,   Louise   E.   Léon   Blum: Evolution   of   a
        Socialist.   New York, 1963.   #286.

701.   David, André.   "Anatole de Monzie et Georges
        Mandel."   Nouvelle Revue des Deux Mondes 10
        (1976): 98-101.   #s 522 and 694.

702.   Debû-Bridel, Jacques.   "La vrai figure d'André
        Tardieu."   Société d'histoire de la troisième
        République.   Bulletin 13 (1955): 247-60.   See
        Appendix B and #372.

703.   ── "Edouard   Herriot   (l'écrivain)."   Revue   des
        lettres 104 (1969): 24-26.   See Appendix B.

704.   Demey, Evelyne.   Paul Reynaud, mon père.   Paris,
        1980.   See Appendix B.

705.   Devillers, Philippe.   "Henry Lémery, 1874-1972."
        Comptes rendus mensuels des séances de l'Académie
        des sciences d'Outre-Mer 34 (1974): 415-35.
        #477.

706.   Diriart, Henri. "Léon Bérard, Béarnais." Revue de
        Pau et de Béarn 5 (1977): 249-53. #666.

707.   Docteur, Admiral Jules T. La grande énigme de la
        guerre: Darlan, amiral de la Flotte. Paris,
        1949. See Appendix B.

708.   Dollet, René. "Charles Loiseau." R.H.D. 74
        (1960): 97-99. #480.

709.   Dominique, Pierre. Clemenceau. Paris, 1964.
        #352.

710.   Droit, Michel, ed. L'homme du destin, Charles de
        Gaulle. 2 vols. Paris, 1971-72. #418.

711.   Ducla, Louis. "Le centenaire de Louis Barthou."
        Revue régionaliste des Pyrénées 46 (1962): 1-17.
        See Appendix B.

712.   — "Le centenaire de Louis Barthou au musée
        béarnais." Revue régionaliste des Pyrénées 47
        (1963): 17-22.

713.   — and Maurice Bellan. "Hommage à Louis Barthou."
        Revue régionaliste des Pyrénées 50 (1968): 1-12.

714.   Duroselle, J.B. "Herriot dans la France de XXe
        siècle." In Edouard Herriot: études et
        témoignages, 17-36. Paris, 1975. See Appendix
        B.

715.   Elesha, Achille. Aristide Briand; discours et
        écrits de politique étrangère. Paris, 1965. See
        Appendix B.

716.   Erlanger, Philippe. Clemenceau. Paris, 1968.
        #352.

717.   Escaich, René. "Georges Bonnet que j'ai connu."
        Ecrits de Paris 327 (1973): 19-22. See Appendix
        B.

718.   Esme, Jean d'. De Gaulle. Paris, 1959. #418.

719.   — "Le président Albert Sarraut." Comptes rendus
        mensuels des séances de l'Académie des sciences
        d'Outre-Mer 22 (1962): 431-34.

Deputy (1902-24); senator (1926-45); minister of
Colonies (1920-24, 1932-33), of Interior (1926-28,
1934, 1938, 1938-40); of Navy (1930-33, 1933-34);
premier (1933, 1936); of State (1937-38); of
National Education (March-June 1940); Governor-
General of Indochina (1916-19); ambassador to Turkey
(1925-26).

720.   Eubank, Keith. Paul Cambon: Master Diplomatist.
        Norman, Okla., 1960. #325.

721.   Favreau, Bertrand. Georges Mandel, un clemenciste
        en Gironde. Paris, 1969. #694.

722.   Ford, Franklin L. and Carl E. Schorske. "The Voice
        in the Wilderness: Robert Coulondre." In The
        Diplomats, 1919-1939, 555-78. Edited by Gordon
        A. Craig and Felix Gilbert. Princeton, 1953.
        See Appendix D.

723.   Ford, Franklin L. "Three Observers in Berlin:
        Rumbold, Dodd, and François-Poncet." In The
        Diplomats, 1919-1939, 437-74. Edited by Gordon
        A. Craig and Felix Gilbert. Princeton, 1953.
        See Appendix D.

724.   Frossard, André and Jean Mauriac. Charles de
        Gaulle, 1890-1970. Paris, 1973. #418.

725.   Funk, Arthur Layton. Charles de Gaulle: The Crucial
        Years, 1943-1944. Norman Okla., 1959. #418.

726.   Galante, Pierre. Le Général. Paris, 1968. #418.

727.   Gillet-Maudot, M.J. Paul Claudel. Paris, 1966.
        #350.

728.   Gounelle, Claude. Le dossier Laval. Paris, 1969.
        See Appendix B.

729.   Grawitz, Madeleine. "Léon Blum." Etudes offertes à
        Achille Mestre (1956): 267-78. #286.

730.   Griffiths, Richard. Marshal Pétain. London, 1970.
        #552.

731.   Grinnell-Milne, Duncan. The Triumph of Integrity: A
        Portrait of Charles de Gaulle. New York, 1962.
        #418.

732.   Guéhenno, Jean.   Discours prononcé à l'occasion de la mort de ... Wladimir d'Ormesson et de Georges Izard. Paris, 1973. #541.

733.   Guitton, Jean.   "Le centenaire de Léon Bérard." Nouvelle Revue des Deux Mondes 10 (1976): 20-25. #666.

734.   Hadancourt, Gaston.   Clemenceau, homme d'état, homme d'esprit. Paris, 1958. #352.

735.   Harrar, Georges.   Edouard Herriot et la République. Casablanca, 1955. See Appendix B.

736.   Harrity, Richard and Ralph Martin.   Man of Destiny, De Gaulle of France. New York, 1961. #418.

737.   Héring, General Pierre.   La vie exemplaire de Philippe Pétain. Paris, 1956. #552.

738.   Herzog, W.   Barthou.   Zurich, 1938.   See Appendix B.

739.   Hoffmann, Stanley and Inge Hoffmann.   De Gaulle, artiste de la politique. Paris, 1973.   #418.

740.   Holt, Edgar.   The Tiger: The Life of Georges Clemenceau, 1841-1929.   London, 1976.   #352.

741.   Huddleston, Sisley.   Poincaré: A Biographical Portrait. London, 1924. See Appendix B.

742.   Isorni, Jacques.   Philippe Pétain.   2 vols.   Paris, 1972-73.   #552.

743.   Jacquemin, Gaston.   La vie publique de Pierre Laval (1883-1945). Paris, 1973. See Appendix B.

744.   Jeanneney, Jean-Noel.   François de Wendel en république: l'argent et le pouvoir, 1914-1940. 3 vols. Lille, 1976.

       Iron industrialist from Lorraine, and president of the Comité des Forges in the 1930s; deputy (1924-33), and senator thereafter; principal shareholder in Journal des Débats, and Le Temps.

745.   Jessner, Sabine.   Edward Herriot; Patriarch of the Republic. New York, 1974. See Appendix B.

746. Joll, James. Intellectuals in Politics: Léon Blum, Walter Rathenau and F.T. Marinetti; three biographical essays. London, 1960. #286.

747. Kupferman, Fred. Pierre Laval. Paris, 1976. See Appendix B.

748. Lacouture, Jean. De Gaulle. Paris, 1965. #418.

749. — Léon Blum. Paris, 1977. #286.

750. La Gorce, Paul Marie de. De Gaulle entre deux mondes. Une vie et une époque. Paris, 1964. #418.

751. Langlois-Berthelot, Daniel. "Philippe Berthelot (1886-1934)." Nouvelle Revue des Deux Mondes 6 (1976): 574-82. See Appendix C.

752. Lapaquellerie, Yvon. Edouard Daladier. Paris, 1939. See Appendix B.

753. Lapie, Pierre-Olivier. Herriot. Paris, 1967. See Appendix B.

754. — "Herriot, humaniste." Revue des lettres 107 (1972): 14-24.

755. Laure, General Auguste Marie. Pétain. Paris, 1942. #552.

755A. Léger, Alexis Saint-Léger. Briand. New York, 1943. See Appendix B.

756. Léon-Bérard, Marguerite. "Souvenir de mon père (Léon Bérard)." R.D.D.M. (1968): 43-56. #666.

757. Lévis Mirepoix, Antoine-Pierre, duc de. Inauguration d'un monument à la mémoire de Léon Bérard. Discours prononcé à Pau, le 19 octobre 1968. Paris, 1968. #666.

758. Levy, Roger. "Albert Sarraut." Politique étrangère 27 (1962): 480-83. #719.

759. Logue, William. Léon Blum: The Formative Years, 1872-1914. De Kalb, Ill., 1973. #286.

760. Magnien, G. "Edouard Herriot." Bulletin de la Société historique, archéologique et littéraire de Lyon 20 (1958): xii-xv. See Appendix B.

761.   Mallet, Alfred. Pierre Laval. 2 vols. Paris,
        1955. See Appendix B.

762.   Malone, G.P.   "Briand: Architect   of   U.N.O."
        Contemporary Review 189 (1956):   31-36.   See
        Appendix B.

763.   Mannoni, Eugène. Moi, Général de Gaulle. Paris,
        1964. #418.

764.   Marchat, Henry.   "Briand, pèlerin de la paix."
        Revue de défense nationale 18 (1962): 1330-48.
        See Appendix B.

765.   — "Eloge de M. Emmanuel de Peretti de La Rocca."
        Comptes rendus mensuels des séances de l'Académie
        des sciences d'Outre-Mer 31 (1971): 531-42. See
        Appendix C.

766.   Marie, Yvonne. Edouard Herriot et Dieu. Paris,
        1965. See Appendix B.

767.   Marmisse, Jean.   "Henry   de   Jouvenel."   Revue
        littéraire sous l'égide de la Société d'études
        historiques et archéologiques de la Moyenne-
        Corèze 57 (1976): 300-28. See Appendix D.

768.   Martel, Francis. Pétain: Verdun to Vichy.   New
        York, 1943. #552.

769.   Martin, Jacques, Jacques de Lacretelle and Pierre de
        Boisdeffre.   "Hommage   à   Wladimir   d'Ormesson."
        Nouvelle Revue des Deux Mondes 11 (1973):
        302-17. #541.

770.   Martinaud-Deplat, Leon.   "Un parlementaire (Paul
        Reynaud)." R.D.D.M. (1966): 3-8. See Appendix B.

771.   Mauriac, François. De Gaulle. Paris, 1964. #418.

772.   Mendès-France, Pierre. "Edouard Herriot." Reflets
        de la vie lyonnaise 140 (1967): 24-27.   See
        Appendix B.

773.   — "Un hommage à Edouard Herriot."   In Edouard
        Herriot: études et témoignages, 172-75. Paris,
        1975.

774.   Middleton, W.L. "Aristide Briand." Contemporary
        Review 201 (1962): 129-33. See Appendix B.

775. Mikes, G. <u>Darlan: A Study</u>. London, 1943. See
Appendix B.

776. Millet, Pierre. "Henri Bonnet (1888-1978);
ambassadeur de France." <u>Nouvelle Revue des Deux
Mondes</u> 12 (1978): 581-84.

Diplomat; attached to League secretariat (1920-31);
director of Institut de Coopération Intellectuelle
(1931-40); commissioner, then minister, of
Information (1943-44); ambassador to Washington
(1944-55).

777. Minart, Colonel Jacques. <u>Charles de Gaulle, tel que
je l'ai connu</u>. Paris, 1945. #418.

778. Miquel, Pierre. <u>Poincaré</u>. Paris, 1961. See
Appendix B.

779. ── "Le centenaire de Raymond Poincaré." <u>Revue
politique et parlementaire</u> 63 (1961): 63-68.

780. Monnerville, Gaston. <u>Clemenceau</u>. Paris, 1968. #352.

781. Monticone, Ronald C. <u>Charles de Gaulle</u>. Boston,
1975. #418.

782. Montmorency, Alec de. <u>The Enigma of Admiral
Darlan</u>. New York, 1943. See Appendix B.

783. Morand, Paul. <u>Giraudoux. Souvenirs</u>. Geneva,
1948. #s 424, 524.

784. Mordacq, General Henri. <u>Clemenceau au soir de sa
vie, 1920-1929</u>. Paris, 1933. #352.

785. Moulis, André. <u>Un destin hors série: Anatole de
Monzie, 1876-1947. Avec des inédits de Monzie</u>.
Brive, n.d. #522.

786. Nachin, Lucien. <u>Charles de Gaulle</u>. Nancy, 1971.
#418.

787. Nicolet, Claude. <u>Pierre Mendès-France ou le métier
de Cassandre</u>. Paris, 1959. #504.

788. Offroy, Raymond. "De Gaulle 1940-1944." <u>De Gaulle
et le service de l'Etat</u> (1977): 21-66. #418.

789.   Ormesson, Wladimir d'. "Deux grandes figures de la
        diplomatie française: Paul et Jules Cambon."
        R.H.D. 57-59 (1943-45); 33-71. See Appendices C
        and D.

790.   — "Claudel diplomate." Bulletin de la société Paul
        Claudel 43 (1971): 9. #350.

791.   Ory, Pascal. De Gaulle ou l'ordre du discours.
        Paris, 1978. #418.

792.   Ott, Barthélemy. Georges Bidault: l'Indomptable.
        Annonay, 1975. See Appendix B.

793.   Persil, Raoul. Alexandre Millerand, 1859-1943.
        Paris, 1949. See Appendix B.

794.   Pierre-Bloch, Jean. De Gaulle ou le temps des
        méprises. Paris, 1969. #418.

795.   Plaisant, Marcel. "Un portrait inédit de Paul
        Reynaud." Revue politique et parlementaire 68
        (1966): 38-48. See Appendix B.

796.   — "Raymond Poincaré, orateur." R.D.D.M. (1958):
        605-13. See Appendix B.

797.   Planté, Louis. Un grand seigneur de la politique:
        Anatole de Monzie. Paris, 1955. #522.

798.   Plumyène, Jean. Pétain. Paris, 1964. #552.

799.   Pomaret, Charles. "Un destin hors-série: Anatole de
        Monzie." Annales du Centre Universitaire
        Méditerranéen 14 (1960-61): 85-100. #522.

800.   Privat, M. Pierre Laval, cet inconnu. Paris,
        1941. See Appendix B.

801.   Prouteau, Gilbert. Le dernier défi de Georges
        Clemenceau. Paris, 1979. #352.

802.   Ratinaud, Jean. Clemenceau, ou la colère et la
        gloire. Paris, 1959. #352.

803.   Ray, Oscar. The Life of Edouard Daladier. London,
        1940. See Appendix B.

804.   Ritter, Raymond. "Louis Barthou et le Béarn."
        Pyrénées: organe du musée pyrénéen de Lourdes 54
        (1963): 73-81. See Appendix B.

805.   Robuchon, Jean. <u>Les grandes heures de Georges Clemenceau.</u> Fontenay-le-Comte, 1967. #352.

806.   Roche, Emile. "Joseph Caillaux et Georges Mandel." <u>Nouvelle Revue des Deux Mondes</u> 10 (1977): 61–65. #s 323 and 694.

807.   —— "Joseph Caillaux et Léon Blum." <u>Nouvelle Revue des Deux Mondes</u> (1977): 606–10. #s 323 and 286.

808.   Saint-Connat, Hughes. "Monzie, ministre des Affaires étrangères." <u>Ecrits de Paris</u> (1955): 57–64. #522.

809.   Sarraute, Claude. "Mme Georges Bidault, ministre plénipotentiaire." <u>Le Monde diplomatique</u> (Sept. 1956): 4. #280.

810.   Sarrazin, Bernard and Jean d'Auvergne. <u>Edouard Herriot.</u> Saint-Etienne, 1957. See Appendix B.

811.   Saulière, Pierre. <u>Clemenceau.</u> Paris, 1979. #352.

812.   Schaper, B.W. <u>Albert Thomas: Trente ans de réformisme social.</u> Assen, 1959.

        Deputy (1910-21); minister of Armaments (1916-17); ambassador to Moscow (1917-18); member of the Peace Conference (1918-19); director of the International Labor Bureau (1920-1932).

813.   Schillemans, G.T. <u>Philippe Pétain: le prisonnier de Sigmaringen.</u> Paris, 1965. #552.

814.   Schoenbrun, David. <u>Les trois vies de Charles de Gaulle.</u> Paris, 1965. #418.

815.   Sebastien, A. and J. Philippe. <u>Pétain -- de Gaulle. Pourquoi amis? Pourquoi ennemis? Etude psychologique.</u> Paris, 1965. #s 552 and 418.

816.   Sherwood, John. <u>Georges Mandel and the Third Republic.</u> Stanford, 1970. #694.

817.   Siebert, Ferdinand. <u>Aristide Briand, 1867-1932. Ein Staatsmann zwischen Frankreich und Europa.</u> Zurich, 1973. See Appendix B.

818.   Soulas,   •   "Anatole   de   Monzie   (1876-1947)."
        Mémoires de la Société d'agriculture, sciences,
        belles-lettres   et   arts   d'Orléans   35   (1970):
        121-23. #522.

819.   Soulié, Michel.   La   vie   politique   d'Edouard
        Herriot. Paris, 1962. See Appendix B.

820.   — "Herriot, la France et la République."   Revue
        politique et parlementaire 64 (1962): 23-29.

821.   Spears, Sir Edward.   Two Men Who Saved France:
        Pétain, De Gaulle.   London, 1966.   #s 552 and
        418.

822.   Stokes, R.L. Léon Blum: Poet to Premier. New York,
        1937. #286.

823.   Suarez, Georges.   Herriot, 1924, suivie d'un récit
        historique de R. Poincaré.   Paris, 1932.   See
        Appendix B.

824.   — Le maréchal Pétain. Paris, 1941. #552.

825.   — Briand. Sa vie. Son oeuvre, avec son journal et
        de nombreux documents inédits.   6 vols.   Paris,
        1938-52. See Appendix B.

826.   Suffert, Georges. Charles de Gaulle. Paris, 1970.
        #418.

827.   Thomson, David.   Two Frenchmen: Pierre Laval and
        Charles de Gaulle.   Westport, Conn., 1975.   See
        Appendix B and #418.

828.   Torrès, H. Pierre Laval, La France trahie.   New
        York, 1941. See Appendix B.

829.   Tournoux, Jean-Raymond.   Pétain et de Gaulle.
        Paris, 1968. #s 552 and 418.

830.   Vallat, Xavier, ed. "L'Homme Pierre Laval." Ecrits
        de Paris 314 (1972): 20-28. See Appendix B.

831.   Varenne, François.   Mon patron, Georges Mandel.
        Paris, 1945. #694.

832.   Vichniac, M. Léon Blum. Paris, 1937. #286.

833.   Waline, Marcel. Notice sur la vie et les travaux de
         Gabriel Puaux, 1883-1970; lue dans la séance du
         18 avril 1972. Institut de France, Académie des
         sciences morales et politiques. Paris, 1972.
         #567.

834.   Warner, Geoffrey. Pierre Laval and the Eclipse of
         France. London, 1968. See Appendix B.

835.   Watson, David. Georges Clemenceau: A Political
         Biography. London, 1974. #352.

836.   Williams, Wythe. The Tiger of France. New York,
         1949. #352.

837.   Wormser, Georges. La république de M. Clemenceau.
         Paris, 1961. #352.

838.   — Georges Mandel. Paris, 1967. #694.

838A.   — Clemenceau vu de près. Paris, 1979. #352.

839.   Wurstemberger, Jean-Pierre de. "André François-
         Poncet." La revue universelle 40 (1978): 65-69.
         See Appendix D.

840.   Ziebura, Gilbert. Léon Blum, Theorie und Praxis
         einer sozialistischen Politik. Berlin, 1963.
         #286.

841.   Zizine, Pierre. Le citoyen Lémery. Paris, 1972.
         #477.

842.   Unsigned. Anatole de Monzie; tel qu'en lui-même
         (documents inédits). Saint-Jean-Lespinasse,
         1963. #522.

843.   — "André Laboulaye." R.H.D. 80 (1966): 357-58.
         #459.

844.   — "Charles de Gaulle, 1890-1970." France-
         Informations 32 (1971): 1-42. #418.

845.   — Claudel diplomate. Paris, 1962. #350.

846.   — "Henry de Jouvenel, journaliste, parlementaire,
         homme d'état aurait eu cent ans en 1976."
         Bulletin de la Société scientifique, historique
         et archéologique de la Corrèze 98 (1976):
         237-45. #767.

847.   — <u>Hommage à Albert Lebrun</u>. Paris, 1960. #476.

848.   — "Hommage à Raymond Poincaré." <u>Reflets de la
         Meuse</u> 10 (1968): 16-33. See Appendix B.

849.   — "Joseph Paul-Boncour, 1873-1972." <u>Cahiers des
         Nations Unies</u> numéro spécial (1972), 34 pp. See
         Appendix B.

850.   — "Numéro consacré à Edouard Herriot." <u>Ecrivains
         contemporains</u> 10 (1954): 1-20. See Appendix B.

851.   — "Philippe Berthelot." <u>Bulletin de la Société
         Paul Claudel</u> 28 (1967): 1-67. See Appendix C.

852.   — <u>Quand mourut Aristide Briand</u>. Liège, 1967. See
         Appendix B.

853.   — Société des amis d'Albert Thomas. <u>Un grand
         citoyen du monde: Albert Thomas vivant. Etudes,
         témoignages, souvenirs</u>. Geneva, 1957. #812.

F. CONTEMPORARY STUDIES (published 1918-1945)

854.   Allard, P. Le Quai d'Orsay. Paris, 1938.

855.   — Les favorites de la troisième république. Paris,
        1942.

856.   Archimbault, Léon. La conférence de Washington (12
        novembre 1921-6 février 1922). Paris, 1923.

857.   Bardoux, Jacques. Lloyd George et la France.
        Paris, 1921.

858.   Barrès, Maurice. L'appel du Rhin, la France dans
        les pays rhénans. Paris, 1919.

859.   — La politique rhénane. Paris, 1922.

860.   — Le génie du Rhin. Paris, 1921.

861.   — Les grands problèmes du Rhin. Paris, 1930.

862.   Barthélemy, Joseph. Essai sur le travail
        parlementaire et le système des commissions.
        Paris, 1934.

863.   Barthou, Louis. Le traité de paix. Paris, 1919.

864.   Beauvais, Armand P. Attachés militaires, attachés
        navals et attachés de l'air. Paris, 1937.

865.   Bernus, P. "La grande crise de la diplomatie
        française." R.D.D.M. 58 (Aug. 1940): 254-264.

866.   Bourgeois, Léon. Le traité de paix de Versailles.
        Paris, 1919.

867.   Briey, R. de. Le Rhin et le problème d'occident.
        Paris, 1922.

868.   Cambon, Jules. Le diplomate. Paris, 1926.

869.   Cameron, Elizabeth. Prologue to Appeasement: A
        Study in French Foreign Policy. Washington,
        1942.

870. Chow, S.R. Le contrôle parlementaire de la
      politique étrangère en Angleterre, en France et
      aux Etats-Unis. Paris, 1920.

871. Clémentel, Etienne. Inventaire de la situation
      financière au début de la treizième législature.
      Paris, 1924.

872. Comité des Forges de France. La métallurgie et le
      traité de paix. Paris, 1920.

873. Coquet, James de. Le procès de Riom. Paris, 1945.

874. Daniélou, Charles. Les Affaires étrangères. Paris,
      1927.

875. Driault, Edouard. La question d'Orient, 1918-1937:
      la paix de la Méditerranée. Paris, 1937.

876. Duval, General Maurice. "La convention aérienne."
      l'Esprit International 9 (July 1935): 306-19.

877. Echeman, Jacques. Les ministères en France de 1914
      à 1932. Paris, 1932.

878. Fabry, Jean. "La 'stratégie générale', affaire de
      gouvernement." Revue Militaire Générale 1 (April
      1937): 387-390.

879. François-Marsal, Frédéric. Les dettes interalliées.
      Paris, 1927.

880. Genet, Raoul. Traité de diplomatie et de droit
      diplomatique. 3 vols. Paris, 1931-32.

881. Géraud, André (Pertinax). Les fossoyeurs. Défaite
      militaire de la France. 2 vols. New York,
      1944. Translated as The Gravediggers of France.
      New York, 1944.

      A journalist's shrewd if partisan indictment of the
      "gravediggers", Gamelin, Daladier, Reynaud, Pétain
      and Laval.

882. —— "France and the Anglo-German Naval Treaty."
      Foreign Affairs 14 (1935-36): 51-61.

883. —— "France, Russia and the Pact of Mutual
      Assistance." Foreign Affairs 13 (1935): 226-35.

884.   — "The Anglo-French Alliance." Foreign Affairs 18
        (1939-40): 601-613.

885.   — "What England Means to France." Foreign Affairs
        17 (Jan. 1939): 362-73.

886.   Gontaut-Biron, Comte R. de. Comment la France s'est
        installée en Syrie (1918-1919). Paris, 1922.

887.   Gooch, R.K. The French Parliamentary Committee
        System. New York, 1935.

888.   Gruben, Hervé de. La crise allemande et
        l'occupation rhénane, 1923-1924. Brussels,
        1925.

889.   Hanotaux, Gabriel. Le traité de Versailles du 28
        juin 1919: l'Allemagne et l'Espagne. Paris,
        1919.

890.   Heinberg, J.G. "The Personnel of French Cabinets,
        1871-1930." American Political Science Review 25
        (May 1931): 389-96.

891.   Kérillis, Henri de. Français, voici la vérité. New
        York, 1942.

892.   — and Cartier, Raymond. Laisserons-nous démembrer
        la France? Paris, 1939.

893.   Knapton, E.J. "Duel for Central Europe: Some
        Aspects of French Diplomacy, 1938-1939." Journal
        of Central European Affairs 2 (April 1942):
        1-19.

894.   Leeds, Stanton B. These Rule France. New York,
        1940.

        Included among these sketches are politicians like
        Daladier, Herriot, Tardieu and Chautemps; financiers
        and businessmen like de Wendel and Schneider; press
        people like Daudet, Bailby and Galtier-Boissière;
        and officers from Pétain through Gamelin and
        Darlan.

895.   Lévis-Mirepoix, Emmanuel de. Le Ministère des
        Affaires étrangères: organisation de
        l'administration centrale et des services
        extérieurs, 1793-1933. Angers, 1934.

896.   Lombard, Paul. Le chemin de Munich. Paris, 1938.

897.   Marin, Louis. Le traité de paix. Paris, 1920.

898.   Mazé, P. and Genebrier, R. Les grandes journées du
        procès de Riom. Paris, 1945.

899.   Montigny, Jean and Kayser, Jacques. Le drame
        financier: les responsables. Paris, 1925.

900.   Mousset, Albert. La France vue de l'étranger; ou le
        déclin de la diplomatie et le mythe de la
        propagande. Paris, 1926.

901.   Norton, Henry Kittredge. "Foreign Office
        Organization. A Comparison of the Organization
        of the British, French, German and Italian
        Foreign Office with that of the Department of
        State of the U.S.A." The Annals. American
        Academy of Political and Social Science.
        Supplement to vol. 143 (1929). 83 pp.

902.   Pange, Jean de. Les libertés rhénanes: pays rhénans
        Sarre-Alsace. Paris, 1922.

903.   Pinon, René. L'avenir de l'entente franco-anglaise.
        Paris, 1924.

904.   — La bataille de la Ruhr, 1923. Chroniques du
        ministère Poincaré. Paris, 1924.

905.   — Le redressement de la politique française, 1922
        Paris, 1923.

906.   Recouly, Raymond. La barrière du Rhin: Droits et
        devoirs de la France pour assurer sa sécurité.
        Paris, 1923.

907.   — La Ruhr. Paris, 1923.

908.   Reibel, Charles. Pourquoi nous avons été à deux
        doigts de la guerre. Paris, 1938.

909.   Reynaud, Paul. Jeunesse, quelle France veux-tu?
        Paris, 1936.

910.   Roques, Paul. Le contrôle militaire interallié en
        Allemagne, septembre 1919-janvier 1927. Paris,
        1927.

911.   Rousseau, Jean. La haute commission interalliée des territoires rhénans. Mayence, 1923.

912.   Schuman, F.L. War and Diplomacy in the French Republic. New York, 1931.

913.   — Europe on the Eve: The Crises of Diplomacy, 1933-1939. New York, 1939.

914.   Selsam, Jon P. The Attempts to Form an Anglo-French Alliance, 1919-1924. Philadelphia, 1936.

915.   Seydoux, Jacques. "Suggestions pour une réorganisation du Ministère des Affaires étrangères." l'Europe Nouvelle (26 March 1927): 428-30.

916.   Sharp, Walter Rice. The French Civil Service: Bureaucracy in Transition. New York, 1931.

917.   — The Government of the French Republic. New York, 1938.

918.   Simone, André (Otto Katz). J'Accuse. New York, 1940.

919.   Tabouis, Geneviève. Blackmail or War. London, 1938.

920.   Tardieu, André. France in Danger. London, 1935.

921.   Vogel, L. "Cartoons in Writing: Notes on France's Foreign Policy, 1935-1940." Free World 2 (1942): 71-6.

922.   Werth, Alexander. France and Munich. London, 1939.

923.   — The Destiny of France. London, 1937.

G. HISTORICAL ARTICLES

Colloquia Collections

924.   Centenaire de la Troisième République.   Colloque,
         Rennes, 1975. Paris, 1975.

925.   Centre de relations internationales.   Université de
         Metz. Colloque, Otzenhausen, 1974. Metz, 1975.

926.   Colloque Franco-Allemand.   La France et l'Allemagne
         (1932-1936). Paris, 1980.

927.   Colloque Franco-Allemand.   La France et l'Allemagne
         (1936-1939), Bonn. To be published.

928.   Edouard Herriot.   Etudes et Témoignages.   Paris,
         1975.

929.   Fondation Nationale des Sciences Politiques.   La
         Politique Etrangère et ses Fondements.   Paris,
         1954.

930.   Fondation   Nationale   des   Sciences   Politiques.
         Edouard   Daladier,   chef   du   gouvernement.
         Colloque, Paris, 1975. Paris, 1977.

931.   Français et Britanniques dans la drôle de guerre.
         Colloque Anglo-Français, 1975. Paris, 1979.

932.   Guerre en Méditerranée.   Colloque, Paris, 1971.
         Paris, 1971.

933.   La France et l'Italie pendant la première guerre
         mondiale.   Colloque, Grenoble, 1973.   Paris,
         1976.

934.   La Libération de la France. Colloque international,
         Paris, 1974. Paris, 1976.

935.   La politique française et les Balkans, 1933-1936.
         1ᵉʳ Colloque historique franco-bulgare, Paris
         1973. Paris, 1975.

Colloquia Collections

936.   La position internationale de la France. 2e Congrès
         national. Association française des historiens
         économistes, Paris, Nanterre. Paris, 1977.

937.   Léon Blum, chef du gouvernement. Colloque, Paris,
         1965. Paris, 1967.

938.   Les relations franco-allemandes, 1933-1939.
         Colloque, Strasbourg, 1975. Paris, 1976.

939.   Les relations franco-belges de 1830 à 1934.
         Colloque, Metz, 1974. Metz, 1975.

940.   Les relations franco-britanniques, 1935-1939.
         Colloques Anglo-Français, 1971, 1972. Paris,
         1975.

941.   Les relations militaires franco-belges, 1936-1940.
         Paris, 1968.

942.   L'Industrie. Colloque, Metz, 1972. Metz, 1974.

943.   Mélanges offerts à V.-L. Tapié. Paris, 1973.

944.   Mélanges Pierre Renouvin. Etudes d'histoire des
         relations internationales. Paris, 1966.

945.   Institut d'Etudes Juridiques de Nice. Les Affaires
         étrangères. Paris, 1959.

946.   Institut national d'études slaves. Munich 1938:
         Mythes et Réalités. Colloque, Paris, 1978.
         Revue des études slaves 52 (1979).

947.   Université de Metz. Les relations
         franco-luxembourgeoises: De Louis XIV à Robert
         Schuman. Colloque, Luxembourg, 1977. Metz,
         1978.

948.   Université des sciences juridiques, politiques et
         sociales (Strasbourg). Cent ans de relations
         franco-allemandes, 1871-1971. Colloque,
         Strasbourg, 1971. Revue d'Allemagne 4 (1972).

General (1918-1945)

949.   Ageron, Charles. "L'idée d'Eurafrique et le débat
        colonial franco-allemand de l'entre-deux-
        guerres." R.H.M.C. 22 (1975): 446-75.

950.   Albrecht-Carrié, René. "France in Europe: prospect
        and retrospect." Political Science Quarterly 69
        (1954): 161-85.

951.   — "Perspectives sur un quart de siècle, 1914-1939."
        Politique étrangère 23 (1958): 269-93.

952.   — "For an End to the Hundred Years War." Orbis 14
        (1970): 627-41.

953.   Alexandrov, Victor. "Les relations franco-
        soviétiques à travers l'histoire." Année
        politique et économique 154 (1960): 145-62.

954.   Andrew, C. "Déchiffrement et Diplomatie: Le cabinet
        noir du Quai d'Orsay sous la Troisième
        République." R.I. 5 (1976): 37-64.

955.   Berstein, S. "Les conceptions du parti radical en
        matière de politique économique extérieure."
        R.I. 13 (1978): 71-89.

956.   Bled, Jean-Paul. "Charles de Gaulle et l'Europe de
        Versailles." Etudes gaulliennes 3 (1975):
        37-46.

957.   Bordeaux, Henry. "Freycinet, Clemenceau, Foch."
        Ecrits de Paris 157 (1958): 34-47.

958.   Břachová, Věra. "Francouzská Vojenská Mise V
        Československu." (The French military mission in
        Czechoslovakia) Historie a Vojenosti 6 (1967):
        883-910.

959.   Bruckmüller, Ernst. "Österreich, die
        Tschechoslowakei und Frankreich in der
        Zwischenkriegszeit." Österreich in Geschichte
        und Literatur 16 (1972): 417-31.

960.   Brunschwig, Henri. "Un Dialogue de Sourds: un
        siècle de rapports franco-allemands." Politique
        étrangère 20 (1955): 575-90.

General (1918-1945)

961.   Cairns, John C. "Along the Road Back to France
         1940." American Historical Review 64 (1959):
         583-603.

962.   ── "De Gaulle Confronts the British: The Legacy of
         1940." International Journal 23 (1968):
         187-210.

963.   ── "A Nation of Shopkeepers in Search of a Suitable
         France: 1919-1940." A.H.R. 79 (1974): 710-43.

964.   Capelle, Comte Robert. "Versailles (1919),
         Berchtesgaden (1940)." Histoire de notre temps 6
         (1968): 103-32.

965.   Craig, Gordon A. "The Professional Diplomat and his
         Problems, 1919-1939." In War, Politics and
         Diplomacy, pp. 207-219. Edited and written by
         Gordon Craig. New York, 1966.

966.   Crouzet, François. "Problèmes de la communication
         franco-britanniques aux XIXe et XXe siècles."
         R.H. 254 (1975): 105-34.

967.   Croy-Chanel, Etienne de. "L'école des diplomates."
         Hommes et Mondes 9 (1954): 488-95.

968.   Dhers, Pierre. "Du 7 mars 1936 à l'Ile d'Yeu."
         R.H.D.G.M. 5 (1952): 17-26.

         Reflections of a member of the 1946 Serre commission
         of inquiry.

969.   Droz, Jacques. "Les relations franco-allemandes
         dans l'oeuvre des historiens allemands et
         français de 1918 à nos jours." Revue d'Allemagne
         4 (1972): 600-02.

970.   Duclos, Jacques and others. "Le cinquantenaire de
         l'établissement des relations franco-
         soviétiques." Annuaire d'études françaises
         (1976): 5-63.

971.   Duroselle, Jean-Baptiste. "French Diplomacy in the
         Postwar World." In Diplomacy in a Changing
         World, pp. 204-48. Edited by S. Kertesz and M.
         Fitzsimmons. Notre Dame, 1959.

General (1918-1945)

972. — "L'évolution des formes de la diplomatie et son effet sur la politique étrangère des Etats." #929, pp. 325-49.

973. — "La politique extérieure de la Troisième République: ses traits originaux." #924, pp. 130-40.

974. Fischer-Galati, Stephen. "France and Rumania: A Changing Image." East European Quarterly 1 (1967): 107-21.

975. Géraud, André. "Diplomacy, Old and New." Foreign Affairs, 23 (January 1945): 256-70.

976. — "Rise and Fall of the Anglo-French Entente." Foreign Affairs 32 (1954): 374-83.

977. Gorce, Paul Marie de la. "Le rôle de l'Armée dans l'élaboration de la politique étrangère." In l'Elaboration de la politique étrangère, 223-238. Issued by the Centre d'Etudes des relations politiques (Université de Dijon). Paris, 1969.

978. Gros, André. "La négociation diplomatique." #945, 135-43.

979. Grunewald, Jacques. "L'influence des facteurs économiques sur les décisions dans la politique étrangère de la France." #929, 3-32.

980. Hayter, Sir William. "French Diplomacy." In his The Diplomacy of the Great Powers, pp. 33-41. London, 1960.

981. Hoffmann, Stanley. "Quelques aspects du rôle du droit international dans la politique étrangère des Etats." #929, 239-77.

982. Klein, Fritz. "Zur deutsch-französischen Auseinandersetzung zwischen 1919 und 1939 über die Ursprünge des Ersten Weltkrieges." Revue d'Allemagne 4 (1974): 47-57.

983. Lebel, Claude. "L'organisation et les services du Ministère des Affaires étrangères." #945, 57-96.

General (1918-1945)

984.   Mares, Antoine. "La faillite des relations franco-tchécoslovaques: la mission militaire française à Prague (1926-1938)." R.H.D.G.M. 28 (1978): 45-71.

985.   Narotchnitsky, A. "Deux tendances dans l'histoire des relations franco-russes." R.H. 237 (1967): 99-124.

986.   Néré, Jacques. "Le problème de la sécurité française entre les deux guerres mondiales." L'Information Historique 29 (1967): 113-116.

987.   Noel, Léon. "Politique extérieure et diplomatie." #945, pp. 97-134.

988.   Olenev, S. "Dans les coulisses de la politique extérieure officielle. Faits nouveaux sur l'activité du comité franco-allemand d'information et de documentation, 1925-1939." (In Russian) Meždunarodnaja žisń 6 (1958): 73-82.

989.   Osgood, S.M. "Le mythe de 'la perfide Albion' en France 1919-1940." Cahiers d'Histoire 20 (1975): 5-20.

990.   Outrey, Amédée. "Histoire et principes de l'administration française des affaires étrangères." Revue française de science politique 3 (1953): 298-318; 491-510; 714-738.

991.   Pelletier, Pierre. "Le fonctionnement d'un ministère des Affaires étrangères et d'une grande ambassade." In Session d'Etudes administratives, diplomatiques et économiques. Paris, 1959.

992.   Scherer, André. "Le problème des 'Mains libres' à l'Est." R.H.D.G.M. 32 (1958): 1-25.

993.   Schuman, Robert. "Le Ministre des Affaires Etrangères." #945, 11-20.

994.   Schumann, Maurice. "La commission des affaires étrangères et le contrôle de la politique extérieure en régime parlementaire." #945, pp. 21-55.

HISTORICAL ARTICLES

General (1918-1945)

995.   Simmert, Dietrich. "Les influences et les intérêts
        de la France, de l'Allemagne et de l'U.R.S.S. en
        Europe sud-est." Problèmes soviétiques 15
        (1968): 52-61.

1918-1920s

996.   Alexander, Manfred. "Die Reise von Marschall Foch
        nach Warschau und Prag im Frühjahr 1923."
        Bohemia. Jahrbuch des Collegium Carolinum 14
        (1973): 289-319.

997.   Ambrosius, Lloyd E. "Wilson, Clemenceau and the
        German Problem at the Paris Peace Conference of
        1919." Rocky Mountain Social Science Journal 12
        (1975): 69-80.

998.   Andrew, Christopher and Kanya-Forstner, A.S.
        "France and the Repartition of Africa,
        1914-1922." Dalhousie Review 57 (1977): 475-93.

999.   Artaud, Denise. "A propos de l'occupation de la
        Ruhr." R.H.M.C. 17 (1970): 2-21.

1000.   — "Les dettes de guerre de la France, 1919-1929."
        #936, 313-18.

1001.   — "La question des dettes interalliées et la
        reconstruction de l'Europe." R.H. (1979):
        363-82.

1002.   — "Le gouvernement américain et la question des
        dettes de guerre au lendemain de l'armistice de
        Rethondes (1919-1920)." R.H.D.G.M. 20 (1973):
        201-29.

1003.   Bariéty, Jacques. "L'appareil de presse de Joseph
        Caillaux et l'argent allemand, 1920-1932." R.H.
        247 (1972): 375-406.

1004.   — "Les réparations allemandes 1919-1924: Objet ou
        prétexte à une politique rhénane de la France."
        Bulletin de la Société d'Histoire Moderne 72
        (1973): 21-33.

1005.   — "L'administration des territoires rhénans occupés
        pendant la période de l'armistice, 11 novembre
        1918-18 juin 1919." Travaux et Recherches
        (Metz), (1974): 59-78.

1918-1920s

1006. — "Le rôle d'Emile Mayrisch entre les sidérurgies allemandes et françaises après la première guerre mondiale." R.I. 1 (1974): 123-34.

1007. — "Industriels allemands et industriels français à l'époque de la République de Weimar." Revue d'Allemagne 6 (1974): 1-16.

1008. — "Sidérurgie, littérature, politique et journalisme: ...les Mayrisch entre l'Allemagne et la France après la première guerre mondiale." Bulletin de la Société d'Histoire Moderne 68 (1969): 7-13.

1009. — "La Haute Commission interalliée des territoires rhénans." #925, 15-28.

1010. — "Le projet de rétrocession d'Eupen Malmédy par la Belgique à l'Allemagne et la France (1925-1926)." #939, 325-48.

1011. — "Les livraisons en nature allemandes à la France au titre des réparations après la première guerre mondiale (1919-1924)." #942, 143-53.

1012. — "Finances et relations internationales: A propos du 'plan de Thoiry' (Septembre 1926)." R.I. 21 (1980): 51-70.

1013. Baumont, Maurice. "La Belgique, la France et le Luxembourg en 1919-1920." Annales d'Etudes Internationales 1 (1970): 171-79.

1014. — "The Rhineland crisis: 7 March 1936." In Troubled Neighbours, pp. 158-69. Edited by Neville Waites. London, 1971.

1015. — "Les relations franco-belges après 1917." #939, 295-302.

1016. Bierzanek, R. "La Pologne dans les conceptions politiques des puissances occidentales en 1918-1919." R.H.M.C. 15 (1968): 273-303.

1017. Birn, Donald S. "Open Diplomacy at the Washington Conference of 1921-22: The British and French Experience." Comparative Studies in Society and History 12 (1970): 297-319.

1918-1920s

1018.   Bonnet, Serge.   "La tentative d'instaurer la
          république à Luxembourg en 1919: Le rapport du
          général Roques, envoyé de Clemenceau."   Hémecht.
          Zeitschrift für luxemburger Geschichte 26 (1974):
          169-86.

1019.   Bordeaux, Henry.   "Le traité de Versailles (28 juin
          1919)."   R.D.D.M. 20 (1960): 617-27.

1020.   Borisov, I.V.   "L'établissement des relations
          diplomatiques   entre   la   France   et   l'Union
          soviétique."   Annuaire d'études françaises,
          (1962): 289-331.

1021.   Boyce, R.W.   "Britain's First 'No' to Europe:
          Britain and the Briand Plan, 1929-1930."
          European Studies Review 4 (1980): 17-46.

1022.   Brach, R.   "Francouzský Alianční Systém A
          Československo Na Počátku Roku 1924."   (The
          French system of alliances and Czechoslovakia at
          the beginning of 1924.) Historie a Vojeností 1
          (1968): 1-21.

1023.   Bradley, J.   "L'intervention française en Sibérie
          (1918-1919)."   R.H. 234 (1965): 375-388.

1024.   Buthak, Henryk. "Rozmowy Sztabowe Polsko-Francuskie
          W Paryzu."   (Franco-Polish Staff Talks in Paris,
          September-October 1922.) Przegląd Historyczny 60
          (1969): 363-74.

1025.   — "Rozmowy   Polsko-Francuskie   w   Paryzu."
          (Franco-Polish talks in Paris, October-November
          1924.) Przegląd Historyczny 61 (1970): 680-83.

1026.   — and Stawecki, P.   "Rozmowy Sztabowe Polsko-
          Francuskie w Paryzu."   (Polish-French military
          negotiations in Paris, May 1924.) Przegląd
          Historyczny 67 (1976): 55-70.

1027.   Carley, Michael J.   "The Politics of Anti-
          Bolshevism: The French Government and the Russo-
          Polish War, December 1919 to May 1920."
          Historical Journal 19 (1976): 163-89.

1028.   — "The Origins of the French Intervention in the
          Russian Civil War, January-May 1918: A
          Reappraisal."   J.M.H., (1976): 413-39.

1918-1920s

1029. Carlton, David. "The Anglo-French Compromise on Arms Limitation, 1928." Journal of British Studies 8 (1969): 141-62.

1030. Cassels, Alan. "Repairing the Entente Cordiale and the New Diplomacy." Historical Journal 23 (1980): 133-53.

1031. Chastenet, Jacques. "Une occasion manquée; l'affaire de la Ruhr." Revue de Paris 66 (1959): 5-19.

1032. — "Les années d'illusion (1918-1939)." Revue de Paris 67 (1960): 3-10.

1033. Chevallaz, Georges-André. "Le traité de Versailles, paix carthaginoise." Etudes de Lettres 3 (1960): 138-58.

1034. Crouzet, François. "Réactions françaises devant les conséquences économiques de la paix de Keynes." R.H.M.C. 19 (1972): 6-26.

1035. Debeir, Jean-Claude. "Le problème des exportations de capitaux français de 1919 à 1930." R.I., (1976): 171-82.

1036. — "La crise du franc de 1924. Un exemple de spéculation 'internationale'." R.I. 13 (1978): 29-49.

1037. Debo, Richard K. "Mésentente Glaciale: Great Britain, France, and the Question of Intervention in the Baltic, 1918." Canadian Journal of History 12 (1977): 65-86.

1038. Defoort, Eric. "Rapports diplomatiques français, 1918-1919." In De France Nederlanden. Les Pays-Bas français, pp. 174-92.

1039. Degros, Maurice. "Les delibérations du Conseil des Quatres (24 mars-28 juin 1919)." R.H.D. 69 (1955): 154-58.

1040. Duroselle, Jean-Baptiste. "Pro und Contra in Frankreich. Versailles nach 35 Jahren." Monat 70 (1954): 352-60.

1918-1920s

1041.   — "Reconsiderations — The Spirit of Locarno:
         Illusions of Pactomania." Foreign Affairs 50
         (1972): 752-64.

1042.   — "Clemenceau et la Belgique (de 1917 a 1920)."
         #939, 245-50.

1043.   — "Clemenceau et l'Italie." #933, 492-511.

1044.   Einzig, Paul. "Behind the Scenes of International
         Finance." Fortnightly, (1954): 160-65.

1045.   Fabrègues, Jean de. "The Reestablishment of
         Relations between France and the Vatican in
         1921." Journal of Contemporary History 2 (1967):
         163-82.

1046.   Fritz, Stephen E. "La politique de la Ruhr and
         Lloyd Georgian Conference diplomacy: the tragedy
         of Anglo-French relations, 1919-1923."
         Proceedings of the 3rd Annual Meeting of the
         Western Society for French History 3 (1975):
         566-82.

1047.   Gajan, Koloman. "La politique étrangère de la
         Tchécoslovaquie et les relations franco-
         tchécoslovaques (1918-1924)." #943, 476-88.

1048.   Goold, J. Douglas. "Lord Hardinge as Ambassador to
         France, and the Anglo-French Dilemma over Germany
         and the Near East, 1920-1922." Historical
         Journal 21 (1978): 913-37.

1049.   Grant, Philip. "Naval Disarmament, War Debts, and
         Franco-American Relations, 1921-1928."
         Mid-America 60 (1978): 37-44.

1050.   Guillen, Pierre. "L'échec des tentatives d'entente
         économique avec l'Italie (1922-1929)." R.I. 13
         (1978): 51-69.

1051.   — "La politique douanière de la France dans les
         années vingt." R.I. 16 (1978): 315-31.

1052.   Hall, Hines. "The Growth of Anglophobia and Foreign
         Policy-Making in France, 1919-1923." Proceedings
         of the Annual Meeting of the Western Society for
         French History 4 (1976): 423-31.

1918-1920s

1053.   — "Lloyd George, Briand and the Failure of the
         Anglo-French Entente." J.M.H. 50 (1978)
         microfiche.

1054.   Hamon, Léo. "Un précédent: La tentative d'Union
         Européenne d'Aristide Briand." Année politique
         et économique 28 (1955): 28-52.

1055.   Helmreich, J. "The Negotiation of the
         Franco-Belgian Military Accord of 1920." F.H.S.
         3 (1964): 360-78.

1056.   Hoop, Jean Marie d'. "Le maréchal Foch et la
         négociation de l'accord militaire franco-belge de
         1920." #944, 191-98.

1057.   Hubert, Lucien. "A la commission sénatoriale des
         affaires étrangères." R.H.D. 81 (1967): 233-53.

         Based on the notes of the author's father who was a
         member of the senate commission from 1915 to 1938.

1058.   Iordan-Sima, Constantin. "La Roumanie et les
         relations franco-italiennes dans les années
         1926-1927. Une page de l'histoire de la
         diplomatie roumaine." Revue Roumaine d'Histoire
         14 (1975): 317-40.

1059.   Jacobson, Jon and Walker, John T. "The Impulse for
         a Franco-German Entente: The Origins of the
         Thoiry Conference, 1926." Journal of
         Contemporary History 10 (1975): 157-81.

1060.   Jeanmougin, Gaston. "Les relations franco-turques
         en 1925; une amitié à l'épreuve." R.H.D. 84
         (1970): 108-146.

1061.   Jeanneney, Jean-Noel. "De la spéculation financière
         comme arme diplomatique. A propos de la première
         bataille du franc (novembre 1923-mars 1924)."
         R.I. 13 (1978): 5-27.

1062.   Karpova, R.F. "L'établissement des relations
         diplomatiques entre l'U.R.S.S. et la France."
         (in Russian) Annuaire d'études françaises,
         (1973): 202-15.

1918-1920s

1063. l'Huillier, Fernand. "Jacques Rivière et les rapports franco-allemands de 1921 à 1924." Cahiers de l'Association interuniversitaire de l'Est 6 (1964): 106-12.

1064. — "Locarno." Revue d'Allemagne 4 (1972): 558-68.

1065. Lindner, Heinz. "Zu einigen Problemen der deutsch-französischen Verständigung nach dem Ersten Weltkrieg." Revue d'Allemagne 6 (1974): 29-37.

1066. McCrum, Robert. "French Rhineland Policy at the Paris Peace Conference, 1919." Historical Journal 21 (1978): 623-48.

1067. McDougall, W.A. "Political Economy versus National Sovereignty: French Structures for German Economic Integration after Versailles." J.M.H. 51 (1979): 4-23.

1068. Magos, S. "Tratativele Franco-Ungare din 1920." (The Franco-Hungarian negotiation of 1920). Studii Revistă de Istorie 9 (1956): 73-86.

1069. Manévy, Raymond. "Une interview inédite de Raymond Poincaré par Maurice Bunau-Varilla, le 9 mai 1920." Etudes de Presse 5 (1953): 174-86.

1070. Maurois, André. "Briand à Genève (1929)." Revue de Paris 67 (1960): 3-17.

1071. Milhaud, Albert. "Herriot au Quai d'Orsay." Revue Politique et Parlementaire, (1953): 13-19.

1072. Mouton-Brady, Jean. "Un Francese a Roma (1897-1924): l'ambasciatore Barrère." Il Veltro 3 (1971): 353-72.

1073. Murphy, Francis J. "The Poet and the Pact: Paul Claudel and the Kellogg-Briand Pact." Mid-America 60 (1978): 45-50.

1074. Neveu, Bruno. "Louis Canet et le service du conseiller technique pour les affaires religieuses au ministère des Affaires étrangères." R.H.D. 82 (1968): 134-180.

1918-1920s

Louis Canet (1883-1958) was appointed expert on
Vatican affairs at the Quai d'Orsay in 1920.

1075. Nouschi, André. "La Francia, il Petrolio e il
       Vicino Oriente (1918-1919)." Studi Storici 7
       (1966): 97-127.

1076. — "Les relations franco-belges de 1919 à 1924."
       #939, 315-24.

1077. — "L'Etat français et les pétroliers Anglo-Saxons:
       La naissance de la compagnie française des
       pétroles (1923-1924)." R.I. 7 (1976): 241-59.

1078. Orde, Anne. "France and Hungary in 1920:
       Revisionism and Railways." Journal of
       Contemporary History 15 (July 1980): 475-92.

1079. Ormesson, Wladimir d'. "Une tentative de
       rapprochement franco-allemand entre les deux
       guerres." Revue de Paris 69 (1962): 18-27.

1080. Pastor, Peter. "The Vix Mission in Hungary,
       1918-1919: A Reexamination." Slavic Review 29
       (1970): 481-98.

1081. Peron, Jean Paul. "Les relations franco-allemandes,
       de l'entrée en vigueur du traité de Versailles
       (10 janvier 1920) à l'avènement de Hitler."
       Information Historique 34 (1972): 240-45.

1082. Poulain, Marc. "L'Italie, la Yugoslavie, la France
       et le Pacte de Rome, Janvier 1924: La Comédie de
       l'Accord à Trois." Balkan Studies 16 (1975):
       93-118.

1083. Pourtalès, Guy de. "1918-1919. Visite du président
       de la République (Poincaré) et mission sur le
       Rhin. Notes inédites presentées par Pierre
       Lyautey." Saisons d'Alsace 13 (1968): 449-69.

1084. Renouvin, Pierre. "Le destin du pacte d'assistance
       américain à la France en 1919." Annales d'Etudes
       Internationales 1 (1970): 9-22.

1085. — "Aux origines de la Petite Entente: les
       hésitations de la politique française dans l'été
       1920." #943, 489-500.

1918-1920s

1086.   Ristelhueber, René. "Deux missions en Moyen-Orient
        de général Catroux (1919-1922)." R.H.D. 73
        (Jan.-Mars. 1959): 82-86.

1087.   Ruge, Wolfgang. "Stresemann und Briand. Zu den
        deutsch-französischen Beziehungen in den
        zwanziger Jahren des 20. Jahrhunderts."
        Zeitschrift für Geschichtswissenschaft 17 (1970):
        178-184.

1088.   Rupieper, Hermann J. "Die britische Reinlandpolitik
        im Spannungsfeld der anglo-französischen
        Beziehungen, 1919-1924." #925, 89-107.

1089.   Sault, Jean du. "Les relations diplomatiques entre
        la France et le Saint-Siège." R.D.D.M. 10
        (1971): 115-22.

1090.   Schram, Stuart R. "Christian Rakovsky et le premier
        rapprochement franco-soviétique (1924-1927)."
        Cahiers du Monde Russe et Soviétique 1 (1960):
        205-37, 584-629.

1091.   Senn, Alfred E. "The Rakovsky Affair: A Crisis in
        Franco-Soviet Relations, 1927." Etudes Slaves et
        Est-Européennes 10 (1965): 102-17.

1092.   Sieburg, Heinz-Otto. "Les Entretiens de Thoiry
        (1926)." Revue d'Allemagne 4 (1972): 520-46.

1093.   Sorre, []. "Herriot et la Ruhr." Cahiers de la
        République 2 (1957): 81-92.

1094.   Soutou, Georges. "La politique économique de la
        France en Pologne (1920-1924)." R.H. 251 (1974):
        85-116.

1095.   —— "Problèmes concernant le rétablissement des
        relations économiques franco-allemandes après la
        première guerre mondiale." Francia 2 (1974):
        580-96.

1096.   —— "Les mines de Silésie et la rivalité
        franco-allemande, 1920-1923. Arme économique ou
        bonne affaire?" R.I. 1 (1974): 135-54.

1097.   —— "La politique économique de la France à l'égard
        de la Belgique (1914-1924)." #939, 257-74.

1918-1920s

1098.   —— "Die   deutschen   Reparationen   und   das
         Seydoux-Projekt 1920-21." Vierteljahrshefte für
         Zeitgeschichte 23 (1975): 237-70.

1099.   —— "Une autre politique?   Les tentatives français
         d'entente   économique   avec   l'Allemagne
         (1919-1921)."   Revue d'Allemagne 8 (1976):
         21-34.

1100.   —— "L'impérialisme   du   pauvre: la   politique
         économique de gouvernement français en Europe
         Centrale et Orientale de 1918 à 1929."   R.I.
         (1976): 219-39.

1101.   Taboulet, Georges.   "Le retour de l'Alsace-Lorraine
         à la France."   Miroir de l'histoire 108 (1958):
         696-702.

1102.   Trachtenberg, Marc.   "A New Economic Order: Etienne
         Clémentel and French Economic Diplomacy during
         the First World War."   F.H.S. (Fall 1977):
         315-341.

1103.   —— "Reparations at the Paris Peace Conference."
         J.M.H. (March 1979): 24-55.

1104.   Trausch, Gilbert.   "Les relations franco-belges à
         propos   de   la   question   luxembourgeoise
         (1914-1922)."   #939, 275-94.

1105.   Vaisse, Maurice.   "Le désarmement en question:
         l'incident de Saint-Gothard (1928)."   R.H.M.C. 22
         (1975): 530-548.

1106.   Vanlangenhove, Fernand.   "L'accord militaire
         franco-belge de 1920 à la lumière des documents
         diplomatiques belges."   Académie royale de
         Belgique. Bulletin de la classe des lettres et
         des sciences morales et politiques 53 (1967):
         520-35.

1107.   Wandycz, Piotr.   "Sojusz Polsko-Francuski Z 1921."
         (The Polish-French Alliance of 1921). Kultura 13
         (1959): 108-22.

1108.   —— "General Weygand and the Battle of Warsaw of
         1920."   Journal of Central European Affairs 19
         (1960): 357-65.

1918-1920s

1109. —— "Henrys i Niessel, Dwaj Pierswi Szefowie
Francuskiej Misji Wojskowej w Polsce, 1919-1921."
(Henrys and Niessel, the first two chiefs of the
French military mission in Poland, 1919-1921).
Bellona 44 (1962): 3-19.

1110. —— "French Diplomats in Poland, 1919-1926." Journal
of Central European Affairs 23 (1964): 440-50.

The two in question are Eugène Pralon (1919-20) and
Hector de Panafieu (1920-26).

1111. Watson, D.R. "The Making of the Treaty of
Versailles." In Troubled Neighbours, pp. 67-99.
Edited by Neville Waites. London, 1971.

1112. Willequet, Jacques. "Problèmes économiques
franco-belges en 1919 et 1920." #939, 303-14.

1930s

1113. Adamthwaite, A.P. "Bonnet, Daladier and French
Appeasement, April-September 1938."
International Relations 3 (April 1967): 226-41.

1114. —— "Reactions to the Munich Crisis." In Troubled
Neighbours, 170-99. Edited by Neville Waites.
London, 1971.

1115. —— "The Franco-German Declaration of 6 December
1938." #938, 395-409.

1116. —— "Le facteur militaire dans la décision
franco-britannique avant Munich." #946, 59-66.

1117. Ageron, Charles. "L'opinion publique française
pendant les crises internationales de septembre
1938 à juillet 1939." Cahiers de l'histoire de
la presse et de l'opinion, (1974-75): 203-223.

1118. —— "A propos d'une prétendue politique de 'repli
impérial' dans la France des années 1938-1939."
Revue d'histoire maghrébine 12 (1978): 225-37.

1119. Askew, W.C. "The Secret Agreement between France
and Italy on Ethiopia, January 1935." J.M.H.,
(March 1953): 47-48.

1930s

1120. Bariéty, Jacques. "Les relations franco-allemandes de 1924 à 1933." Annales de la Société d'Histoire de la IIIᵉ République, (1962-63): 57-68.

1121. — "Idée européenne et relations franco-allemandes." Bulletin de la Faculté des lettres de Strasbourg 46 (1968): 571-84.

1122. — "Léon Blum et l'Allemagne, 1930-1938." #938, 33-55.

1123. — "La France et le problème de l'Anschluss, mars 1936-mars 1938." #927.

1124. — and Bloch, Charles. "Une tentative de réconciliation franco-allemande et son échec (1932-1933)." R.H.M.C. 15 (1968): 433-65.

1125. Basler, Werner. "Die britisch-französisch-sowjetischen Militärbesprechungen im August 1939." Zeitschrift für Geschichtswissenschaft 5 (1957): 18-59.

1126. Batowski, Henryk. "Les traités d'alliance polono-britannique et polono-français de 1939." La Pologne et les affaires occidentales, (1973): 89-108.

1127. — "Le dernier traité d'alliance franco-polonais (4 septembre 1939)." #938, 353-62.

1128. Baumont, Maurice. "French Critics and Apologists Debate Munich." Foreign Affairs 25 (July 1947): 685-90.

1129. Bédarida, François. "La 'gouvernante anglaise'." #930, 228-40.

1130. — "Convergences et divergences stratégiques franco-britanniques." #931, 359-79.

1131. Beloglovski, E.S. "Contribution à l'histoire de la préparation du pacte franco-soviétique d'assistance mutuelle de 1935." Annuaire d'études françaises, (1963): 175-210.

1930s

1132.   Belousova, Z.S. "Die sowjetisch-französischen Beziehungen in den zwanziger und dreissiger Jahren und die Frage der kollektiven Sicherheit in Europa." Zeitschrift für Geschichtswissenschaft 17 (1969): 1533-53.

1133.   Bernardi, Giovanni. "La dibattuta questione della parita navale tra l'Italia e la Francia nel periodo tra le due guerre Mondiale." Revue Internationale d'Histoire Militaire 39 (1978): 64-97.

1134.   Bishop, Larry V. "England, France, and the Rhineland Crisis of 1936." Research Studies 34 (1966): 219-29.

1135.   Bled, Jean-Paul. "L'image de l'Allemagne chez Charles de Gaulle avant juin 1940." Etudes gaulliennes 5 (1977): 59-68.

1136.   Bloch, Charles. "Les relations franco-allemandes et la politique des puissances pendant la guerre d'Espagne." #927.

1137.   Blumé, Daniel. "Contribution à l'histoire de la politique de la non-intervention (en Espagne): documents inédits de Léon Blum." Cahiers Léon Blum (1977-78): 5-93.

1138.   Bouvier, Jean. "Contrôle des changes et politique économique extérieur de la S.F.I.O. en 1936." R.I. 13 (1978): 111-15.

1139.   Bozinov, V. "Certains aspects des relations franco-bulgares, 1933-1935." #935.

1140.   Braddick, Henderson B. "The Hoare-Laval Plan: A Study in International Politics." Review of Politics 24 (1962): 342-64.

1141.   Braubach, M. "Hitlers Machtergreifung. Die Berichte des französischen Botschafters François-Poncet über der Vorgänge in Deutschland von Juli 1932 bis Juli 1933." Festschrift für L. Brandt, pp. 443-64. Cologne, 1968.

1142.   Buckley, P.N., Haslam, E.B., and Neave-Hill, W. "Anglo-French Staff Conversations, 1938-1939." #940, 91-118.

1930s

1143.   Buffotot, Patrice. "Le réarmament aérien allemand et l'approche de la guerre vus par le 2e Bureau Air français (1936-39)." #927.

1144.   Butterworth, S.B. "Daladier and the Munich Crisis: A Reappraisal." Journal of Contemporary History 9 (July 1974): 191-216.

1145.   Cairns, John C. "March 7, 1936: The View from Paris." International Journal 20 (Spring 1965): 230-46.

1146.   Campus, Eliza. "La diplomatie roumaine et les relations franco-allemandes pendant les années 1933-1939." #938, 335-52.

1147.   Carlton, D. "Eden, Blum and the Origins of Non-Intervention." Journal of Contemporary History 6 (1971): 40-55.

1148.   Castellan, Georges. "Les Balkans dans la politique française à la réoccupation de la Rhénanie (7 mars 1936)." Studia Balcanica, 33-44. Sofia, 1973.

1149.   — "L'alerte du 21 mai 1938 vue par le 2e Bureau de l'E.M. Français." #943, 556-66.

1150.   — "Le réarmement clandestin de l'Allemagne dans l'entre-deux-guerres." Revue d'Allemagne 8 (1976): 61-82.

1151.   Celli, Arrigo L. "Joseph Paul-Boncour e l'avvio della collaborazione politica franco-sovietica nel 1933." Storia e Politica 15 (1976): 646-87.

1152.   — "L'Italia, Barthou e il progetto di une locarno orientale nel 1934." Storia e politica 17 (1978): 48-50, 241-78.

1153.   Chabord, T. "Les services français de l'information de 1936 à 1947." R.H.D.G.M. 16 (1966): 81-87.

1154.   Chastenet, Jacques. "Défense de Munich." Nouvelle Revue des Deux Mondes 12 (1975): 534-43.

1155.   Christienne, C. and Buffotot, P. "L'Armée de l'Air Française et la crise du 7 mars 1936." #926, 315-32.

1930s

1156. Claque, Monique. "Vision and myopia in the new politics of André Tardieu." F.H.S. 8 (1973): 105-29.

1157. Clemens, Walter C. "Great and Small Power Collaboration to Enforce the Status Quo: France and Czechoslovakia against the Vienna Protocol." East European Quarterly 2 (1969): 385-412.

1158. Cot, Pierre. "De l'affaire des dettes au pacte franco-soviétique." #928, 37-83.

1159. Culen, Constantine. "Osusky after March 14, 1939." Slovakia 9 (1959): 69-75.

Osusky being the Czech ambassador to Paris in the late 1930s.

1160. Daneva-Mihova, Christine. "La diplomatie française et la préparation du Pacte balkanique (1934)." #935.

1161. Deakin, M.F.W. "Anglo-French policy in relation to South-East Europe, 1936-1939." #940, 63-90.

1162. — "Les relations franco-anglaises et le problème de la neutralité italienne (septembre 1939-juin 1940)." #931, 309-25.

1163. Debicki, R. "The Remilitarization of the Rhineland and its Impact on the French-Polish Alliance." Polish Review 14 (Autumn 1969): 45-55.

1164. Deborine, G. "Les négociations anglo-franco-soviétiques de 1939 et le traité de non-agression germano-soviétique." Recherches internationales à la lumière du marxisme, (Jan.-April 1961): 139-66.

1165. Defrasne, Jean. "L'événement du 7 mars 1936: la réalité et la portée de l'opération allemande, la réaction de la France dans le cadre de ses alliances." #938, 247-76.

Colonel Defrasne served with army intelligence (the 2e Bureau) between 1936 and 1940.

1930s

1166.   Deuerlein, Ernst. "Die gescheiterte Anti-Hitler Koalition: Die politischen und militärischen Verhandlungen zwischen Grossbritannien, Frankreich und der Sowjetunion im Frühjahr und Sommer 1939." Wehrwissenschaftliche Rundschau 9 (1959): 634-50.

1167.   Dominique, Pierre. "Psychologie de Pierre Laval." Ecrits de Paris 123 (1955): 48-54.

1168.   —— "L'ambassade du maréchal Pétain en Espagne et l'échec du 'Plan Félix'." Ecrits de Paris 313 (1972): 37-43.

1169.   Dreifort, John. "France, Britain and Munich: An Interim Assessment." Proceedings of the First Annual Meeting of the Western Society for French History, 356-75. New Mexico, 1973.

1170.   —— "The French Popular Front and the Franco-Soviet Pact, 1936-1937: A Dilemma in Foreign Policy." Journal of Contemporary History 11 (1976): 217-36.

1171.   —— "France, the Powers and the Far Eastern Crisis, 1937-1939." Historian 39 (1977): 733-53.

1172.   Dugowson, J. "La déclaration franco-allemande du 6 décembre 1938." Recherches internationales à la lumière du marxisme, (Jan.-April 1961): 113-38.

1173.   Du Réau, Elisabeth. "Edouard Daladier et les problèmes de mobilisation industrielle au moment de Munich." #946, 71-90.

1174.   Duroselle, Jean-Baptiste. "Louis Barthou et le rapprochement franco-soviétique en 1934." Cahiers du monde russe et soviétique 3 (1962): 525-45.

1175.   —— "L'influence de la politique intérieure sur la politique extérieure de la France; l'exemple de 1938 et 1939." #940, 225-41.

1176.   —— "Les ambassadeurs français." R.I. 7 (1976): 283-92.

1177.   —— "Les milieux gouvernementaux français en face de problème allemand en 1936." #926, 373-96.

1930s

1178. — "Inspecteurs des finances et politique étrangère dans les années 30." R.I. 13 (1978): 117-22.

1179. Fergusson, G. "Munich: The French and British Roles." International Affairs 44 (Oct. 1938): 649-65.

1180. Flottes, Pierre. "Tchécoslovaquie, France et Pologne en 1938." Revue Politique et Parlementaire 56 (1954): 345-53.

1181. Frankenstein, Robert. "L'intervention étatique et réarmement en France 1935-1939." Revue Economique 31 (July 1980): 743-81.

1182. — "Le financement français de la guerre et les accords avec les Britanniques (1939-1940)." #931, 461-89.

1183. French, G.S. "Louis Barthou and the German Question in 1934." Canadian Historical Association Annual Report, (1964): 120-35.

1184. Fridenson, P. "Forces et faiblesses des conversations aériennes franco-britanniques." #940, 359-72.

1185. — "L'épreuve de l'attente: la coopération aérienne franco-britannique de septembre 1939 au 10 mai 1940." #931, 529-53.

1186. Gacon, Jean. "De nouveau sur Munich: une semaine décisive." La Nouvelle Critique 11 (1959): 122-34.

1187. Gallagher, M.D. "Leon Blum and the Spanish Civil War." Journal of Contemporary History 6 (1971): 56-64.

1188. Garnier, Jean-Paul. "Autour d'un accord (franco-italien 1935)." Revue de Paris 9 (1961): 102-114.

1189. Geigenmüller, Ernst. "Botschafter von Hoesch und der Deutsch-Österreichische Zollunionsplan von 1931." Historische Zeitschrift 195 (1962): 581-95.

Von Hoesch being the German ambassador in Paris.

1930s

1190.   Giradet, R. "La vision du monde extérieur dans la
         France des années 30." Bulletin de la Société
         d'Histoire Moderne. 67 (1968): 14-19.

1191.   Girault, René. "Léon Blum, la dévaluation de 1936
         et la conduite de la politique extérieure de la
         France." R.I. 13 (1978): 91-109.

1192.   — "Les relations internationales et l'exercice du
         pouvoir pendant le Front populaire, juin
         1936-juin 1937." Cahiers Léon Blum, (May 1977):
         15-46.

1193.   — "Les relations franco-soviétiques à la veille de
         la seconde guerre mondiale: bilan des années
         1937-1940." Revue des études slaves 50 (1977):
         417-28.

1194.   — "La décision gouvernementale en politique
         extérieure." #930, 209-227.

1195.   — "La politique française de Munich au 15 mars
         1939." #927.

1196.   — "Les relations franco-soviétiques après septembre
         1939." #931, 263-81.

1197.   Gowing, Margaret. "Anglo-French economic
         collaboration before the Second World War: oil
         and coal." #940, 263-75.

1198.   — "Anglo-French economic collaboration up to the
         outbreak of the Second World War." #940,
         179-88.

1199.   Haight, J. McVickar. "France, the United States and
         the Munich Crisis." J.M.H., (Dec. 1960):
         340-58.

1200.   — "France and the Aftermath of Roosevelt's
         'Quarantine' Speech." World Politics 14 (1962):
         283-306.

1201.   — "Les négociations relatives aux achats d'avions
         américains par la France pendant la période qui
         précède immédiatement la guerre." R.H.D.G.M.,
         (1965): 1-34.

1930s

1202. —— "France's Search for American Military Aircraft: Before the Munich Crisis." Aerospace Historian 25 (1978): 141-52.

1203. Haslam, E.B. "Anglo-French Conversations: Air Staff Views on Preparations for the North East Theatre of Operations." #940, 373-82.

1204. Hauner, Milan. "La Tchécoslovaquie en tant que facteur militaire." #946, 179-90.

1205. Hiegel, Henri. "La France et l'Allemagne de 1933 à 1945, d'après les discours et déclarations de Hitler." Information Historique 29 (1967): 118-22.

1206. Hildebrand, K. "L'Allemagne et la France de 1936 à 1939." R.H.D.G.M., (July 1979): 89-94.

1207. Hohne, Roland R. "Die aussenpolitische Neuorientierung Frankreichs 1934-1936." #938, 209-31.

1208. Hoop, J.M. d'. "Frankreichs Reaktion auf Hitlers Aussenpolitik 1933-1939." Geschichte in Wissenschaft und Unterricht 15 (1964): 211-23.

1209. —— "Les rapports militaires franco-belges de mars 1936 au 1er septembre 1939." #941, 15-73.

1210. —— "La politique militaire de la France dans les Balkans de l'accord de Munich au début de la deuxième guerre mondiale." Studia Balcanica, (1973): 79-89.

1211. —— "La France, la Grande-Bretagne et les pays balkaniques de 1936 à 1939." #940, 53-61.

1212. —— "La coopération franco-britannique devant le problème italien." #931, 293-309.

1213. Jiru, Jaroslav. "From Delbos to Bonnet: development of French-Czechoslovak relations from January until April 1938." (In Czech) Československý Časopis Historický 15 (1967): 35-50.

1214. Keserich, Charles. "The Popular Front and the Rhineland crisis of March 1936." International Review of History and Political Science 7 (1970): 87-102.

1930s

1215. Knipping, Franz. "Frankreich in Hitlers Aussenpolitik, 1933-1939." In Hitler, Deutschland und die Mächte. Edited by M. Funke. Dusseldorf, 1976.

1216. ── "La diplomatie allemande et la France, 1933-1936." #926, 213-232.

1217. ── "Der deutsch-französische Erklärung vom 6. Dezember 1938." #927.

1218. Kovrig, Bennett. "Mediation by Obfuscation: The Resolution of the Marseille Crisis, October 1934 to May 1935." Historical Journal 19 (1976): 191-221.

1219. Kvaček, Robert. "Delbos' Political Journey to Prague." (in Czech). Československý Časopis Historický 26 (1978): 507-30.

1220. Laloy, Jean. "Remarques sur les négociations anglo-franco-soviétiques de 1939." #940, 403-13.

1221. Lazea, Alvina. "Problems of Franco-Roumanian Military Cooperation." (in Roumanian). Studii R. de Istorie 22 (1969): 105-127.

1222. Lecuir, Jean and Fridenson, Patrick. "L'organisation de la coopération aérienne franco-britannique." R.H.D.G.M., (1969):43-71.

1223. Le Goyet, Colonel P. "Les conversations de 1939 sur la coopération franco-britannique en temps de guerre." #940, 127-48.

1224. ── "Les relations économiques franco-britanniques à la veille de la deuxième guerre mondiale." #940, 189-200.

1225. l'Huillier, Fernand. "Les français et l'accord du 6 décembre 1938." #938, 411-424.

1226. Lindner, Heinz. "Die deutsch-französische Erklärung vom 6. Dezember 1938." Zeitschrift für Geschichtswissenschaft 16 (1968): 884-93.

1930s

1227. Longéanie, Christian. "La politique du repli impérial devant l'opinion parlementaire (1937-1939)." Cahiers de l'Institut d'Histoire de la presse et de l'opinion 44 (1977): 163-77.

1228. MacDonald, C.A. "Britain, France and the April Crisis of 1939." European Studies Review 2 (1972): 151-69.

1229. Markus, Gertrud. "Die deutsch-französischen Auseinandersetzungen und das Saargebiet 1933 bis 1935." Wissenschaftliche Zeitschrift der Humboldt-Universität Berlin 22 (1973): 103-114.

1230. Marseille, J. "Le commerce entre la France et l'Allemagne pendant les années 30." #926, 279-284.

1231. Masson, Philippe. "Les conversations militaires franco-britanniques (1935-1938)." #940, 119-26.

1232. — "La marine française et la crise de mars 1936." #926, 333-38.

1233. Maurois, André. "Notes sur une conférence: Lausanne 1932." Revue de Paris 67 (1960): 5-14.

1234. Mazurowa, K. "La politique allemande des gouvernements des principaux partis et groupements français dans les années 1938-1939." #938, 57-74.

1235. Miceva, Z. "La France et les rapports bulgaro-yougoslaves (1933-1935)." #935.

1236. Michel, Bernard. "L'ambassadeur Osusky et son action en France." Revue des études slaves 52 (1979): 125-34.

1237. Michel, Henri. "Le Front Populaire et l'U.R.S.S." #940, 215-221.

1238. — "France, Grande-Bretagne et Pologne (mars-août 1939." #940, 383-401.

1239. Michel-Durandin, C. "La France et les Balkans en 1934." #935.

1930s

1240.   Neave-Hill, W.B.R.   "L'évolution de la stratégie
         franco-anglaise (1939-1940)."   #931, 333-59.

1241.   Niedhart, Gottfried.   "Die britisch-französische
         Garantieerklärung für Polen vom 31. März 1939."
         Francia 2 (1974): 597-618.

1242.   Parker, R.A.C.   "The First Capitulation.   France and
         the Rhineland Crisis of 1936."   World Politics 8
         (April 1956): 355-73.

1243.   — "Great Britain, France and the Ethiopian Crisis,
         1935-1936."   English Historical Review 89 (1974):
         293-332.

1244.   — "Anglo-French Conversations, April and September
         1938."   #938, 371-79.

1245.   — "Grande-Bretagne,   France   et   Scandinavie   en
         1939-1940:   la   politique,   les   hommes   et   la
         stratégie."   #931, 561-82.

1246.   Perett, W. Gregory.   "Naval Policy in French Foreign
         Affairs, 1930-1939."   Proceedings of the Annual
         Meeting of the Western Society for French History
         4 (1976): 432-41.

1247.   Perfetti, Francesco.   "Alle origini degli accordi
         Laval-Mussolini, alcuni contatti italo-francesi
         del   1932   in   materia   coloniale."   Storia
         contemporanea 8 (1977): 683-748.

1248.   Poidevin, Raymond.   "Vers une relance des relations
         économiques   franco-allemandes   en   1938-1939."
         #927.

1249.   Pressnel, L.S.   "Les finances de guerre britanniques
         et la coopération économique franco-britannique
         en 1939 et 1940."   #931, 489-511.

1250.   Quartararo, Rosario.   "Le origini del piano Hoare-
         Laval."   Storia contemporanea 8 (1977): 749-90.

1251.   Rain, Pierre.   "Une date fatidique, le 7 mars 1936."
         R.D.D.M. 21 (1964): 95-107.

1252.   Ratcliff, Ann.   "Les relations diplomatiques entre
         la France et les Etats-Unis (du 29 septembre 1938
         au 16 juin 1940)."   R.H.D.G.M. 19 (1969): 1-40.

1930s

1253. Rémond, René. "Politique extérieure et politique intérieure française, à la fin de la IIIe République." #944, 177-89.

1254. Renouvin, Pierre. "La politique extérieure de la France de 1933 à 1939." Bulletin de l'Académie Royale de Belgique, Classe des lettres et des sciences morales et politiques. 49 (1963): 199-221.

1255. — "La politique extérieure du premier gouvernement Léon Blum." #937, 329-75, 407-11.

1256. — "La place du Pacte balkanique de février 1934 dans la politique extérieure française." #935.

1257. — "Les relations de la Grande-Bretagne et de la France avec l'Italie en 1938-1939." #940, 295-317.

1258. — "Les relations franco-anglaises (1935-1939): Esquisse provisoire." #940, 15-51.

1259. — "Rapport général présenté à la séance de clôture, 28 septembre 1972." #940, 415-29.

1260. Robertson, J.C. "The Hoare-Laval Plan." Journal of Contemporary History 10 (July 1975): 433-64.

1261. Ruby, Edmond. "Hitler réoccupe la Rhénanie (7 mars 1936)." Ecrits de Paris 249 (1966): 29-43.

1262. Sakwa, George. "The 'Renewal' of the Franco-Polish Alliance of 1936 and the Rambouillet Agreement." Polish Review 16 (1971): 45-66.

1263. — "The Franco-Polish Alliance and the Remilitarization of the Rhineland." Historical Journal 16 (1973): 125-46.

1264. Sbacchi, Alberto. "Toward the recognition of the Italian empire: Franco-Italian negotiations, 1936-1940." Africa. Rivista mensile di Studi...dell'Istituto Italo-Africana 30 (1975): 373-92.

1930s

1265.   Schützler, Horst. "Die politischen Verhandlungen der Sowjetunion mit Grossbritannien und Frankreich im Frühjahr und Sommer 1939." Zeitschrift für Geschichtswissenschaft 7 (1959): 1716-42.

1266.   Scott, William E. "Balance of Power as a Perennial Factor: French Motives in the Franco-Soviet Pact." In Foreign Policy in the Sixties. Essays in Honor of Arnold Wolfers, pp. 207-28. Edited by R. Hilsman and R.C. Good. Baltimore, 1965.

1267.   Stawecki, Piotr. "The French Loan of 1936." (In Polish, but with summary in French). Kwartalnik Historyczny 74 (1967): 49-68.

1268.   Szaluta, Jacques. "Marshal Pétain's Ambassadorship to Spain: Conspiratorial or Providential Rise toward Power?" F.H.S. 8 (1974): 511-33.

1269.   Taboulet, Georges. "La France et l'Angleterre face au conflit sino-japonais (1937-1939)." R.H.D. 88 (1974): 112-44.

1270.   Vaisse, Maurice. "Le procès de l'aviation de bombardement." Revue Historique des Armées 4 (1977): 41-61.

1271.   — "Continuité et discontinuité dans la politique française en matière de désarmement; l'exemple du contrôle (février 1932-juin 1933)." #926, 27-48.

1272.   Vanlangenhove, Fernand. "La crise fatidique du 7 mars 1936." Académie royale de Belgique. Bulletin de la classe des lettres... 53 (1967): 17-39.

1273.   Vasilev, V.A. "La France, la Petite Entente et la Bulgarie (1933-1934)." #935.

1274.   Vnuk, Francis. "Stephen Osusky and March 1939." Slovakia 9 (1959): 65-68.

1275.   Wandycz, Piotr. "More concerning the mission of Jerzy Potocki in 1933." (In Polish). Zeszyty Hist. 18 (1970): 81-83.

1276.   Wanty, Emile. "Les relations militaires franco-belges: 1936-octobre 1939." R.H.D.G.M., (1958): 12-23.

1930s

1277.   Warner, Geoffrey. "France and Non-Intervention in
         Spain, July-August 1936." International Affairs
         38 (April 1962): 203-220.

1278.   Watt, Donald C.   "The Secret Laval-Mussolini
         Agreement of 1935 on Ethiopia." The Middle East
         Journal 15 (1961): 69-78.

1279.   — "Britain, France and the Italian Problem,
         1937-1939." #940, 277-94.

1280.   Willequet, J.   "Les relations franco-belges,
         1936-1940." Travaux et Recherches. Centre de
         Relations internationales. Université de Metz.
         1973, 112-22.

1281.   Wisniewska, K.   "La Pologne, la France et la
         Tchécoslovaquie au printemps 1938." (In Polish).
         Studia historyczne 16 (1973): 81-89.

1282.   Young, Robert J.   "French Policy and the Munich
         Crisis of 1938.   A Reappraisal."   Canadian
         Historical Association, Historical Papers, 1970,
         186-206.

1283.   — "Le haut commandement français au moment de
         Munich." R.H.M.C. 24 (Jan.-March 1977): 110-29.

1284.   — "The Aftermath of Munich: The Course of French
         Diplomacy, October 1938 to March 1939." F.H.S. 8
         (Fall 1973): 305-22.

1285.   Unsigned.   "Les negociations militaires entre
         l'U.R.S.S., la Grande-Bretagne et la France en
         août 1939."   Recherches internationales à la
         lumière de marxisme (March-April 1959): 130-220.

1286.   — "Protocols of the Polish-French General Staff
         Conferences in Paris, May 1939."   Bellona,
         (1958): 165-79.

1287.   — "The negotiations between the U.S.S.R., Great
         Britain and France in 1939." (In Polish). Sprawy
         Miedzynarodowe 23 (1970): 101-114, no. 2,
         89-106.

Wartime Diplomacy, 1940-1945

1288.   Aimel, Georges.   "La dernière mission de Général
        Weygand (Afrique, 1940-41)."   Ecrits de Paris 244
        (1966): 32-40.

1289.   Albord, Tony and Dillemann, Louis.   "Le facteur
        allemand dans l'affaire de Syrie, 1941."   Ecrits
        de Paris 311 (1972): 66-78.

1290.   Aldus   (pseud.)   "La   rettifica   della   frontiera
        Italo-Francese."   R.   di   Studi   Politici
        Internazionali 29 (1962): 520-32.

1291.   Avantaggiato, Franca.   "Gli Armistizi Francesi del
        1940: La Testimonianza di Chautemps."   Storia e
        Politica 4 (1965): 94-109.

1292.   Bédarida, François. "France, Britain and the Nordic
        Countries."   Scandinavian Journal of History 2
        (1977): 7-27.

1293.   Bell, P.M.H.   "Prologue   de   Mers-El-Kébir."
        R.H.D.G.M. 9 (1959): 15-36.

1294.   — "The Breakdown of the Alliance in 1940."   In
        Troubled Neighbours, 200-227.   Edited by Neville
        Waites.   London, 1971.

1295.   Beloff, M.   "The Anglo-French Union Project of June
        1940."   #944, 199-219.

1296.   Blumenson, Martin.   "La place de la France dans la
        stratégie et dans la politique des Alliés."
        #934, 191-208, 239-40.

1297.   Bo Rasmussen, Lars.   "Les   relations   franco-
        britanniques   pendant   la   deuxième   guerre
        mondiale."   Etudes gaulliennes 3 (1975): 71-85.

1298.   Borisov, I.V.   "The Soviet Union and France in the
        years of the Second World War (1941-45)."   (In
        Russian).   Novaia i Noveishaia Istoriia 3 (1960):
        92-103.

1299.   Cairns, John C.   "Great Britain and the Fall of
        France: A Study in Allied Disunity."   J.M.H. 27
        (1955): 365-409.

HISTORICAL ARTICLES

Wartime Diplomacy, 1940-1945

1300.   Dethan, Georges. "La politique étrangère française
         au lendemain de la Libération." Storia e
         Politica 14 (1975): 318-26.

1301.   Facon, Patrick and Ruffray, Françoise de. "Aperçus
         sur la collaboration aéronautique franco-
         allemande (1940-1943)." R.H.D.G.M. 27 (1977):
         85-102.

1302.   Ferro, Maurice. "La France libre et les Etats-Unis
         de Londres à Alger." Etudes gaulliennes 1
         (1973): 43-81.

1303.   Fontaine, André. "Potsdam: A French View."
         International Affairs 46 (1970): 466-74.

1304.   Funk, Arthur. "La 'reconnaissance' du C.F.L.N.
         (Comité Français de la Libération Nationale)."
         R.H.D.G.M. 9 (1959): 37-48.

1305.   ─ "Negotiating the 'Deal with Darlan'." Journal of
         Contemporary History 8 (1973): 81-117.

1306.   Gait, Maurice. "Mission spéciale de René de
         Chambrun aux Etats-Unis en 1940." Ecrits de
         Paris 344 (1975): 5-15.

1307.   Garrett, Charles W. "In Search of Grandeur: France
         and Vietnam, 1940-1946." Review of Politics 29
         (1967): 303-23.

1308.   Girault, René. "Les relations franco-soviétiques
         après septembre 1939." Cahiers du monde russe et
         soviétique 17 (1976): 27-42.

1309.   Graham, Robert A. "La missione di W. d'Ormesson in
         Vaticano nel 1940: intervista inedita." La
         Civiltà Cattolica 124 (1973): 145-48.

1310.   Guillen, Pierre. "Les relations franco-italiennes
         de 1943 à 1949." R.H.D. 90 (1976): 112-60.

1311.   Haight, J. McVickar. "France's First War Mission to
         the United States." Airpower Historian 11
         (1964): 11-15.

197

Wartime Diplomacy, 1940-1945

1312.   Hoisington, William A.   "The Struggle for Economic
         Influence in Southeastern Europe: The French
         Failure in Rumania, 1940." J.M.H. 43 (1971):
         468-82.

1313.   Jiline, General. "La coopération franco-soviétique
         durant la seconde guerre mondiale." #934, 209-21.

1314.   Johnson, Douglas. "Britain and France in 1940."
         Transactions of the Royal Historical Society 22
         (1972): 141-57.

1315.   — "Le général de Gaulle et M. Winston Churchill."
         Etudes gaulliennes 3 (1975): 87-93.

1316.   Krautkrämer, Elmar.   "Die Entmachtung Lavals im
         Dezember 1940.   Ein aussenpolitisches Kalkül
         Vichys." Vierteljahrshefte für Zeitgeschichte 27
         (1979): 79-112.

1317.   Le Goyet, Pierre and Vanwelkenhuyzen, Jean.   "Les
         rapports militaires franco-belges du premier
         septembre au 10 mai 1940." #941, 75-193.

1318.   Lipgens, Walter. "Innerfranzösische Kritik an der
         Aussenpolitik   de   Gaulles   1944-1946."
         Vierteljahrshefte für Zeitgeschichte 24 (1976):
         136-98.

1319.   Melka, Robert L.   "Darlan Between Britain and
         Germany, 1940-1941." Journal of Contemporary
         History 8 (1973): 57-80.

1320.   Michel, Henri. "Les relations franco-italiennes de
         l'armistice de juin 1940 à l'armistice de
         septembre 1943." #932, 485-511.

1321.   — "Le régime de Vichy et la république de Salo."
         Convegno storica italo-francese.   Storia e
         Politica 14 (1975): 3-20.

1322.   Mickelson, Martin L.   "Another Fashoda: the
         Anglo-Free French Conflict over the Levant,
         May-September, 1941." Revue Française d'Histoire
         d'Outre-Mer 63 (1976): 75-100.

1323.   Mourin, Maxime. "Pouvait-on faire la paix pendant
         'la drôle de guerre'?"   Revue de Défense
         Nationale 17 (1961): 853-73.

HISTORICAL ARTICLES

Wartime Diplomacy, 1940-1945

1324.   Parker, R.A.C.   "Britain, France and Scandinavia,
         1939-40." History 61 (1976): 369-87.

1325.   Pavlowitch, Stevan K.   "Le général de Gaulle, la
         France libre et la Yougoslavie (1940-1945)."
         Espoir. Revue de l'Institut Charles de Gaulle 25
         (1978): 38-55.

1326.   Queuille, Pierre.   "Le   décisif   armistice
         franco-italien 23-24 juin 1940."   R.H.D. 90
         (1976): 100-111.

1327.   Sainsbury, Keith.   "The second wartime alliance."
         In Troubled Neighbours, pp. 228-58.   Edited by
         Neville Waites. London, 1971.

1328.   Salewski, M.   "De Mers-el-kébir à Toulon: les
         grandes lignes de la politique maritime
         franco-allemande de 1940 à 1942."   Travaux et
         Recherches. Université de Metz, (1973): 123-50.

1329.   Schmitt, General C.   "Les   accords   secrets
         franco-anglais de fin 1940.   Les télégrammes
         secrets envoyés par le Maréchal à Alger en
         novembre 1942."   Bulletin de la Société
         d'Histoire Moderne 56 (1957): 13-16.

1330.   Schneider, Fernand-Thiebaut.   "Les entretiens de
         Hitler avec Laval, Pétain et Darlan en 1940-41."
         Revue Militaire Générale 10 (1969): 654-68.

1331.   Thomson, David.   "La proposition d'union
         franco-britannique en 1940."   La Table Ronde
         (1966): 56-88.

1332.   Toscano, Mario.   "La Ripresa delle Relazioni
         Diplomatiche fra l'Italia e la Francia nel corso
         della seconda guerre mondiale."   Storia e
         Politica 1 (1962): 523-604.

1333.   Vaccarino, Giorgio.   "Le relazioni franco-italiane
         dopo l'8 Settembre 1943."   Movimento di
         Liberazione in Italia 21 (1969): 103-115.

1334.   Vanwelkenhuyzen, Jean.   "Les contacts militaires
         franco-belges pendant la 'drôle de guerre'."
         Revue du Nord 53 (1971): 247-52.

Wartime Diplomacy, 1940-1945

1335.   Viault, Birdsall S.   "Les démarches pour le
        rétablissement de la paix (septembre 1939-août
        1940)."   R.H.D.G.M. 17 (1967): 13-30.

1336.   Villate, R.   "Roosevelt contre De Gaulle."
        R.H.D.G.M. 6 (1956): 17-31.

1337.   Warner, Geoffrey.   "The Decline and Fall of Pierre
        Laval."   History Today 9 (Dec. 1961): 817-27.

1338.   Wheatly, R.   "La guerre russo-finlandaise, les plans
        d'intervention   alliés   et   les   relations
        britanniques avec la Russie."   #931, 245-63.

1339.   White, Dorothy S.   "Charles de Gaulle et Franklin
        Roosevelt. Les chemins de la discorde."   Espoir.
        Revue de l'Institut Charles de Gaulle,   (1974):
        20-44.

1340.   Wright, Gordon.   "Ambassador Bullitt and the Fall of
        France."   World Politics 10 (1957): 63-90.

1341.   Unsigned.   "Les entretiens Staline-De Gaulle, 1944."
        Contrat Social 10 (1966): 171-84.

H. HISTORICAL STUDIES

General: Third Republic

1342.   Agulhon, Maurice and Nouschi, André. La France de
        1914 à 1940. Paris, 1971.

1343.   Aron, Robert. Les grandes heures de la Troisième
        République. 6 vols. Paris, 1967-68.

1344.   Auffret, Marc. La France de L'entre-deux-guerres.
        Paris, 1972.

1345.   Azéma, Jean-Pierre and Winock, Michel. La IIIe
        République. Paris, 1969.

1346.   Baumont, Maurice. La Troisième République. Paris,
        n.d.

1347.   Bonnefous, Edouard and Georges. Histoire politique
        de la Troisième République. 7 vols. Paris,
        1956-67.

1348.   Bouju, Paul M. and Dubois, Henri. La Troisième
        République: 1870-1940. Paris, 1967.

1349.   Brissac, Pierre de Cossé, duc de. En d'autre temps,
        i, 1900-1939, ii, 1939-1958. Paris, 1972-74.

1350.   Brogan, D.W. France under the Republic: The
        Development of Modern France (1870-1939).
        Westport, Conn., 1974.

1351.   — The French Nation, 1814-1940. New York, 1958.

1352.   Brunet, Jean-Paul and Launay, Michel. D'une guerre
        à l'autre, 1914-1945. Paris, 1974.

1353.   Bury, J.B. La Troisième République: Dans l'Europe
        de Versailles. Paris, 1972.

1354.   Cairns, John C., ed. Contemporary France: Illusion,
        Conflict and Regeneration. New York, 1978.

1355.   Challener, Richard D. The French Theory of the
        Nation in Arms. New York, 1955.

201

General: Third Republic

1356.   Chapman, Guy. Why France Collapsed. London, 1968.

1357.   Chastenet, Jacques. Histoire de la Troisième République. 7 vols. Paris, 1960-63.

1358.   Dansette, Andrien. Histoire des présidents de la République. Paris, 1960.

1359.   Earle, E.M., ed. Modern France: Problems of the Third and Fourth Republics. Princteon, 1951.

1360.   Fohlen, Claude. La France de l'entre-deux-guerres (1917-1939). Paris, 1966.

1361.   Greene, Nathaniel. From Versailles to Vichy: The Third French Republic, 1919-1940. New York, 1970.

1362.   Herzog, Wilhelm. From Dreyfus to Pétain: The Struggle of a Republic. New York, 1976.

1363.   Hoffmann, Stanley, et al. In Search of France. Cambridge, Mass., 1963.

1364.   Horne, Alistair. To Lose a Battle: France 1940. London, 1969.

1365.   Joll, James, ed. The Decline of the Third Republic. London, 1959.

1366.   Miquel, Pierre. La IIIe République. Paris, 1971.

1367.   Néré, Jacques. La Troisième République: 1914-1940. Paris, 1967.

1368.   Ouston, Philip. France in the Twentieth Century. New York, 1972.

1369.   Rials, Stéphane. Administration et Organisation, 1919-1930. Paris, 1977.

1370.   Shirer, William. The Collapse of the Third Republic. London, 1970.

1371.   Tint, Herbert. The Decline of French Patriotism, 1870-1940. London, 1964.

1372.   Wright, Gordon. France in Modern Times. Chicago, 1974.

General: International Relations

1373.   Adamthwaite, A.P.   The Making of the Second World War. London, 1977.

1374.   Albrecht-Carrié, R.   France, Europe and the Two World Wars. New York, 1961.

1375.   Aster, Sidney.   1939: The Making of the Second World War. London, 1973.

1376.   Baillou, J. and Pelletier, P.   Les Affaires Etrangères. Paris, 1962.

1377.   Bankwitz, P.C.F.   Maxime Weygand and Civil-Military Relations in Modern France. Cambridge, Mass., 1967.

1378.   Barbier, J.B.   La politique étrangère de la France, de 1914 à 1945. Paris, 1962.

1379.   Baumont, Maurice.   La faillite de la paix, 1918-1939. I, De Réthondes à Stresa, 1918-1935. Paris, 1951.

1380.   — Les origines de la deuxième guerre mondiale. Paris, 1969.

1381.   Berger, Gaston and Trotabas, Louis.   Les affaires étrangères. Paris, 1959.

1382.   Berlia, Georges.   Cours de grands problèmes politiques contemporains, le problème international de la sécurité et la France, étude politique et juridique (1918-1966). Paris, 1967.

1383.   Binoche, Jacques.   L'Allemagne et le général de Gaulle, 1924-1970. Paris, 1975.

1384.   Binoux, P.   Les Pionniers de l'Europe et le rapprochement franco-allemand: J. Caillaux, A. Briand, R. Schuman, K. Adenauer, J. Monnet. Paris, 1975.

1385.   Cartier, Raymond.   Le monde entre deux guerres, 1919-1939. Paris, 1977.

1386.   Castillon, Richard.   Les réparations allemandes. Deux expériences (1919-31 et 1945-52). Paris, 1953.

General: International Relations

1387.   Cialowicz, Jan. Polsko-Francuski Sojusz Wojskowy,
         1921-1939. Warsaw, 1970.

1388.   Craig, Gordon and Gilbert, Felix. The Diplomats
         1919-1939. 2 vols. Princeton, 1953.

1389.   Dischler, Ludwig. Der Auswärtige Dienst
         Frankreichs. 2 vols. Hamburg, 1952.

1390.   Duroselle, Jean-Baptiste. Les relations
         franco-allemandes de 1918 à 1950. 5 vols.
         Paris, 1966-67.

1391.   —— France and the United States: From the Beginnings
         to the Present. Chicago, 1978.

1392.   —— Histoire diplomatique de 1919 à nos jours. 7th
         edition. Paris, 1978.

1393.   —— La politique extérieure de la France de 1914 à
         1945. Paris, 1965.

1394.   Faculté de droit du Maroc. Session d'études
         administratives, diplomatiques et économiques,
         Rabat, 1958. Paris, 1959.

1395.   Gatzke, H. European Diplomacy between Two Wars,
         1919-1939. Chicago, 1972.

1396.   Girault, René. Diplomatie Européenne et
         Impérialismes 1871-1914. Paris, 1980.

1397.   Gombin, R. Les socialistes et la guerre. La
         S.F.I.O. et la politique étrangère française
         entre les deux guerres mondiales. Paris, 1970.

1398.   Grunwald, Constantin de. Les alliances
         franco-russes. Neuf siècles de malentendus.
         Paris, 1965.

1399.   Howard, J.E. Parliament and Foreign Policy in
         France. London, 1948.

1400.   Jordan, W.M. Great Britain, France and the German
         Problem, 1919-1939. London, 1954.

1401.   Laroche, Carlo. La diplomatie française. Paris,
         1946.

General: International Relations

1402.   Lauren, Paul Gordon. Diplomats and Bureaucrats: The
         First Institutional Responses to Twentieth-
         Century   Diplomacy   in   France   and   Germany.
         Stanford, 1976.

1403.   Leffler, Melvyn. The Elusive Quest: America's
         Pursuit of European Stability and French
         Security, 1919-1933. Chapel Hill, N.C., 1979.

1404.   Marks, Sally. The Illusion of Peace: International
         Relations in Europe, 1918-1933. London, 1976.

1405.   Milza, Pierre. De Versailles à Berlin, 1919-1945.
         Paris, 1968.

1406.   Minart, Jacques. Le drame du désarmement français,
         1919-1939. Paris, 1960.

1407.   Mourin, Maxime. Les relations franco-soviétiques,
         1917-1967. Paris, 1967.

1408.   Néré, Jacques. The Foreign Policy of France from
         1914 to 1945. London, 1975.

1409.   Poidevin, Raymond. Les relations économiques et
         financières entre la France et l'Allemagne de
         1898 à 1914. Paris, 1969.

1410.   — and   Bariéty,   Jacques.   Les   relations
         franco-allemandes, 1815-1975. Paris, 1977.

1411.   Renouvin, Pierre.   Histoire des relations
         internationales: Les crises du XXe siècle, ii, De
         1929 à 1945. Paris, 1958.

1412.   Sallet, Richard. Der diplomatische Dienst. Seine
         Geschichte   und   Organisation   in   Frankreich,
         Grossbritannien und den Vereinigten Staaten.
         Stuttgart, 1953.

         For France, see pages 21-130.

1413.   Struye, Paul. Problèmes internationaux, 1927-1972.
         Brussels, n.d.

1414.   Tournoux,   General   P.E.   Haut   Commandement:
         Gouvernement et Défense des Frontières du Nord et
         de l'Est, 1919-1939. Paris, 1960.

General: International Relations

1415.   Waites,   Neville,   ed.   Troubled   Neighbours:
         Franco-British   Relations   in   the   Twentieth
         Century. London, 1971.

1416.   Watt, Donald C.   Too Serious a Business: European
         Armed Forces and the Approach to the Second World
         War. London, 1975.

1417.   Wolfers, A.   Britain and France between the Wars.
         New York, 1963.

1418.   Wullus-Rudiger, J.   Français et Allemands: ennemis
         héréditaires. Paris, 1965.

1918-1920s

1419.   Artaud, Denise.   La question des dettes interalliées
         et la reconstruction de l'Europe: 1917-1929.   2
         vols. Paris, 1978.

1420.   Baas, Geneviève.   Le malaise alsacien, 1919-1924.
         Strasbourg, 1972.

1421.   Bariéty, Jacques.   Les relations franco-allemandes
         après la première guerre mondiale: 10 novembre
         1918-10 janvier 1925, de l'exécution à la
         négociation. Paris, 1977.

1422.   Bernard, Philippe.   La fin d'un monde, 1914-1929.
         Paris, 1975.

1423.   Bobrie, François and Gaston, Pierre.   L'opinion et
         les groupes de pression face à la politique
         financière et monétaire de Poincaré.   Paris,
         1973.

1424.   Boisvert, Jean-Jacques.   Les relations franco-
         allemandes en 1920. Quebec, 1977.

1425.   Bournazel, Renata.   Rapallo: naissance d'un mythe.
         La politique de la peur dans la France du Bloc
         national. Paris, 1974.

1426.   Buccianti, G.   L'egemonia sull'Etiopia (1918-1923).
         La scontro diplomatico tra Italia, Francia e
         Inghilterra. Milan, 1977.

1918-1920s

1427.   Delbreil, Jean-Claude. Les catholiques français et
         les tentatives de rapprochement franco-allemand
         (1920-1933). Metz, 1972.

1428.   Duroselle, Jean-Baptiste. La France et les
         français, 1914-1920. Paris, 1972.

1429.   Elcock, Howard. Portrait of a Decision: The Council
         of Four and the Treaty of Versailles. London,
         1972.

1430.   Hermans, Jules. L'évolution de la pensée européenne
         d'Aristide Briand. Nancy, 1965.

1431.   Hughes, Judith. To the Maginot Line: The Politics
         of French Military Preparation in the 1920's.
         Cambridge, Mass., 1971.

1432.   King, Jere Clemens. Foch Versus Clemenceau: France
         and German Disarmament, 1918-1919. Cambridge,
         Mass., 1960.

1433.   Kukulka, J. Francja a Polska po Traktacie
         Wersalskim, 1919-1922. Warsaw, 1970.

1434.   Lagana, Marc Laurent. Quest for Unity: Aristide
         Briand and European Integration, 1929-1930. San
         Jose (Cal.), 1968.

1435.   Leonhardt, Fritz H. Aristide Briand und seine
         Deutschlandpolitik. Heidelberg, 1951.

1436.   L'Huillier, F. Dialogues franco-allemands, 1925-
         1933. Paris, 1971.

1437.   McDougall, Walter A. France's Rhineland Diplomacy,
         1914-1924: The Last Bid for a Balance of Power in
         Europe. Princeton, 1978.

1438.   Mäelo, Meemo. Briands plan om Europas forenta
         staler 1929-30. Uppsala, 1968.

1439.   Maier, Charles S. Recasting Bourgeois Europe:
         Stabilization in France, Germany and Italy in the
         Decade after World War I. Princeton, 1975.

1440.   Mantoux, Etienne. The Carthaginian Peace, or the
         Economic Consequences of Mr. Keynes. London,
         1946.

1918-1920s

1441.   Marchese, S. La Francia e il probleme dei rapporti
        con la Santa Sede (1914–1924). Naples, 1969.

1442.   Miquel, Pierre. La paix de Versailles et l'opinion
        publique française. Paris, 1972.

1443.   Mittelstadt, Axel. Frankreichs Währungspolitik von
        Poincaré zu Rueff. Frankfurt, 1967.

1444.   Mordal, Jacques. Versailles ou la paix impossible.
        Paris, 1970.

1445.   Nelson, Keith. Victors Divided: America and the
        Allies in Germany, 1918–1923. Berkeley, 1975.

1446.   Néré, Jacques. La crise de 1929. Paris, 1968.

1447.   Renouvin, Pierre. L'armistice de Rethondes. Paris,
        1975.

1448.   — Le traité de Versailles. Paris, 1969.

1449.   Schmidt, Royal J. Versailles and the Ruhr: Seedbed
        of World War II. The Hague, 1968.

1450.   Schuker, Stephen A. The End of French Predominance
        in Europe: The Financial Crisis of 1924 and the
        Adoption of the Dawes Plan. Chapel Hill, 1976.

1451.   Tanenbaum, Jan K. France and the Middle East,
        1914–1920. Philadelphia, 1978.

1452.   Trachtenberg, Marc. Reparation in World Politics:
        France and European Economic Diplomacy,
        1916–1923. New York, 1980.

1453.   Wandycz, Piotr. France and Her Eastern Allies,
        1919–1925. Minneapolis, 1962.

1454.   Weill-Raynal, Etienne. Les réparations allemandes
        et la France. 3 vols. Paris, 1947.

1455.   Wormser, Georges. La république de Clemenceau.
        Paris, 1961.

1456.   — Le septennat de Poincaré. Paris, 1977.

1457.   Wroniak, Z. Polska-Francja, 1926–1932. Poznan,
        1971.

1918-1920s

1458.   Yates, L.   United States and French Security,
         1917-1921: A Study in American Diplomatic
         History. New York, 1957.

1459.   Zimmermann, Ludwig.   Frankreichs Ruhrpolitik von
         Versailles bis zum Dawesplan. Göttingen, 1971.

1930s

1460.   Adamthwaite, A.P.   France and the Coming of the
         Second World War, 1936-1939. London, 1977.

1461.   Azeau, Henri.   Le pacte franco-soviétique, 2 mai
         1935. Paris, 1968.

1462.   Azéma, Jean-Pierre.   De Munich à la Libération,
         1938-1944. Paris, 1979.

1463.   Belousova, Z.S.   Francija i Europejskaja bezoposnot,
         1929-1939. Moscow, 1976.

1464.   Berthelot, Jean.   Sur les rails de pouvoir: de
         Munich à Vichy. Paris, 1967.

1465.   Bouillon, Jacques and Vallette, G.   Munich 1938.
         Paris, 1964.

1466.   Brancion, Yves.   Munich, crise européenne. Paris,
         1969.

1467.   Broche, François.   Assassinat d'Alexandre 1er et de
         Louis Barthou. Paris, 1977.

1468.   Castellan, Georges.   Le réarmement clandestin du
         Reich 1930-1935. Paris, 1954.

1469.   Cienciala, Anna M.   Poland and the Western Powers,
         1938-1939. London, 1968.

1470.   Colombani, Roger et Laplayne, Jean.   La mort d'un
         roi; la vérité sur l'assassinat d'Alexandre de
         Yougoslavie. Paris, 1971.

1471.   Cuvillier, Jean-Pierre.   Vincent Auriol et les
         finances publiques du Front populaire ou
         l'alternative du contrôle et de la liberté:
         1933-1939. Toulouse, 1979.

1930s

1472. Dreifort, John. Yvon Delbos at the Quai d'Orsay: French Foreign Policy during the Popular Front, 1936-1938. Lawrence, Kansas, 1973.

1473. Dubief, Henri. Le déclin de la Troisième République, 1929-1938. Paris, 1976.

1474. Duroselle, Jean-Baptiste. La Décadence, 1932-1939. Paris, 1979.

1475. Emmerson, James T. The Rhineland Crisis, 7 March 1936: A Study in Multilateral Diplomacy. London, 1977.

1476. Fridenson, Patrick and Lecuir, Jean. La France et la Grande-Bretagne face aux problèmes aériens, 1935-mai 1940. Vincennes, 1976.

1477. Furnia, A.H. The Diplomacy of Appeasement: Anglo-French Relations and the Prelude to World War II, 1931-1938. Washington, 1960.

1478. Hoggan, David L. Frankreichs Widerstand gegen den zweiten Weltkrieg. Die französische Aussenpolitik von 1934 bis 1939. Tübingen, 1963.

1479. Jäckel, Eberhard. Frankreich in Hitlers Europa. Stuttgart, 1966. La France dans l'Europe de Hitler. Paris, 1968.

1480. Komjathy, A.T. The Crises of France's East Central European Diplomacy, 1933-1938. Boulder, Colorado, 1977.

1481. Kuźmiński, T. Polska, Francja, Niemcy, 1933-1935: Z dziejów sojuszu polsko-francuskiego. (Poland, France and Germany, 1933-1935. On the history of the Polish-French alliance). Warsaw, 1963.

1482. Laurens, F.D. France and the Italo-Ethiopian Crisis, 1935-1936. The Hague, 1967.

1483. Le Goyet, Pierre. Le Mystère Gamelin. Paris, 1975.

1484. McVickar Haight, John. American Aid to France, 1938-1940. New York, 1970.

1930s

1485. Massip, Roger and Descola, Jean. Il y a 40 ans, Munich. Paris, 1978.

1486. Noguères, Henri. Munich ou la drôle de paix (29 septembre 1938). Paris, 1963. Munich: The Phoney Peace. London, 1965.

1487. Pike, David Wingate. Conjecture, Propaganda, and Deceit, and the Spanish Civil War: The International Crisis over Spain, 1936-1939 as Seen by the French Press. Stanford, 1968.

1488. Reussner, A. Les conversations franco-britanniques d'Etat-Major (1935-1939). Vincennes, Service Historique de la Marine, 1969.

1489. Scheler, Eberhard. Die politischen Beziehungen zwischen Deutschland und Frankreich zur Zeit der aktiven Aussenpolitik Hitlers, Ende 1937 bis zum Kriegsausbruch. Frankfurt, 1962.

1490. Scott, William E. Alliance Against Hitler: The Origins of the Franco-Soviet Pact. Durham, N.C., 1963.

1491. Steinert, M.G. Les origines de la seconde guerre mondiale. Paris, 1974.

1492. Wathen, Sister Mary. The Policy of England and France toward the 'Anschluss' of 1938. Washington, 1954.

1493. Weygand, Jacques. Weygand, Mon Père. Paris, 1970.

1494. Young, Robert J. In Command of France: French Foreign Policy and Military Planning, 1933-1940. Cambridge, Mass., 1978.

Wartime, 1940-1945

1495. Adès, Lucien. L'aventure algérienne, 1940-1944. Pétain, Giraud, de Gaulle. Paris, 1979.

1496. Amouroux, Henri. La France et les Français de 1939 à 1945. Paris, 1970.

1497. — La grande histoire des français sous l'Occupation. Currently 4 vols. Paris, 1976-.

Wartime, 1940-1945

1498.　—— and Melchoir-Bonnet, Christian, eds. Les années
　　　　40: La vie des français de l'Occupation à la
　　　　Libération. Paris, 1978.

1499.　Anglin, Douglas G. The St. Pierre and Miquelon
　　　　Affair of 1941. A Study in Diplomacy in the
　　　　North Atlantic Quadrangle. Toronto, 1966.

1500.　Aron, Robert. Dossiers de la seconde guerre
　　　　mondiale. Paris, 1976.

1501.　—— and Elgey, G. The Vichy Regime, 1940-1944.
　　　　London, 1958.

1502.　—— Histoire de Vichy. Paris, 1960.

1503.　—— Histoire des années 40. 7 vols. Paris,
　　　　1976-1977.

1504.　—— Histoire de la Libération de la France. 2 vols.
　　　　Neuilly-sur-Seine, 1975.

1505.　Bédarida, François. La Stratégie secrète de la
　　　　Drôle de guerre. Le conseil suprême interallié,
　　　　septembre 1939-avril 1940. Paris, 1979.

1506.　Bell, P.M.H. A Certain Eventuality: Britain and the
　　　　Fall of France. London, 1974.

1507.　Béteille, Pierre and Rimbaud, Christianne. Le
　　　　Procès de Riom. Paris, 1973.

1508.　Blumenson, Martin. The Duel for France: 1944. New
　　　　York, 1963.

1509.　Bond, Brian. France and Belgium, 1939-1940.
　　　　London, 1975.

1510.　Boutron, Jean. De Mers-el-Kébir à Londres,
　　　　1940-1944. Paris, 1980.

1511.　Carmoy, Guy de. The Foreign Policies of France,
　　　　1944-1968. Chicago, 1970.

1512.　Crémieux-Brilhac, Jean-Louis, ed. Ici Londres: Les
　　　　voix de la liberté, 1940-1944. 4 vols. Paris,
　　　　1975.

Wartime, 1940-1945

1513. De Porte, A.W. De Gaulle's Foreign Policy, 1944-1946. Cambridge, Mass., 1967.

1514. Farmer, Paul. Vichy: Political Dilemma. New York, 1977.

1515. Fritsch-Estrangin, Guy. New York entre de Gaulle et Pétain, les Français aux Etats-Unis de 1940 à 1946. Paris, 1969.

1516. Funk, Arthur L. The Politics of Torch: The Allied Landings and the Algiers Putsch, 1942. Lawrence, Kansas, 1974.

1517. Furniss, Edgar S. France, Troubled Ally. De Gaulle's Heritage and Prospects. New York, 1960.

1518. Gandin, Robert. Darlan, Weygand, Cunningham: Artisans de la victoire, 1939-1944. Paris, 1977.

1519. Gillois, André. Histoire secrète des Français à Londres: de 1940 à 1944. Paris, 1973.

1520. Gounelle, Claude. De Vichy à Montoire. Paris, 1966.

1521. — Le dossier Laval. Paris, 1969.

1522. Gun, Nerin E. Les secrets des archives américaines. Pétain, Laval, De Gaulle. Paris, 1979.

1523. Hostache, René. De Gaulle 1944, victoire de la légitimité. Paris, 1978.

1524. Hytier, A.D. Two Years of French Foreign Policy: Vichy, 1940-1942. Paris, 1958.

1525. Jeantet, Gabriel. Pétain contre Hitler. Paris, 1966.

1526. Kaspi, André. La mission de Jean Monnet à Alger, mars-octobre, 1943. Paris, 1971.

1527. Launay, Jacques de. La France de Pétain. Paris, 1972.

Wartime, 1940-1945

1528.   —— Le dossier de Vichy. Paris, 1967.

1529.   Laurens, Anne. Les Rivaux de Charles de Gaulle: la
          bataille de la légitimité en France de 1940 à
          1944. Paris, 1977.

1530.   Laurent, Jacques. Année 40 Londres, De Gaulle,
          Vichy. Paris, 1965.

1531.   Lipschits, Isaac. La politique de la France au
          Levant, 1939-1941. Amsterdam, 1962.

1532.   Marder, Arthur. Operation 'Menace'. The Dakar
          Expedition and the Dudley North Affair. London,
          1976.

1533.   Michel, Henri. La drôle de guerre. Paris, 1971.

1534.   —— La seconde guerre mondiale. Paris, 1975.

1535.   —— Pétain et le régime de Vichy. Paris, 1978.

1536.   —— Pétain, Laval, Darlan: Trois politiques? Paris,
          1972.

1537.   Milward, Alan S.   The New Order and the French
          Economy. London, 1970.

1538.   Ordioni, Pierre. Le secret de Darlan, 1940-1942: le
          vrai rival de de Gaulle. Paris, 1974.

1539.   —— Tout commence à Alger, 1940-1944. Paris, 1972.

1540.   Paillat, Claude. L'échiquier d'Alger. 2 vols. I,
          Avantage à Vichy, juin 1940-novembre 1942. II,
          De Gaulle joue et gagne, novembre 1942-août
          1944. Paris, 1966-67.

1541.   Paxton, Robert O.   Parades and Politics at Vichy:
          The French Officer Corps under Marshal Pétain.
          Princeton, 1966.

1542.   —— Vichy France: Old Guard and New Order,
          1940-1944. New York, 1972.

1543.   Queuille, Pierre-François. Histoire diplomatique de
          Vichy: Pétain diplomate. Paris, 1976.

214

Wartime, 1940-1945

1544.   Raissac, Guy. Un combat sans merci: l'affaire
         Pétain-de Gaulle. Paris, 1966.

1545.   Sala, Admiral Antoine. L'amiral Georges Durand-
         Viel. Paris, 1960.

1546.   Saurel, Louis. La fin de Pierre Laval. Paris,
         1965.

1547.   Schmitt, General G. Les accords secrets
         franco-britanniques de novembre-décembre 1940.
         Paris, 1957.

1548.   Tesson, Philippe. De Gaulle 1er. La révolution
         manquée. Histoire du premier gouvernement de
         Gaulle (août 1944-janvier 1946). Paris, 1965.

1549.   Thomas, R.T. Britain and Vichy: The Dilemma of
         Anglo-French Relations, 1940-1942. New York,
         1979.

1550.   Thomson, David. The Proposal for Anglo-French Union
         in 1940. Oxford, 1966.

1551.   ── Two Frenchmen: Laval and de Gaulle. London,
         1951.

1552.   Tompkins, Peter. The Murder of Admiral Darlan: A
         Study in Conspiracy. New York, 1965.

1553.   Viorst, Milton. Hostile Allies: F.D.R. and de
         Gaulle. New York, 1965.

1554.   White, Dorothy S. Seeds of Discord: De Gaulle, Free
         France, and the Allies. Syracuse, 1964.

42.	Daladier	10 April 1938 – 20 March 1940
43.	Reynaud	21 March 1940 – 16 June 1940
44.	Pétain	16 June 1940 – 12 July 1940
45.	Pétain	12 July 1940 – 17 April 1942
46.	Laval	18 April 1942 – 17 August 1944
47.	De Gaulle	September 1944 – November 1945

APPENDIX B

French Foreign Ministers, 1918-1945

1. PICHON, Stéphen [16 November 1917 - 18 January 1920]
   b.1857; d.1933; journalist and diplomat; deputy for Seine (1885-93); senator for Jura (1906-24); previously foreign minister (October 1906-February 1911) (March-December 1913).

2. MILLERAND, Alexandre [20 January - 23 September 1920]
   b.1859; d.1943; lawyer; deputy for Seine (1885-1920); senator for Seine (1925-27) for Orne (1927-43); several cabinet posts pre-1914; war minister (Aug. 1914-Oct. 1915); commissioner general of Strasbourg (March-Sept. 1919); premier and foreign minister (Jan.-Sept. 1920); President of the Republic (Sept. 1920-June 1924).

3. LEYGUES, Georges [24 September 1920 - 12 January 1921]
   b.1857; d.1933; lawyer, deputy for Lot-et-Garonne (1885-1933); several prewar cabinet posts; minister of Interior (Dec. 1930-Jan. 1931); of Navy (Nov. 1917-Jan. 1920) (Nov. 1925-July 1926) (July 1926-Feb. 1930) (June 1932-Sept. 1933); premier and foreign minister (Sept. 1920-Jan. 1921).

4. BRIAND, Aristide [16 January 1921 - 15 January 1922]
   b.1862; d.1932; lawyer and journalist; deputy for Saint-Etienne (1902-19) and for Loire-Inférieure (1919-32); several prewar cabinet posts, including Premiership, Interior and Justice; held latter portfolio, then premiership and foreign ministry in wartime cabinets (1914-17); premier and foreign minister (Jan. 1921-Jan. 1922); foreign minister (April-Nov. 1925); premier and foreign minister (Nov. 1925-July 1926) (July 1926-Jan. 1932).

5. POINCARE, Raymond [15 January 1922 - 1 June 1924]
   b.1860; d.1934; lawyer; deputy for Meuse (1887-1903); senator for Meuse (1920-34); several prewar cabinet posts, including premiership and foreign ministry (1912-13); President of the Republic (Feb. 1913-Feb. 1920); premier and foreign minister (Jan. 1922-June 1924); premier and finance minister (July 1926-Nov. 1928); premier (Nov. 1928-July 1929).

219

6. LEFEBVRE du PREY, Edmond [9 - 14 June 1924]
   b.1866; lawyer; deputy for Pas-de-Calais (1909-27);
   then senator (1927-44); minister of Agriculture
   (Jan. 1921-Jan. 1922); of Justice (March-June 1924);
   foreign minister in short-lived François-Marsal
   government of June 1924.

7. HERRIOT, Edouard [14 June 1924 - 10 April 1925]
   b.1872; d.1957; professor of Literature; senator for
   Rhône (1912-19), then deputy (1919-42, 1945-54);
   president of Chamber of Deputies (1925-26, 1936-40);
   president of National Assembly (1947-54); premier and
   foreign minister (June 1924-April 1925) (July 1926)
   (June-Dec. 1932); also minister of Public Instruction
   (July 1926-Nov. 1928); and minister of State (Feb.
   1934-Jan. 1936).

8. BRIAND, Aristide [17 April 1925 - 18 July 1926]
   See earlier entry.

9. HERRIOT, Edouard [19 - 23 July 1926]
   See earlier entry.

10. BRIAND, Aristide [23 July 1926 - 12 January 1932]
    See earlier entry.

11. LAVAL, Pierre [13 January - 16 February 1932]
    b.1883; d.1945; lawyer; deputy for Seine (1914-19,
    1924-27); then senator (1927-36) and for Puy-de-Dôme
    (1936-44); minister of Public Works (April-Oct.
    1925); Justice (March-July 1926); Labor (March 1930);
    premier and Interior (Jan. 1931-Jan. 1932); Labor and
    Social Security (Feb.-June 1932); Colonies
    (Feb.-Oct. 1934); State, and vice-premier (June-July
    1940); premier (June 1935-Jan. 1936) (April
    1942-Aug. 1944). Several times foreign minister
    (Jan.-Feb. 1932) (Oct. 1934-Jan. 1936) (Oct.-Dec.
    1940) (April 1942-Aug. 1944).

12. TARDIEU, André [20 February - 2 June 1932]
    b.1876; d.1945; inspector general of administration
    in Interior ministry, and writer on foreign policy;
    deputy for Seine-et-Oise (1914-24) and Territory of
    Belfort (1926-36); minister of Liberated Regions
    (Nov. 1919-Jan. 1920); Public Works (July 1926-Nov.
    1928); Interior (Nov. 1928-Feb. 1930); premier and
    Interior (March-Dec. 1930); Agriculture (Jan.
    1931-Jan. 1932); War (Jan.-Feb. 1932); premier and
    foreign minister (Feb.-June 1932); State (Feb.-Nov.
    1934).

13. HERRIOT, Edouard [3 June - 14 December 1932]
    See earlier entry.

14. PAUL-BONCOUR, Joseph [31 December 1932 - 27 January
    1934] b.1873; d. 1972; lawyer; deputy for
    Loir-et-Cher (1909-14), for Seine (1919-24) for Tarn
    (1924-31); senator for Loir-et-Cher (1931-41); member
    of provisional Consultative Assembly (1944-45);
    minister of War (June-Dec. 1932); premier and foreign
    minister (Dec. 1932-Jan. 1933); foreign minister
    (Jan. 1933-Jan. 1934) (March 1938); National Defense
    and War (Feb. 1934); State, and delegate to League of
    Nations (Jan.-June 1936).

15. DALADIER, Edouard [30 January - 7 February 1934]
    b.1884; d.1970; professor of History and Geography;
    deputy for Vaucluse (1919-42, 1946-58); minister of
    Colonies (June 1924-April 1925); War (Oct.-Nov. 1925)
    (Dec. 1932-Jan. 1934); Public Instruction (Nov.
    1925-March 1926); Public Works (Feb. 1930-Jan. 1931);
    National Defense (June 1936-March 1940); premier and
    foreign minister (Jan.-Feb. 1934); premier and
    National Defense (April 1938-March 1940) and
    including foreign ministry (Sept. 1939-June 1940).

16. BARTHOU, Louis [9 February - 9 October 1934]
    b.1862; d.1934; lawyer and man of letters; deputy for
    Basses-Pyrénées (1889-1922); then senator (1922-34);
    several prewar cabinet posts, including Justice, and
    the premiership (1913); minister of State and foreign
    minister (Oct.-Nov. 1917); War (Jan. 1921-Jan. 1922)
    (Dec. 1930-Jan. 1931); president of Reparations
    Commission (1922-26); Justice (July 1926-Oct. 1929);
    foreign minister from February 1934 until his
    assassination in October 1934.

17. LAVAL, Pierre [13 October 1934 - 22 January 1936]
    See earlier entry.

18. FLANDIN, Pierre-Etienne [24 January - 4 June 1936]
    b.1889; d.1958; lawyer; deputy for Yonne (1914-42);
    under-secretary for Public Works (Feb. 1920-Jan.
    1921); minister for Commerce and Industry (June 1924)
    (Nov. 1929-Feb. 1930); Finance (Jan. 1931-May 1932);
    Public Works (Feb.-Nov. 1934); premier (Nov. 1934-May
    1935); foreign minister (Jan.-June 1936) (Dec.
    1940-Feb. 1941).

19. DELBOS, Yvon [4 June 1936 - 10 March 1938]
    b.1885; d.1956; teacher and journalist; deputy for
    Dordogne (1924-40, 1946-55); under-secretary for
    Technical Education and Fine Arts (April-Oct. 1925),
    then minister (Oct.-Nov. 1925); Justice and
    vice-premier (Jan.-June 1936); foreign minister
    (1936-38); National Education (Sept. 1939-March 1940)
    (June 1940) (1948-50).

20. PAUL-BONCOUR, Joseph [13 March - 8 April 1938]
    See earlier entry.

21. BONNET, Georges [10 April 1938 - 13 September 1939]
    b.1889; d.1973; lawyer; deputy for Dordogne (1924-28,
    1929-42, 1956-68); under-secretary to premier
    Painlevé (April-Oct. 1925); minister of the Budget
    (Oct.-Nov. 1925); Pensions (July 1926); Commerce and
    Industry (Feb.-March 1930) (June 1935-June 1936);
    P.T.T. (Dec. 1930-Jan. 1931); Public Works (Dec.
    1932-Jan. 1933); Finance (Jan. 1933-Jan. 1934) (June
    1937-Jan. 1938); State (Jan.-March 1938); foreign
    minister (1938-39); Justice (Sept. 1939-March 1940).

22. DALADIER, Edouard [13 September 1939 - 20 March 1940]
    See earlier entry.

23. REYNAUD, Paul [21 March - 18 May 1940]
    b.1878; d.1966; lawyer; deputy for Basses-Alpes
    (1919-24) for Seine (1928-42) for Nord (1946-62);
    minister of Finance (March-Dec. 1930) (Nov.
    1938-March 1940); Colonies (Jan. 1931-Feb. 1932);
    Justice and vice-premier (Feb.-June 1932); Justice
    (April-Nov. 1938); premier and foreign minister
    (March-May 1940); premier and defense minister
    (May-June 1940); premier, defense and foreign
    minister (June 1940); Finance and Economic Affairs
    (1948); vice-premier (1953-54).

24. DALADIER, Edouard [18 May - 5 June 1940]
    See earlier entry.

25. REYNAUD, Paul [5 - 16 June 1940]
    See earlier entry.

26.   BAUDOUIN, Paul [16 June - 12 July 1940]
      b.1894; d.1964; financial administrator and banker;
      under-secretary to premier Reynaud and secretary to
      war cabinet and war committee (March-June 1940);
      under-secretary for foreign affairs (June 1940);
      minister of foreign affairs in Pétain's cabinet, the
      last of the Third Republic (June-July 1940);
      minister-secretary of State for foreign affairs
      (July-October 1940); minister-secretary of State to
      the premier's office (October 1940-January 1941).

                      Vichy France

27.   BAUDOUIN, Paul [12 July - 28 October 1940]
      See above.

28.   LAVAL, Pierre [28 October - 13 December 1940]
      See earlier entry.

29.   FLANDIN, Pierre [14 December 1940 - 9 February 1941]
      See earlier entry.

30.   DARLAN, Admiral François [10 February 1941 - 17 April
      1942] b.1881; d.1942; naval officer; commanded Rhine
      Flotilla (1918-20); served in naval minister Leygue's
      personal cabinet (1926-29); headed military cabinet
      of successive naval ministers (1929-34, 1936); chief
      of naval staff (1937); commander-in-chief of naval
      forces (1939); minister of Navy and Merchant Marine
      (June-July 1940) (July 1940-April 1942); Foreign
      Affairs, Interior and Information (Feb. 1941-April
      1942); National Defense (Aug. 1941-April 1942);
      commander-in-chief of Vichy's armed forces
      (April-Nov. 1942); high commissioner in North Africa
      (Nov.-Dec. 1942).

31.   LAVAL, Pierre [17 April 1942 - 17 August 1944]
      See earlier entry.

                      Free France

32.   DEJEAN, Maurice [September 1941 - October 1942]
      b.1899; head of press service in Berlin embassy
      (1930-39); deputy head, then head of foreign
      minister's cabinet (Sept. 1939-June 1940); Free
      French director of political affairs (Feb.-Sept.
      1941); national commissioner for foreign affairs
      (1941-42); diplomatic counselor for CFLN in Algiers
      (1943); minister on mission to allied governments in
      London (1943-44); director-general of political
      affairs at Quai d'Orsay (1944-45); distinguished
      postwar diplomatic and business career.

33. PLEVEN, René [October 1942 - June 1943]
b.1901; businessman in international
telecommunications (1926-39); assistant to president
of Anglo-French Coordinating Committee (1939-40); as
secretary-general, rallied French Equatorial Africa
to de Gaulle (1940); national commissioner for
Economy, Finance and Colonies (Sept. 1941-Oct. 1942);
commissioner for Economy, Colonies, Merchant Marine,
and Foreign Affairs (Oct. 1942-June 1943); CFLN
commissioner for Colonies (June 1943-Oct. 1944);
minister of Finance (Oct. 1944-Oct. 1945);
distinguished postwar career as deputy and frequent
cabinet minister under the 4th Republic, including
the foreign minister's portfolio very briefly in May
1958.

34. MASSIGLI, René [June 1943 - September 1944]
b.1888; secretary-general of Conference of
Ambassadors (1920) and Lausanne Conference (1922-23);
head of League service at Quai d'Orsay (1928); deputy
director of political affairs (1933-37); then
director (1937-38); ambassador to Turkey (1938-40);
CFLN commissioner for Foreign Affairs (1943-44);
ambassador to London (1944-55); secretary-general at
Quai d'Orsay (1955-56).

35. BIDAULT, Georges [September 1944 - 1948]
b.1899; professor of History; succeeded Jean Moulin
as head of National Resistance Council (1943-44);
first post-Liberation foreign minister (Sept. 1944);
deputy for the Loire (1945); premier (1949-50);
minister of national defense (1951-52); of foreign
affairs (1953) (1954); resisted 5th Republic's policy
toward Algeria; exile from France (1962-68).

Note   The foregoing data on the foreign ministers has been
assembled from a variety of sources, not all of which
agree on every detail. Apart from my bibliographical
entries #15 to #25, I have also drawn upon The
International Who's Who (London, 1938, 1947), and Qui
Etes-Vous? Annuaire des Contemporains (Paris, 1924).

APPENDIX C

Quai d'Orsay Administrators

I   Secrétaire Général, 1918-1945

CAMBON, Jules [30 October 1915-1917]
   b.1845; d.1935; lawyer, prewar ambassador to
   Washington (1897-1902); Madrid (1902-07); Berlin
   (1907-14); appointed by Briand the first Secretary
   General in the foreign ministry; delegate to the
   Peace Conference (1919); retired from diplomacy
   (1922) but continued active business career until his
   death.

PALEOLOGUE, Maurice [June-September 1920]
   b.1859; d.1944; professional diplomat; director of
   political and commercial affairs (1912-14);
   ambassador to Petrograd (1914-17); appointed
   Secretary General in June 1920.

BERTHELOT, Philippe [September 1920-January 1922]
                         and
              [April 1925-February 1933]
   b.1866; d.1934; entered diplomatic service in 1889,
   six years before father Marcelin became foreign
   minister (1895); frequent head of foreign minister's
   cabinets before 1914 (e.g. Rouvier, Bourgeois,
   Pichon); deputy-director of political and commercial
   affairs (1914), and director (1919); appointed
   Secretary General by Leygues (1920); post vacated
   between the first Poincaré cabinet of 1922 and the
   first Painlevé cabinet of 1925.

LEGER, Alexis [February 1933-May 1940]
   b.1885; d.1975; entered foreign ministry in 1914;
   secretary in Peking (1916-21); attached to political
   affairs directorate and Asia subdivision (1922-25);
   Briand's chef de cabinet (1925); deputy director,
   then director of political affairs (1927-33);
   Secretary General (1933-40); resided in United States
   after 1940, where he continued his literary career as
   Nobel prize-winning poet Saint-John Perse.

225

CHARLES-ROUX, François [July-October 1940]
b.1879; entered diplomatic service in 1902; prewar postings to St. Petersbourg, Constantinpole, Cairo, London; Rome (1916-24); minister to Prague (1927-32); ambassador to the Vatican (1932-40); placed on inactive service (October 1940).

ROCHAT, Charles [November 1940-August 1944]
b.1892; attached to missions in Petrograd and Vienna in early 1920s; secretariat at The Hague (1926); embassy in Rome (1930); early 1930s was posted to Europe sous-direction, then to Washington embassy (1936); director of political and commercial affairs (1940), and Secretary General shortly thereafter; condemned to death in absentia (1946).

CHAUVEL, Jean [January 1945-February 1949]
b.1897; entered diplomatic service in 1921; served in China, Syria and Lebanon in 1920s and early 1930s; deputy director of Asia-Oceania sous direction (1938-40); director of Far East sous direction for Vichy foreign ministry (1940-42); escaped to Algiers in spring 1944; became secretary general for CFLN commissariat for foreign affairs; became first post-Liberation Secretary General.

II   Directeur des Affaires politiques et commerciales

MARGERIE, Pierre de [1912-1919]
b.1861; entered diplomatic service in 1883; secretary in Copenhagen, Constantinople, Washington and Madrid (1883-87); minister in Siam and China (1887-89); director of political and commercial affairs (1912-19); ambassador to Belgium (1919-22), and Germany (1922-31).

BERTHELOT, Philippe [1919-1920]
See earlier entry.

PERETTI de la ROCCA, Emmanuel [1920-1924]
b.1870; entered diplomatic service in 1894; chargé d'affaires in Rio de Janeiro (1901-02), and Mexico (1926); first secretary in Washington (1910-14); directed African sous direction (1914); director of political affairs (1920-24); ambassador to Spain (1924-29) and Belgium (1929-31).

LAROCHE, Jules [1924-1925]
b.1872; entered diplomatic service in 1897; director of sous-direction Europe (1918); president of Commission for Revision of Treaties (1920); political and commercial affairs director (1924-25); ambassador to Poland (1925-35) and to Belgium (1935-37).

CORBIN, Charles [1927-1929*]
*It appears as if the post was not formally filled in 1926, as Berthelot tried to add the duties involved here to those of the Secretary General.
b.1881; attaché to Rome embassy (1906); head of press service at Quai (1919); counselor in Madrid (1923); director of European sous-direction (1924-27); director of political and commercial affairs (1927-29); ambassador to Spain (1929-31), Belgium (1931-33), Britain (1933-40).

LEGER, Alexis [1929-33]
See earlier entry.

BARGETON, Paul [1933-1937]
b.1882; entered diplomatic service in 1905; French delegate to Eastern Peace Conference (1922-23); director of Information at Quai (1926-29); directed European sous-direction (1929); delegate to Hague and London conferences (1930); political and commercial affairs director (1933-37); ambassador to Belgium (1937-40).

MASSIGLI, René [1937-1938]
See Appendix B.

CHARVERIAT, Emile [1938-1940]
b.1889; entered diplomatic service in 1914; deputy head of minister's cabinet (1928); directed Asian sous-direction (1933-33) and that of Europe (1933-37); deputy director of political and commercial affairs (1937-38); director (1938-40).

III Directeur-adjoint des Affaires politiques et commerciales

SEYDOUX, Jacques [1924-1926]
b.1870; directed Blockade (1918); rank of minister plenipotentiary (1924); delegate to Spa (1920), London (1921), Cannes (1922), Genoa (1922); deputy director of political affairs (1924-26).

LEGER, Alexis [1927-1929]
See earlier entry.

LABOULAYE, André [1929-1933]
b.1876; prewar posting to embassy at Vatican; postwar postings to Bucharest, Berlin, Moscow, Washington, before becoming deputy director; ambassador to Washington (1933-37).

MASSIGLI, René [1933-1937]
See Appendix B.

COULONDRE, Robert [1933-1936]
b.1885; d.1959; entered diplomatic service in 1909; attached to minister's cabinet in 1910, and to office of Resident General in Morocco (1919-20); deputy head of commercial affairs sous-direction (1920); and head (1927); delegate to Hague conference (1929-30), London (1931), Lausanne (1932); deputy director of political affairs (1933); ambassador to Moscow (1936-38), and Berlin (1938-39); directed minister's cabinet (1939-40); ambassador to Berne (May-Oct.1940).

LABONNE, Erik [1936-1937*]
*Shared with Massigli and Coulondre.
b.1888; entered diplomatic service in 1913; member of mission to Russia (1917-18); headed mission to southern Russia (1919); attached to financial service at Quai (1921-24); posted to Moscow (1925); secretary general for Moroccan Protectorate (1928-32); minister to Mexico (1932); sous-directeur of American department (1933-36); deputy director of political affairs (1936-37); ambassador to Spain (1937); Resident General in Tunisia (1938-40); ambassador to Moscow (1940-41); Resident General of Morocco (1946-47).

CHARVERIAT, Emile [1937-1938]
See earlier entry.

ROCHAT, Charles [1938-1940]
See earlier entry.

LA BAUME, Count Robert Renom de [1937-1940*]
*Shared with Charvériat and Rochat.
b.1885; attached to embassy in Madrid (1912); rank of minister plenipotentiary (1933); deputy director of political affairs (1937-40); attached to directorate of Blockade ministry (1940); ambassador to Madrid (1940) and Berne (1940); head of French delegation to the council for Economic Cooperation (1945).

IV   Sous-Directeur d'Europe

BERTHELOT, Philippe [1914-1920]
See earlier entry.

LAROCHE, Jules [1920-1921]
See earlier entry.

VIGNON, Alfred [1921-1924]
b.1873; attaché to Constantinople (1899), Vatican
(1900); secretary in Peking (1902), Vienna (1906);
head of archival service at Quai (1920); deputy
secretary general for office of President of the
Republic (1920); director of European sub-section
(1921-24); Inspector of diplomatic and consular posts
(1924).

CORBIN, Charles [1924-1927]
See earlier entry.

LABOULAYE, André [1927-1929]
See earlier entry.

BARGETON, Paul [1929-1933]
See earlier entry.

CHARVERIAT, Emile [1933-1937]
See earlier entry.

ROCHAT, Charles [1937-1938]
See earlier entry.

HOPPENOT, Henri [1938-1940]
b.1891; entered diplomatic service in 1917, when he
was attached to Berne embassy; then Teheran (1924),
Rio de Janeiro (1924), Berlin (1925), Peking (1933);
director of European sub-section (1938-40); Vichy
ambassador to Portugal (1940), Uruguay (1940-42);
CFLN representative in Washington (1943-44).

APPENDIX D

A Selection of French Ambassadors in Europe, 1918-1940

I   Berlin

LAURENT, Charles [1920-1922]
b.1856; entered Inspectorate of Finance in 1878;
secretary general of Finance ministry (1898);
financial counselor to Turkish government (1908);
Berlin embassy (1920).

MARGERIE, Pierre de [1922-1931]
See Appendix C.

FRANÇOIS-PONCET, André [1931-1938]
b.1887; d.1978; deputy for the Seine (1924-32);
under-secretary of state in ministry of Public
Instruction and Fine Arts (1928-30); under-secretary
of state in premier's office (1930-31); ambassador to
Berlin (1931-38), to Rome (1938-40); arrested and
deported (1943); liberated (1945); high commissioner
in Germany (1948-53); ambassador (1953-55).

COULONDRE, Robert [1938-1939]
See Appendix C.

II   Rome

BARRERE, Camille [1897-1924]
b.1851; d.1940; embassy secretary in Stockholm and
Munich in early 1880s; delegate to international
commission on Suez canal (1885); ambassador to Berne
(1894), Rome (1897).

BESNARD, René [1924-1928]
b.1879; d. 1952; deputy for Indre-et-Loire (1906-19)
and senator (1920-41); under-secretary of state for
Finance (1911-13); minister of Colonies (1913), Labor
(1913); under-secretary of state for War (1915-16,
1916-17); minister of Colonies (1917), War (Feb.
1930).

231

JOUVENEL, Henry de [1933]
b.1876; d.1935; senator for Corrèze (1921-35); minister of Public Instruction and Fine Arts (1924); Overseas France (1934); longtime member of Senate's foreign affairs commission; delegate to League of Nations (1920-26).

CHAMBRUN, Count Charles Pineton de [1933-1936]
b.1873; d.1952; entered diplomatic service in 1901, with posting to Vatican; attached to embassies in Berlin and Washington before posted to embassy in St. Petersburg (1912-17); head of Information and press service at Quai (1923); minister in Athens (1924), Vienna (1927), Ankara (1928); ambassador to Rome (1933); retired 1936.

BLONDEL, Jules [1936-1938*]
*France and Italy exchanged no ambassadors in this period, but Blondel was left in charge of the embassy.
b.1887; attached to St. Petersburg embassy (1913), London (1914-15), Washington (1916-18), London (1919-21); chargé d'affaires in Mexico (1921-23); counselor in Constantinople (1924), Athens (1925-28), Buenos Aires (1928-34), Rome (1935); minister in Dublin (1939), Sophia (1940); director of CNF in London (1942); CFLN delegate to Rio de Janeiro (1943-44); ambassador to Oslo (1945).

FRANÇOIS-PONCET, André [1938-40]
See earlier entry.

III   London

CAMBON, Paul [1898-1920]
b.1843; d.1924; entered government service in late 1860s; prefect in several departments in 1870s; minister in residence to Tunisia (1882), then resident general (1885); ambassador to Madrid (1896), Constantinople (1898), London (1898).

SAINT-AULAIRE, Count Auguste de [1920-1924]
b.1886; entered diplomatic service in 1892; chargé d'affaires in Lima (1896), Santiago (1897); 1st secretary in Vienna (1909), then minister (1912), Roumania (1917), Poland (1920); ambassador to Spain (1920), England (1920).

FLEURIAU, Aimé-Joseph de [1924-1933]
b.1870; d.1938; entered diplomatic service in 1894;
3rd secretary at Constantinople (1895) and London
(1898), where he became minister (1913); minister in
Peking (1921-24); ambassador to London (1924).

CORBIN, Charles [1933-1940]
See Appendix C.

IV   Moscow

HERBETTE, Jean [1924-1931*]
* After Paléologue's departure in 1917, France and
the Soviet Union did not exchange ambassadors until
Herbette's arrival in 1924.
b. 1878; journalist (1907-24); ambassador to Moscow
(1924), Madrid (1931-Oct. 1937).

DEJEAN, Count François [1931-1933]
b.1871; d.1949; entered diplomatic service in 1894;
posted to Constantinople (1898), Tokyo (1900), Lima
(1904); attached to political affairs directorate at
Quai (1907); posted to Cairo (1908), Tunis (1911);
commercial attaché to United States (1911); attached
to missions in Bucharest (1914), Washington (1915);
chargé d'affaires in Mexico (1918); sous-directeur of
American section (1920); ambassador to Rio de Janeiro
(1928), Moscow (1931).

ALPHAND, Charles [1933-1936]
b.1879; entered diplomatic service in 1902, when he
joined Delcassé's personal secretariat; attached to
President Loubet's staff for visit to Rome (1904);
head of civil cabinet for naval minister (1911);
director of Office des biens et intérêts privés
(1920); delegate to The Hague (1923); consul-general
(1924); headed Herriot's cabinet at Quai (1932);
delegate to disarmament conference; minister to
Dublin (1930); ambassador to Moscow (1933), Berne
(1936).

COULONDRE, Robert [1936-1938]
See Appendix C.

NAGGIAR, Paul [1938-1940]
b.1883; entered diplomatic service (1908); consul at
Shanghai (1913-17), Yunnan (1918); consul-general at
Montreal (1921), Shanghai (1925); sous-directeur of
Asia-Oceania at Quai (1927); minister to Belgrade
(1932-35), Prague (1935-36), China (1938), Russia
(1938-40)

LABONNE, Erik [1940-1941]
  See Appendix C.

VI. SUBJECT INDEX

This index has been prepared principally from the subject matter which is discussed in Section II: The Foreign Ministry and Foreign Policy. Unless otherwise indicated, the following are all page references.